STUDIES IN CHURCH HISTORY
Volume 10

Sanctity and Secularity

Edited by Derek Baker

The relations and interaction of the church and the world in all their complexity is the theme of this tenth volume of *Studies in Church History*. Discussion ranges from the consideration of specific incidents and developments – the allegation of witchcraft made against pope Benedict XIII, the 'business' of victorian religion – to the investigation of wider issues. Contributors discuss the development of a 'secular' theology, consider the institutions and practices of the early Irish church, examine the early quaker programme for overcoming the world (presidential address), investigate the attitudes of eighteenth-century Dutch churchmen, and discourse on 'holy worldliness' in nineteenth-century England. In two important papers with a sociological slant the emergence of a view of the dignity of labour, not in an urban, but a monastic, environment is postulated, and the functions of the local churches in giving cohesion and stability to society are outlined. This collection of papers comprises a wide-ranging discussion of the problems which have arisen, and which still arise, from the need to relate the sacred and the secular, the church and the world.

10

SANCTITY AND SECULARITY:
THE CHURCH AND THE WORLD

SANCTITY AND SECULARITY:
THE CHURCH AND THE WORLD

PAPERS READ AT
THE ELEVENTH SUMMER MEETING AND
THE TWELFTH WINTER MEETING
OF THE
ECCLESIASTICAL HISTORY SOCIETY

EDITED BY

DEREK BAKER

PUBLISHED FOR
THE ECCLESIASTICAL HISTORY SOCIETY
BY
BASIL BLACKWELL · OXFORD
1973

PREFACE

The present volume of *Studies in Church History* is the tenth to be produced by the Ecclesiastical History Society. It includes a selection from the papers presented at the eleventh summer meeting of the Society, held at Newnham College, Cambridge, and at the twelfth winter meeting, on the theme 'Sanctity and Secularity: the Church and the World'.

It is the first volume to appear under the Society's own imprint, in association with Basil Blackwell. By becoming more closely involved in the publishing operation, the Society hopes to stabilise the price of its volumes, and to continue to guarantee the provision of a forum for the younger scholar, and the ready and general availability of the latest research in ecclesiastical history and related studies.

The Society wishes to acknowledge the generous financial help given by the Twenty-Seven Foundation and the British Academy towards the production costs of this Volume.

Derek Baker

CONTENTS

CONTENTS

viii

CONTRIBUTORS

DEREK BAKER, lecturer in history, university of Edinburgh

BRENDA M. BOLTON, senior lecturer in history, polytechnic of north London

JOHN BOSSY, reader in history, Queen's university, Belfast

MARGARET HARVEY, lecturer in history, university of Durham

CHRISTOPHER J. HOLDSWORTH, senior lecturer in history, University College, university of London

KATHLEEN HUGHES, fellow of Newnham College, university of Cambridge

R. BUICK KNOX, Westminster College, university of Cambridge

A. K. MCHARDY, Royal Holloway College, university of London

JANET NELSON, lecturer in history, King's College, university of London

GEOFFREY F. NUTTALL, lecturer in church history, New College, university of London

JOEL T. ROSENTHAL, state university of New York

PATRICK SCOTT, lecturer in English literature, university of Edinburgh

PHILIP SHERRARD, lecturer in the history of the orthodox church, King's College, university of London

J. VAN DEN BERG, professor, free university of Amsterdam

HADDON WILLMER, lecturer in theology, university of Leeds

ABBREVIATIONS

Annales	*Annales: Économies, Sociétés, Civilisations* (Paris 1946–)
ASB	*Acta Sanctorum Ordinis Sancti Benedicti*, ed L. D'Achery and J. Mabillon (Paris 1668–1701)
ASOC	*Analecta Sacri Ordinis Cisterciensis* (*Analecta Cisterciensia* since 1965) (Rome 1945–)
BIHR	*Bulletin of the Institute of Historical Research* (London 1923–)
BJRL	*Bulletin of the John Rylands Library* (Manchester 1903)
BZ	*Byzantinische Zeitschrift* (Leipzig 1892–)
COCR	*Collectanea Ordinis Cisterciensium Reformatorum* (Rome and Westmalle 1934–)
DHGE	*Dictionnaire d'Histoire et de Géographie ecclesiastiques*, ed A. Baudrillart and others (Paris 1912–)
DNB	*Dictionary of National Biography* (London 1885–)
DS	*Dictionnaire de Spiritualité, Ascétique et Mystique*, ed M. Viller (Paris 1932–)
Ec HR	*Economic History Review* (London 1927–)
EETS	*Early English Text Society*
EHD	*English Historical Documents* II, edd D. C. Douglas and G. W. Greenaway (London 1953)
EHR	*English Historical Review* (London 1886–)
FM	*Histoire de l'église depuis les origines jusqu'à nos jours*, edd A. Fliche and V. Martin (Paris 1935–)
HBS	Henry Bradshaw Society
IER	*Irish Ecclesiastical Record* (Dublin 1864–)
HJch	*Historisches Jahrbuch der Görres Gesellschaft* (Cologne 1880 ff, Munich 1950–)
JEH	*Journal of Ecclesiastical History* (London 1950–)
JFHS	*Journal of the Friends Historical Society* (London/Philadelphia 1903–)

ABBREVIATIONS

JRSAI	*Journal of the Royal Society of Antiquaries of Ireland* (Dublin 1871–)
MGH	*Monumenta Germaniae Historica inde ab a. c. 500 usque ad a. 1500*, edd G. H. Pertz and others (Berlin/Hanover 1826–)
Capit	*Capitularia*
SS	*Scriptores*
Moyen Age	*Le moyen âge. Revue d'histoire et de philologie* (Paris 1888–)
NH	*Northern History* (Leeds 1966–)
ns	New series
PG	*Patrologia Graeca*, ed J. P. Migne, 161 vols (Paris 1857–1866)
PL	*Patrologia Latina*, ed J. P. Migne, 217 + 4 index vols (Paris 1841–64)
Potthast	*Regesta Pontificum Romanorum inde ab a. post Christum natum MCXCVIII ad a. MCCCIV*, ed A. Potthast, 2 vols (repr Graz 1957)
PP	*Past and Present* (London 1952–)
PRIA	*Proceedings of the Royal Irish Academy* (Dublin 1836–)
PRO	Public Record Office, London
RB	*Revue Bénédictine* (Maredsous 1884–)
RHE	*Revue d'Histoire Ecclésiastique* (Louvain 1900–)
SA	*Studia Anselmiana* (Rome 1933–)
SCH	*Studies in Church History* (London 1964–)
SM	*Studia Monastica* (Monserrat, Barcelona 1959–)
Speculum	*Speculum, A Journal of Medieval Studies* (Cambridge, Mass 1926–)
SS	*Surtees Society* (Newcastle 1835–)
TRHS	*Transactions of the Royal Historical Society* (London 1871–)

INTRODUCTION

From the time of Constantine the question of the proper relationship of the church to the world has been a subject of debate. How was the church of the elect to adapt to a christian empire and emperor, to a world where it came to be assumed that the boundaries of the faith were coterminous with those of civilisation, and its standards in conformity with those of society, where orthodoxy was not simply an ecclesiastical issue? Should it indeed adapt at all? And if it did, how would its ideals and practice be affected by its involvement in the world?

These are large questions and no definitive treatment of them is possible here, but all are touched upon in the papers collected in this volume. Some, in their examination of alleged papal witchcraft, parliamentary representation, the pattern of benefaction amongst career ecclesiastics, the 'business' of victorian religion, focus on particular instances in the relations of church and world. Others are concerned with wider aspects of these relationships. Could the church only suffer distraction from its essential aims, a debasing of its spiritual standards, an unnecessary ossification of its structures and thought, by pursuing an 'overworldly' rather than an 'otherworldly' policy? Could 'holy worldliness' ever be anything more than an unhappy and uncomfortable compromise? Or can one see a sanctification of the world in the social cohesion and order supplied by the rituals and practices of the church at the grass roots of society, and in the emergence of a doctrine of the dignity of labour within the monastic milieu?

The papers printed here approach these problems from a wide variety of viewpoints—theological, institutional, historical, sociological —and consider them in a broad perspective. Discussion of the English church is set in a wide European context, with particular attention being paid to the fundamental theology of the orthodox church, to the idiosyncracies of early Irish christianity and to the attitudes of eighteenth-century Dutch churchmen. But the relevance and significance of this whole discussion is wider still. Can there be a satisfactory accommodation of sanctity and secularity, or is it true, as one author has commented, that sanctity 'is available only to those who have withdrawn from the *ordo secularis*' and that 'sanctity and secularity are, in effect, mutually exclusive'?

THE DESANCTIFICATION OF NATURE

by PHILIP SHERRARD

THE theme of the environment is one of the most popular and pressing themes of the present time. Somewhat late in the day we have become aware that we have been blindly secreting around ourselves conditions in which it is increasingly difficult for human or any other life to be lived. We have managed to build up a technological and economic order based on machine production and the possession of material goods which inescapably determines to a greater or lesser degree the lives of all the individuals born into it, reducing a great many of them to a state bordering on panic or hysteria. Indeed, we are told that the only real issue before us in this respect is whether uncontrolled technological destruction or uncontrolled population will be the first to tear the fabric of our civilisation to pieces. In spite of this, in the name of a 'war on want' or of developing 'underdeveloped' countries, or simply of progress or evolution or efficiency we go on methodically trying to apply on an even more thorough and extensive scale – on a global scale – exactly the same techniques and habits which have brought about the bleakness of our own world – a bleakness which one might describe as resulting at least in part from a desanctification of nature.

By the phrase, 'the desanctification of nature', I refer to that process whereby the spiritual significance and understanding of the created world has been virtually banished from our minds, and we have come to look upon things and creatures as though they possessed no sacred or numinous quality. It is a process which has accustomed us to regard the created world as composed of so many blind forces, essentially devoid of meaning, personality and grace, which may be investigated, used, manipulated and consumed for our own scientific or economic interest. In short, it has led us to see the world only as so much secularised or desacralised material, with the consequence that we have ruptured the organic links and spiritual equilibrium between man and nature, and have restricted religion more and more to the privacy of the individual conscience or to concern for the beyond of a transcendent God or of an individual salvation after earthly existence is over.

This does not mean of course that people have stopped finding a charm or a beauty in nature, or an outlet from the artificial and suffocating atmosphere of our over-industrialised cities. On the contrary, from the eighteenth century onwards our history has been characterised by periodic 'back to nature' movements, as if nature was a kind of unspoilt paradise ready with ever-open arms to compensate man for all the other losses he has suffered. But what this so often represents is the romantic or sentimental reaction of an exhausted and disillusioned individualism, containing in it very little that may be described as spiritual. In fact, it can very well go, and very often has gone, with an entirely 'atheist' outlook. What is in question here is not this kind of naturalism, but a loss of the sense of the divine in nature – a loss of the sense that the very stuff of the universe has a sacred quality. In what follows I shall try to say something of how this situation has come about and what it means, viewing the question in the perspective of the spiritual insights of the orthodox christian tradition.

There has been a growing tendency within the post-medieval christian world to look upon creation as the artifact of a Maker who, as it were, has produced it from without. This has provided us with a picture of a God in heaven who, having set the cosmic process in motion and having left it to run more or less on its own and according to its own laws, now interferes directly on but rare occasions and then only in the form of special and 'abnormal' acts operated upon the world from without. The result is that the relation between God and creation tends to be seen predominantly as one of cause and effect: God is a world cause, a supreme or first cause or principle of being; and the world and its laws are what He has produced. On this account, it may be possible to speak of some analogy between God and creation. It may be possible to say that creation is a 'moving image of eternity', a kind of projection in corruptible terms of its unmoved perfection, or even that signs and indications of God may be discerned in visible phenomena. But what it is difficult to envisage in this perspective is the idea that creation actually participates in the divine, and is an actual mode of existence or embodiment of the living, ever-present God.

I would like to call this idea that creation is the embodiment of the divine – with its rider that all nature has therefore an intrinsically sacred character – the sacramental idea of creation. This would appear appropriate because what is implied in this idea is that the christian understanding of sacrament, which is usually applied only to the specific rites that go by the name of sacraments in the institutional church, is applied to the realm of nature as a whole. A sacrament, it must be remembered, demands a material expression. In fact, the archetype of all sacramental activity is the Incarnation of Christ Himself. In the Incarnation, the Logos becomes flesh: there is an intimate meeting and inextricable intertwining of the spiritual and the material. In the great christological discussions which resulted in the pronouncements of Nicaea and Chalcedon, what is defended or affirmed is that the two natures in Christ – the divine and the human, the uncreated and the created – are not merely juxtaposed in the person of Christ. There is not simply an interpenetration of the divine and the human, or an assumption by the divine of the human. These ways of regarding the mystery of the two natures in Christ are felt to be inadequate and to fail to do justice to its reality. What is defended or affirmed is the actual union of the two natures – a union 'without confusion, without change, without division, without separation'. In other words, it is maintained that however vast and fundamental the difference between the uncreated and the created may appear, there is ultimately no radical dichotomy between them. If God is God, and if God is manifest in Christ, then creation must be capable of becoming one with the uncreated and it must be possible to transcend the apparent ontological gap between them.

This is why when the Greek Fathers speak of the eucharist, which is the image of the Incarnation – and it must be remembered that for the Greek Fathers the only difference between image and archetype is that the image as such is not the archetype as such – they insist that the material sign of the sacrament is not simply something to which the Spirit is attached, as if the Spirit were an extraneous element added to the matter, or that 'transubstantiates' the matter through His presence. On the contrary, they insist that there is a total integration of the material and the spiritual, so that the elements of bread and wine are an actual mode of existence of the divine and there is a complete union between them. In other words, the sacrament presupposes an actual incarnation of divine power and life; and what is communicated to man in the sacrament is this divine power and life. As St Cyril of Alexandria puts it: 'For the Son is in us on the one hand bodily, as man, united and mixed by means of the eucharist [mystical blessing]; and also spiritually, as God, by the energy and grace of His own Spirit renewing the spirit that is in us for the renewal of life and making us participants in His divinity.'[1]

---

[1] Cyril of Alexandria, *PG* 74 (1863) col 564.

It is now possible to see the consequences of applying the christian understanding of the sacrament to the realm of nature as a whole. It means that nature is regarded not as something upon which God acts from without. It is regarded as something through which God expresses Himself from within. Nature, or creation (the terms are interchangeable in this context), is perceived as the self-expression of the divine, and the divine as totally present within it. It is not a case of complete absorption of the one in the other, or of subservience on the one side and detachment on the other. Moreover, the created depends for its existence on the uncreated, while the uncreated does not depend in the least for its existence on the created. But each finds its own identity in the other, and each at the same time keeps its own identity in the other. In creating what is created, it is Himself that God creates, in another mode. In creation He becomes His own image, in such a way that He enters into it from within, He is its within. Creation is the realm in which God's dynamic, pulsating energies are made manifest. Its apparent stability is simply the flux of these energies, its solidity the result of their ceaseless flow. In this respect the difference between the activity of the Spirit in nature and the activity of the Spirit outside nature is one of degree only, not of kind: it is a difference of the mode in which the Spirit operates. Like the eucharist, nature is a revelation not merely of the truth about God but of God himself. The created world is God's sacrament of Himself to Himself in His creatures: it is the means whereby He is what He is. Were there no creation, then God would be other than He is; and if creation were not sacramental, then God would not be its creator and there would be no question of a sacrament anywhere. If God is not present in a grain of sand then He is not present in heaven either.

It is, then, this sacramental idea of nature which has been eliminated from our minds in order to permit that process of desanctification about which I have spoken. I say 'from our minds' advisedly, because the fact that we do not 'see God in all things' and sense His presence everywhere does not mean that He is not in all things and is not present everywhere. Reality is what it is, and so is revelation. That we fail to perceive them as what they are means that we have lost sight of them, not that the structure of reality has changed. The secular has its origin in man's loss of spiritual vision or – what is the same thing – in the hardening of his heart; and the contraction of the world of nature to a self-contained entity, which is what happens when we ignore its sacred aspect, represents not so much a closing off of nature itself as a closing

4

of our own eyes. We always have to remember that how we see the world about us is but a reflection of the state of our own inner world. Ultimately it is because we see ourselves as existing apart from God that we also see nature as existing apart from God.

This last statement is to the point here because what the building of our modern technological and economic order demonstrates is the triumph of precisely the view in which the world is seen as a self-contained entity, existing in its own right, apart from God, and consequently as something that man is quite entitled to explore, organise and exploit without any reference to the divine. The modern secular world owes its immediate origin not so much to the renaissance and reformation or to Copernicus and Galileo as to the scientific revolution of the seventeenth century, with its 'New Philosophy' as the scientists of the seventeenth century themselves called it. Very briefly and in an over-simplified manner it may be said that this revolution has two main characteristics, which are closely interconnected. The first is that it assumed that knowledge must be based on the observation of external phenomena: it must be based on sense-data without reference to the divine or indeed to any pre-conceived *a priori* ideas. The second is that it concluded that in order to reduce the data obtained from the observation of external phenomena to a coherent and reliable system of knowledge they must be submitted to the discipline of mathematics. This may be illustrated by the theories of two of the leading exponents of this revolution, Francis Bacon and René Descartes.

Bacon's intention was to provide a frame of reference for the whole range of physical phenomena, if not for all knowledge. All possible knowledge must be coordinated, he wrote, into 'a single systematic treatise, a Natural History such as may supply an orderly foundation for philosophy and include material reliable, abundant and well-arranged for the task of interpretation'.[2] But in order for such a task to be carried out there must be a complete separation of religion from 'philosophy': they must not be 'commixed together',[3] because while philosophy follows the light of nature (that is to say, is based upon experiment and observation) religion 'is grounded upon the Word and Oracle of God'.[4] Not only must no metaphysical or theological ideas provide the criteria for assessing the significance of what is

[2] Francis Bacon, Preface to *Parasceve*, in *The Works of Francis Bacon*, edd J. Spedding, R. L. Ellis, D. D. Heath (London 1889) p 393.
[3] Francis Bacon, *Advancement of Learning*, ed W. A. Wright (Oxford 1900) II, 6, i.
[4] *Ibid* II, 24, 3.

observed, but also what is observed must not be thought to provide any evidence or support for metaphysical or theological ideas: 'out of the contemplation of nature to induce any verity or persuasion concerning the points of faith is in my judgement not safe'.[5] The divorce between religion and philosophy is absolute: concern for the spiritual is banished from the study of physical phenomena and all scientific knowledge must be derived from the observation of a natural world regarded as a self-subsistent entity.

Descartes comes in a somewhat different way to much the same conclusion, but with him the emphasis that the knowledge of nature is ultimately a mathematical knowledge is more explicit. This is not the place to retrace the steps by which Descartes arrived at his primal truth, 'I think, therefore I am' – a purely artificial conclusion, because one cannot think without thinking about something; or to retrace the steps by which, having established this initial certainty of self as the basis of thought, he went on to distinguish between ideas that were vague and confused and others that were clear and distinct and to accept the latter as being true apprehensions of and truly applicable to the real world. In this context I wish only to recall that Descartes was a great mathematician and that it was therefore perhaps inevitable that among these clear and distinct ideas which he accepted as true he regarded mathematical ideas as the most important. Mathematical ideas were true in a supreme sense, and it was they that could be taken as providing real knowledge.

This idealising attitude towards mathematics as providing real knowledge, or a knowledge of the real, was not of course new. It was the attitude, for instance, of the Greeks of the pythagorean–platonic tradition. But here it is important to make a distinction. Greek mathematics had no point of contact with sense-data. On the contrary it was held in high esteem precisely because it was thought to provide a way of escape from the physical world. It was seen as a way through which we could learn to leave the world of sense-data behind. In fact, it was because the phenomenal and historical world did not correspond to the ideal of mathematical knowledge that it came to be regarded as more or less unreal. What was real was the realm of entities which could be apprehended by the mind without the inter-position of sense; and this realm of reality was changeless and timeless in the sense of having no reference to the world of change and time at all. Moreover, the geometrical figures in which it could be expressed were related to one

[5] *Ibid* II, 6, i.

6

another not physically but only intelligibly or logically. Hence in the Greek thought of this tradition there is a sharp divide between Being – which is the real world of the basically mathematical entities that constitute true knowledge – and Becoming, which is the phenomenal world of change and about which there can be no true knowledge but only opinion.

For Bacon and for Descartes on the other hand it was precisely this phenomenal world – the world of nature – that was the centre of interest. It was this world which by now was being regarded as virtually the real world, and as the basis of all knowledge – something that Descartes makes completely clear in the third of his four precepts of Logic, where he resolves 'to conduct my thoughts in such order that, by commencing with objects the simplest and easiest to know, I might ascend, little by little and, as it were, step by step, to the knowledge of the more complex'.[6] And if this more complex knowledge was assumed to have pre-eminently a mathematical character, so that mathematical knowledge was held to be the most perfect form of knowledge, this was for a reason more or less opposite to that for which it had been held in such high esteem by the Greeks of the pythagorean–platonic tradition: it was valued by the cartesians precisely because it was thought that it corresponded to or was correlated with the phenomenal world of change and time, the world of sense-data. In fact it was now believed that mathematics, and mathematics alone, could provide the most adequate account of the physical world. For Descartes and his successors, mathematics was the study of the world extended in time and space. It provided a real knowledge of this world. And mathematics, whether concerned with measurement or enumeration, is the application of the science of quantity.

Hence as a result of the scientific revolution of the seventeenth century it came to be thought not only that the world of nature is a self-contained entity, but also that those aspects of its reality which can be known in a true sense and which therefore alone have significance are those susceptible to mathematical or quantitative study and treatment. They are those aspects which can be weighed and measured and numbered – aspects which to all intents and purposes are claimed to constitute the whole of the natural order. It is this conclusion that gives cartesian and post-cartesian science its particular character and explains why the realm of nature apart from the divine has in the end become

6 Descartes, *Discourse on Method*, 2, trans J. Veitch, *The Method, Meditations and Selections from the Principles of Descartes* (London 1899) p 19.

7

identified with the realm of science, and why science itself has been identified with the techniques of weight and enumeration and measurement.

It is in the light of these developments that we can see more clearly how and in what sense the building of our modern secular world has involved the desanctification of nature. First, in order for modern science to come into existence nature had to be regarded as an object divorced from all ontological roots or participation in the non-physical realm of the divine. What was known as formal causation disappears and what is left is the purely mechanistic interpretation of matter, according to which matter contains in itself the efficient causes of its own observable processes. Second, the attribution of value and significance solely to those aspects of the natural order which are susceptible to quantitative study means that what was identified as nature was the realm of matter deprived of all qualitative elements, for the simple reason first that no non-observable qualities were to be taken into account and second that in any case no qualitative elements are susceptible to the kind of observation and analysis which science has adopted and which is, in an inexplicably exclusive manner, called scientific. Hence all spiritual qualities are *ipso facto* excluded from the objects science investigates, and at the same time it is tacitly assumed that there is nothing else to know about these objects except what can be observed by the so-called scientific method. Physical phenomena are to be accounted for in physical categories alone, and that is all there is to be accounted for in them. The idea that every natural effect has a spiritual cause is completely neglected, and the fact that this neglect amounts to a kind of spiritual castration of the natural order seems to be of little or no concern. It is as if one examined and analysed the eucharist according to the scientific method and because one could not discern any trace of the divine in it declared that it was simply composed of its material elements. Having adopted a method of investigation which in its nature precludes the perception of spiritual qualities, it is gratuitous, to say the least, to pronounce that the object one investigates is to be explained in non-spiritual categories alone. Yet it is the conclusions achieved by this kind of circulatory reasoning which for the last three hundred years or more have been regarded as constituting knowledge in a virtually exclusive sense and which moreover have been termed scientific.

Modern science, then, ignoring the sacred aspect of nature as a condition of its own genesis and development, tries to fill the vacuum it has created by producing mathematical schemes whose only function is to help us to manipulate and 'dominate' matter on its own plane, which is that of quantity alone.[7] The physical world, regarded as so much dead stuff, becomes the scene of man's uncurbed exploitation for purely practical, utilitarian or acquisitive ends. It is treated as a de-incarnate world of phenomena that are without interest except in so far as they subserve statistics or fill test-tubes in order to satisfy the scientific mind, or are materially useful to man considered as a two-legged animal with no destiny beyond his earthly existence. This is why the application of science – which is not really the application of science at all but the application of an unbelievable ignorance – has produced such dis-equilibrium, ugliness and even destruction not only in the natural world but in human life as well. Paradoxical as it may seem, through our attempt to achieve a knowledge of the world based on the obser-vation of the physical phenomena of this world, we have reduced our-selves to a chronic state of blindness. We have lost our capacity to see not only the reality of the world about us but even of what was to have been the main purpose of our investigation to start with – the reality of our own presence within the world. If man thinks and acts as if God does not exist and is not present in all things, he thinks and acts a lie; and the result of this is that he reduces his own life to a falsity, which is the same thing as unreality. This dehumanisation of man is an inevitable consequence of man's attempt to live as though he were only human. Man can be truly human only when he is mindful of his theomorphic nature. When he ignores the divine in himself and in other existences he becomes sub-human. And when this happens not merely in the case of a single individual but in the case of society as a whole, then that society disintegrates through the sheer rootlessness of its own structure or through the proliferation of psychic maladies which it is powerless to heal because it has deprived itself of the one medicine capable of healing them.[8]

Much of this is well known and there is no need to insist on it here. Moreover it must be said that many scientists themselves are now aware of it. They have begun to realise that by restricting science to the quantitative study of things they are imposing purely artificial limits on it and that so long as this is the case there can never be any under-standing of the true nature of the objects they study: science under

[7] T. Burckhardt, 'Cosmology and Modern Science', *Tomorrow* (London, Summer 1964) p 186.
[8] Seyyed Hossein Nasr, *The Encounter of Man and Nature* (London 1968) *passim*.

these conditions is forced to remain within the world of 'pointer-readings' and mathematical concepts which are no more than mere hypotheses, or which indeed may not have any reference to the real at all. They are fully aware too that since qualitative or spiritual elements are not subject to verification by the senses, no amount of experimental research can either prove or disprove their presence in the physical world. But it has seemed worth while to recall, however briefly, the main characteristics of cartesian and post-cartesian science for two reasons, the one connected indirectly and the other directly with our theme.

The first reason is that while many scientists themselves have become aware of the impasse into which they have been led by science as conceived and practised in the post-cartesian period, and so have also become conscious that perhaps therefore the assumptions on which that science is based need re-examination, historians of the church and theologians often seem strangely unaware of all this. Indeed, we have developed, really in imitation of scientific practice, such disciplines as biblical criticism or the historical method, and we are ready to 'demythologise' religion in the same imitative spirit; but we have singularly failed (with the exception of representatives of the neo-thomist school and one or two others) to provide any adequate criticism of modern science itself and of the assumptions on which it is based. In fact, the contrary is more nearly the case: theologians and historians – even human intelligence itself – has capitulated to science. To understand the truth of this statement one has only to take into account the degree to which theologians accept the hypothesis of evolution, for instance, as axiomatic, and treat it as a kind of imperative condition to which everything, including theology itself, must accommodate itself. Teilhard de Chardin may be an extreme example of the capitulation of the religious consciousness to this hypothesis, but he is not alone by any means. Some even go so far as to regard the scientific method as a means which can be used in order to get a better understanding of the wisdom of God and the wonder of creation. In this view, the physicist who observes new patterns in the natural order and the technologist who applies these discoveries for practical purposes are both, whatever their attitude, fulfilling a 'high priestly' function, revealing and extending God's glory in the universe.

Indeed, nearly all attempts to reconcile religion and science have been made by theologians, not by scientists (who appear to be more perceptive in this respect). What such a reconciliation generally involves is an

attempt to adapt the principles of religion – transcendent and immu-
table – to the latest findings of science, and so to make religion 'reasonable' or in keeping with the 'spirit of the age' by appearing 'scientific'.
Naturally, the particular scientific hypotheses in the name of which this
adaptation is carried out are often discarded by scientists themselves by
the time the theolgians have completed their task. As professor Mascall
has written, there can be no greater disservice done to the christian
religion than to tie it up with scientific views which in their very nature
are merely temporary.[9] Far from religion and science mutually supporting each other it may be said that the more one is involved with
science and its methods the more likely is one to become impervious to
the experience of those realities which give religion its meaning. This is
one reason why it has seemed worth while to point once again to the
grounds which justify such a statement.

More important in this context is the second reason for indicating
the main characteristics of post-cartesian science and the manner in
which it has so devastatingly contributed to the desanctification of the
natural order. It is that these characteristics and their consequences are
implicit in certain forms of the christian theological tradition itself. An
alleged connection between christianity and modern science has often
been affirmed. 'I am convinced', wrote N. Berdiaev,[10] 'that Christianity
alone made possible both positive science and technics.' Behind this
kind of assumption is the idea that because the central proposition of
christianity is that 'the Logos was made flesh' it tends to be the most
materialistic of all the great religions and so somehow the progenitor
of the natural and materialist sciences. This is as it may be, and in any
case begs many questions. But whether there is some truth in it or not,
it surely cannot be said that the aim of any religion is to produce a world
from which nearly every non-material consideration is excluded, in
which everything is seen as independent of God and in which it is
claimed that things may be understood virtually as though God does
not exist. One wonders whether the greatest deceit of the devil may
not lie in his pretence to an independence of this kind. Yet is it precisely
such an independent world – one in which the sacramental quality of
things has been almost totally obscured – that has grown out of the
western christian matrix.

This may be in some part due to the character of christianity itself
and to the historical conditions in which it appeared. One might, for

9 E. Mascall, *Christian Theology and Natural Science* (London 1956) p 166.
10 N. Berdiaev, *The Meaning of History* (London 1935) p 113.

instance, in this connection point to the early christian reaction against paganism, against the cosmic religion and the naturalism of the hellenistic world, with its tendency to divinise the natural and human order in their own right: a reaction expressed in *Colossians*[11] where the entire cosmos is described as controlled by 'the elemental spirits of the universe' opposed to Christ, although 'created through him and for him'. It has even been said that one of the most characteristic novelties of christianity was that it demystified or, if you wish, secularised the cosmos: the idea that God abides in the elements, in water, in springs, in stars, in the emperor, was from the beginning totally rejected by the apostolic church;[12] and a legacy of this attitude is still evident in the horrified cry of 'pantheism' which tends to greet every suggestion that God does live in His creation. It may in this connection be relevant to point out here that what distinguishes the sacramental view of nature from a point of view which tends to divinise the natural order in its own right, is that while in the first nature is sought and known in the light of God, in the second it is God who is sought and identified in the elements of nature themselves.

Then in addition to this is the fact that christianity is a religion without a sacred law. Unlike judaism or islam or hinduism it possesses no corpus of concrete laws inseparable from its revelation and theoretically applicable to all aspects of human life and human society. It came as a spiritual way without such a corpus, so that when it became the religion of a civilisation it was forced to incorporate Roman and even common law into its structure – law for which, in spite of the efforts of St Thomas and others, it was difficult to claim the authority of the will of God or the divine sanction possessed by the teachings of Christ which are concerned with direct spiritual principles. This has meant that it has always been more easy to detach, so to speak, the political, social and economic sphere of human life from the framework of the christian revelation and so leave it exposed to domination by purely secular interests and influences, than has been the case in the context of the civilisations of other great religions possessing a sacred law supported by the authority of revelation itself.

This being said, however, it still remains true that there is a direct causal connection between the process of desanctification of the natural – and human – order and certain theological limitations within latin christianity. It is not possible here to do more than indicate the character

[11] *Col.*, 1:16; 2:8
[12] J. Meyendorff, 'Orthodox Theology Today', *Sobornost*, 6 series, 1 (London 1970) p 16.

of these limitations. But if it is remembered that a recognition of the
sacramental principle depends upon an understanding that in the
sacrament there is an actual participation of the material in the spiritual,
the created in the uncreated, so that the apparent ontological disparity
between them is somehow transcended – if this is remembered, then
it follows that a failure to perceive the sacramental quality of the
natural order must go with a failure to grasp this participation in all its
fulness. It must go, in other words, with a sense that there is a virtually
unbridgeable ontological gap between the spiritual and the material,
the uncreated and the created. This would indicate that the theological
limitations in question would be those that tend to emphasise the disparity between the uncreated and the created realms and so lead to the
one being regarded as independent of the other in the manner indicated.

The attempt to discern these limitations must of course begin with
St Augustine. Here it must be said that what St Augustine in the first
instance understands by nature is not the physical world as we now
perceive it by means of the senses. Nature signifies for him first of all the
original and uncontaminated state of things as they issued 'in the beginning' from God through the act of divine creation: the world before
the fall, before it became warped and depraved through human defection. But even here, in his conception of the creation of this pre-fallen
world, and moreover in his conception of the creation of its highest
and most perfect beings, the angels, St Augustine already inserts the
thin end of the wedge which, driven further in, produces the sense
of dichotomy between the uncreated and the created to which I have
referred. The quality of grace, St Augustine asserts – the quality of
spiritual illumination – is not something intrinsic to the created nature
of angels as such. It is not their natural element. It is something added
to them as a gift. This giving presupposes the existence of a recipient.
It presupposes the existence of a creature existing in a state other than
that of grace. In other words, in the augustinian perspective one is
invited to envisage a historical phase in which the creature exists in a
state of pure nature without participation in divine grace; and this is so
even though both the creation of a being capable of receiving the gift
of grace and the giving of the gift that is to be received are gratuitous
acts on the part of God.

Moreover, according to St Augustine all created beings – angels and
all beneath angels – are first made (though not created) in the eternal
uttering of their ideas in the Word of God. But these ideas of things as

13

they are in God's mind – these 'principial forms or stable and un-changeable essences of things', as St Augustine calls them[13] – in the light of which all things are created, again are not in Augustinian thought regarded as intrinsic to those things when they are created. They remain extrinsic to their being. They cannot become the core itself of that being, a ray of divine light within the creature. In them-selves, created things must always remain distinct and separate from God ontologically. Rational creatures – angels and men – may appre-hend themselves through intellection as ideas in God's mind. These ideas can be the standards for what each thing ought to be. But they can never become the reality itself of each thing, its own proper subject. The being of each thing in itself is and must remain exterior to the divine idea in the light of which it is created. It can never partici-pate in the inner life of this idea. The separation between Creator and created here appears as radical – a separation not to be bridged by any process of human thought or imagination or by any act of human will: any aspirations towards 'deification' as conceived in the orthodox tradition are by definition chimerical, as is any attempt to see and know the divine through sharing in the life of the divine itself. What man can see or know of God are merely the *vestigia Dei* or traces of the divine visible in creation or impressed on the human mind by the source of divine light which itself must always remain exterior to it.[14]

This, as I said, is the state of affairs in the pre-fallen world. In the fallen world as seen by St Augustine – the world in which we actually live – things are far worse, and this separation between the uncreated and the created is now truly abysmal. Through the fall man and the rest of the natural order are deprived of even that extrinsic participation in grace which they possessed in their pre-fallen state. Their original and true nature is now vitiated, totally corrupt and doomed to destruction. It is a lump of damnation. As for the communication of grace, through which alone man and the world may be redeemed from depravity, this, it was thought by St Augustine and his medieval successors, was confined to the visible church and depended on the performance of certain rites, like baptism, confirmation, ordination and so on, which it was the privilege of the ecclesiastical hierarchy to administer to a submissive and obedient laity. The magnificent scope of the Logos

---

[13] St Augustine, *De Diversis Quaestionibus*, 83, 46, 1–2; *PL* 40 (1887) cols 29–30.
[14] See E. TeSelle, 'Nature and Grace in Augustine's Expositions of Genesis I, 1–5', *Recherches augustiniennes*, 5 (Paris 1968) pp 95–137.

doctrine with its whole 'cosmic' dimension – the idea of God incarnate in all human and created existence – which from the time of the Alexandrians and Cappadocians down to the present day has been one of the major themes of orthodox theology, was tacitly but radically constricted in western thinking. Spontaneous personal participation 'in Christ' became identified with membership of a juristic corporational institution which claimed to be the unique sphere of the Spirit's manifestation, the judge of His presence, and the manipulator of His activity. In these conditions to say that everything in the created order by virtue of the simple fact of its existence possesses, even if unaware of it and so in a potential state, an intrinsically sacramental quality which unites it to the divine, would have been tantamount to blasphemy. Instead, there was a radical separation of the sacred from the secular: everything inside the church (understood as an earthly society) was sacred; outside the formal limits of the church, or in nature, the activity of the Spirit was denied: everything outside these limits was secular, deprived of grace, incurably corrupt and doomed to disintegration.

From St Augustine one must turn to the other major representative of latin theology, St Thomas Aquinas; and it is against this background of the radical disparity in St Augustine's thought between the world and the church, nature and grace, or nature and what is now regarded as the supernatural, that the efforts of St Thomas to 'save' the natural world must be viewed. Unless it is viewed against this background the fact that his thought helped to consolidate the rift between the world of nature and the divine and so contributed to the process of desanctification we are tracing may seem inexplicable. It must be remembered that by the time Aquinas set out upon his attempt to reconcile all views, however contradictory they might appear, in an all-embracing synthesis, the idea of the separation between the natural (understood now in the non-augustinian, aristotelian sense as a physical reality) and the supernatural was so deeply embedded in latin thought that it was impossible to establish any genuine ontological link between them. The only way therefore by which the natural world could be freed from the opprobrium attached to it in augustinian thought and could be accorded a positive status in its own right was, paradoxical as it may sound, to dissociate it altogether from the sphere of theology, to make it independent of theological control, and to substitute for any genuine relationship between the sphere of nature and the sphere of theology the principle of analogy.

It was to this end that St Thomas made his suggestion that there are two levels on which things are viewable, the natural and the supernatural level. The latter is the state in which grace is paramount, and it corresponds to the sphere of theology. But where the efficacy of nature itself is concerned, no grace is necessary, because nature follows its own inherent laws which have nothing to do with grace.[15] All grace does in relation to the natural world is to bring to perfection the operations in nature which have begun without its intervention and exist quite independently of it: grace does not destroy nature but perfects it,[16] and this is to imply that although nature is better with the addition of grace it can exist quite adequately without it. The immediate conclusion is that there must be different principles appertaining to the natural and the supernatural spheres. There must be, as St Thomas put it,[17] a double order in things. This means that nature itself – the natural as such – is now accorded a status of its own, to all intents and purposes independent of the divine; and the augustinian dichotomy between nature and grace is replaced by a dualism between the natural and the supernatural. Assuredly, God is still regarded as the author of nature, but essentially nature works on its own laws, and it is quite sufficient to take account only of these laws in order to discover how nature does work.

Moreover, these laws are thought to be characterised by reasonableness or rationality; and man, defined now as a rational animal, shares in the laws of nature to the fullest extent because he can recognise them through his reasoning faculties. This natural reasoning capacity with which man is endowed operates without any revelation or grace and may pursue its investigations without any reference to the articles of faith. Indeed, the only knowledge which man as a rational creature could effectively obtain was said to be that which he could derive from the observation of phenomena through the senses[18] – a proposition which is at the very basis of the later scientific attitude to knowledge. It is true that St Thomas was constrained to state that the conclusions of natural reason could not affect, and must ultimately conform to, the conclusions of faith. But he was constrained to state this because God Himself – and this is the lynch-pin of the whole system – was now regarded as to the fullest degree a rational being, so that unless something had gone very wrong somewhere there could hardly be any ultimate contradiction between the principles of God's rationality and

15 Aquinas, *Summa Theologica*, I–II, qu 10, art I.
16 *Ibid* I, i, qu 8 ad 2.
17 *Ibid* I, qu 21, art I ad 3.
18 Aquinas, *De Veritate*, ii, 3, obj 19 et ad 19; *Summa Theologica*, 1a, 12, 12.

the laws of nature which He had established to operate on purely rational lines. By means of this kind of argument St Thomas was able to preserve a delicate and correspondingly precarious synthesis between the idea that nature was an integral part of the divine order and yet essentially existed in its own right, autonomous and independent within its own terms of reference, operating according to its own laws, premisses and purposes. Analytical thomist methodology, with its supposition that man is dependent on sense-data for the acquisition of knowledge and that he can apprehend spiritual realities only in so far as he discerns in the natural world evidence of their transcendent and unknowable perfections,[19] effectively promotes the idea that there is an uncrossable boundary between God and man, between the divine and the human. Implicit in it is a failure to grasp the full significance of the unity of the two natures in one person; and the immediate consequence of this was to be the neglect of the possibility of man's personal participation in the divine and a growth in the conviction that he may know the truth concerning God only indirectly by means of his rational faculty operating within the one sphere accessible to it, that of the natural world. And here again what is implicit is not man's supra-rational and personal participation in the inner meaning, the indwelling *logos* of this world, or his disclosure of God's self-expression within it, but a belief that he may decipher, articulate and eventually dominate it as a self-sufficient entity by the use of his individual reason in disregard of, if not in contradiction to, the truths of the christian revelation.

The result could only be that in the following centuries philosophers (like for instance William of Ockham or Marsiglio of Padua) less endowed than St Thomas with a capacity for maintaining his subtle balance between nature and revelation, would break the now tenuous link between nature and the divine, would assert the autonomy of reason, divorce philosophy completely from religion, and claim an unlimited charter to pursue their own methods of inquiry into nature without any reference to metaphysical or theological principles, not because God did not exist or had not created nature but because in practical terms He was no longer present as an immanent, ever-working principle and energy in the natural world. The scene was set for the scientific revolution of the seventeenth century and the emergence of the mechanistic and materialist science of the modern world; and it is not without justice that in a famous passage Alfred North Whitehead traces the origin of the modern scientific movement directly back to the

[19] Aquinas, *Contra Gentiles*, I, 3.

scholastic insistence on the rationality of God and to the concomitant insistence, reached in the way we have described, on the belief that every detailed occurrence in the physical world can be correlated with its antecedents in a perfectly definite and rational manner.[20]

That in trying to rescue nature from the pit of perdition to which it had been consigned by St Augustine, St Thomas should have contributed in this way directly to the formation of the secular mentality and secular approach to nature does, as I said, become understandable when it is remembered that he accepted as virtually axiomatic the conception of a God who by definition cannot be ontologically present in the activities of the world which He has created. But the question remains as to why the presence of God is thought to be limited in this way, and it is in answering this question that it may be possible to specify the limitations within the latin theological tradition more precisely. I would venture to suggest that the answer to this question is related to two interconnected themes, the one metaphysical and the other theological.

The metaphysical theme is connected with a conception of form and matter, basically aristotelian in character but accepted by both St Augustine and St Thomas, according to which God is identified with the formal and active principle and matter is regarded as the principle of formlessness and potentiality. This latter principle, although not opposed explicitly to God, is said to have an absolutely minimal degree of being, and is to such an extent identified with non-being in a purely privative or deficient sense that it can be described as that which is not.[21] In fact, its capacity to be is limited to a capacity to receive form, which comes solely from God, while in itself it tends always, by its formlessness, towards nothingness and non-existence.[22] In short, it is the abyss of disintegration over which every created being is suspended, and as such it is linked with evil, which in its turn may be equated with a disruption of form or a perversity of order, a lapse into non-being.[23]

Moreover, this material principle of formlessness is said to lie at the basis of all formal creation: everything created is regarded as a mixture or composition of matter with form, of an indeterminate substratum with the determination acquired from God. Hence no finite being can ever be 'like' God, still less be 'deified', because by definition all finite

20 A. N. Whitehead, *Science and the Modern World* (New York 1926) p 18.
21 St Augustine, *Confessions*, XII, 6, 6.
22 St Augustine, *De Genesi ad litteram*, I, 4, 9.
23 See E. TeSelle, *Augustine the Theologian* (London 1970) pp 143-4.

beings share in the material substratum with its intrinsic deficiency and 'godlessness'. God – the formal principle and the principle of Being – is pure actuality and there is no potentiality in Him. The material principle on the other hand, which is a formless or deficient cause, coincides with potentiality. Since natural existence also shares in the character of potentiality it can never be a sacramental reality in the full sense of the word unless it becomes other than it is or is, in other words, transubstantiated. One of the limitations in latin theology therefore which would appear to make it difficult, if not impossible, to envisage a full and reciprocal union between God and nature, the uncreated and the created, is that God is conceived solely as the principle of pure actuality, with the consequence that potentiality is regarded as implying a certain lack of being in a negative or deficient sense and so in this respect as outside God; and the same must apply to whatever shares in potentiality.

The theological theme in which a certain limitation in latin christianity is expressed is connected with the doctrine of the Trinity. Here perhaps we reach what is really the crux of the matter. The sacramental understanding of nature depends, as we have seen, upon the recognition of the actual immanence of the divine in nature, the sense that the creative energies of God did not merely produce the created world from without like a builder or an engineer, but are the ever-present, indwelling and spontaneous causes of every manifestation of life within it, whatever form this may take. It depends, in other words, upon the recognition of the continuing, vitalising activity of the Holy Spirit in the world, animating these energies – luminous uncreated radiations of the divine – in the very heart of every existing thing. In its essence therefore the absence of this sacramental understanding must signify a deficiency in the doctrine of the Holy Spirit.

In effect, the doctrine of the Holy Spirit was not fully affirmed in latin christendom. The 'cosmic' significance of pentecost, in which the revelation of the Father and Son is consummated in that of the Spirit, was attenuated, and the full deployment of the doctrine of the Trinity was correspondingly arrested and frozen. The Son was conceived preeminently in the unity of His being with that of the Father; and this emphasis on the transcendent unity and simplicity of the Trinity, confirmed and sealed by the *filioque*, meant that the Spirit was regarded as in ontological dependence on the Son. This in its turn, combined with a failure to distinguish adequately between God's essence and His existence or, in the case of Aquinas, with a conception that actually identifies

PHILIP SHERRARD

God's essence with His existence, prevented it from being possible to understand how God, in the Spirit, 'goes out' of Himself and enters with His uncreated 'existential' energies into creation without either disrupting His unity and simplicity or abandoning His transcendence. Under these conditions it was of course impossible to visualise any real activity of the Spirit in nature or, conversely, any real participation of nature in the divine. This is why I said that those two themes in which the limitations within latin theology are most clearly expressed are interconnected: because unless it is first recognised that God is also the principle of potentiality it cannot be recognised how God may be potentially present in all created existence. Finally, is it accidental that precisely during the centuries in which in the west scholastic and post-scholastic thinkers were preparing the intellectual ground for the emergence of a world from which the sense of the presence of the divine has been increasingly purged, the orthodox east was forging a doctrine of the Holy Spirit as essential for an understanding of the Trinity and the meaning of salvation as the christological formulations of earlier centuries? This great crystallisation of pneumatological thought and its insights has been largely ignored by the theological schools of western Europe down to the present day. Yet it is there that the keys to a comprehensive christian theology of nature may be found – a theology which, deriving from a spiritual penetration into the inner being of creation, affirms the presence of God in all things, and their presence in God.

SANCTITY AND SECULARITY IN THE EARLY IRISH CHURCH

by KATHLEEN HUGHES

IRELAND was odd in the early middle ages. She lay on the outer edge of the world, the survivor of that celtic civilisation which had once covered much of the west. She had never immediately known the pervading influence of Rome, which continued in so many ways for so long after the Roman empire collapsed. Christianity had reached her rather early (there were enough christians to make it worth while to send a continental bishop, Palladius, in 431) and it came before many of the developments which determined the nature of monasticism in early medieval Europe. Ireland's political and social organisation were somewhat different from those of the Germanic peoples of the west; and though the early church in Ireland had an episcopal, diocesan structure, within two hundred years or so of its inception it had been fundamentally modified by native Irish laws and institutions. It is therefore not surprising to find that both Ireland's sanctity and her secularity[1] had peculiar features.

Perhaps the best description of Irish sanctity is in the *Vision of Adamnán*.[2] The family of heaven stand around the throne of God, but separated from it by a veil of glass until the day of judgement. Encircling the throne and separated by a portico from the family of heaven are the saints. It is hard for the visionary to explain the ordering of the saints, for none has his back to another, yet all have their faces toward God. Their delight is to gaze on him. Of that wonderful prince 'None can tell his ardour and energy, his blazing and brilliance, his brightness and beauty, his splendour and his bliss.' 'The saints have need of nothing but to be listening to the music to which they listen and to look on the light which they see, and to be filled with the fragrance which is in the land.'

---

[1] I am taking this word in its moral sense, as meaning worldly, material standards.

[2] *Irische Texte*, ed E. Windisch (Leipzig 1880) I pp 165–96; *Lebor na Huidre*, edd R. I. Best and O. Bergin (Dublin 1929) pp 67–76 for *LU* text only. Translated in W. Stokes, *Adamnán's Vision* (Simla 1870); C. S. Boswell, *An Irish Precursor of Dante* (London 1908); and, in part, K. Jackson, *Celtic Miscellany* (London 1972) pp 290 ff.

Only ascetics and those 'who desire God' can ever reach that land, and even these have climbed through the six lower heavens by a process of purging, for at the gate of each heaven is a guardian. The archangel Michael at the first gate has iron rods, and the archangel Uriel at the second has fiery scourges. The saints have to cross a fiery river which washes their souls free of sin, and a shining well purifies the souls of the just. Comparable trials await them at the gates of the first five heavens, before they are passed into the sixth and so to the welcome of heaven's family in the seventh. These saints have passed, by the trial of asceticism, to the summit of contemplation.

The lyric poetry expresses the same ideals. In one poem the hermit sees himself alone in his cell pursuing the ascetic life, trampling on the body, with passions weak and withered, a cold bed, short sleep and frequent early prayer.[3] But the whole is to be sweetened by a heavenly communion: 'I should love to have Christ son of God visiting me, my Creator, my King, and that my mind should resort to him in the kingdom where he dwells.' Another poem, in which Manchán tells his wish for a tiny community in the wilderness, ends up 'And I to be sitting awhile, praying to God in some place.'[4] (This is a different ideal from that of the English benedictine Wulfstan, who speaks of the glories and joys which God has prepared for those who work his will in the world.) The contemplative ideal continues in some of the later Irish poems: 'Be thou my vision beloved Lord: no other is anything to me but the king of the Seven Heavens', or 'It were my mind's desire to behold the face of God. . . . It were my mind's desire to be for ever in the company of the King.'[5]

Where the poems generally express the aspiration, the monastic rules describe the training in sanctity. So if the poems express the contemplative object, the rules will describe the ascetic practice.[6] The abbot was the legal head of the monastery, and in the early days he was spiritual director of his monks. Later the monk took a 'soul-friend' as his spiritual director who had to be a priest, but was not always the abbot. Ireland had no one monastic rule, so it is easy to see that standards of asceticism might vary. Even in the late sixth and seventh centuries the requirements of Columcille and the *Rule of Cummean* were more humane than the *Rule of Columbanus*.[7] The autocracy of the superior

[3] [G.] Murphy, [*Early Irish Lyrics*] (Oxford 1956) no 9.
[4] *Ibid* no 12.
[5] *Ibid* nos 18, 26.
[6] Asceticism is one of the Irish expressions of martyrdom.
[7] [K.] Hughes, [*The Church in Early Irish Society*] (London 1966) pp 57 ff.

varied. Columbanus ordered his monk 'Not [to] do as he wishes . . .
[to] be subject to whom he does not like. . . . Let him keep silence when
he has suffered wrong, let him fear the superior of his community as a
Lord . . . let him not pass judgement on the opinion of an elder.'
Columcille, on the other hand, was advised by his senior monks, and
his disciples sometimes questioned his actions. There is no suggestion of
harshness deliberately imposed in his practice.

During the late eighth and ninth centuries, when the ascetic movement was at its height, men holding positions of responsibility in the
church or the world might sometimes make confession to some well-
known ascetic leader. The ascetic would give advice and impose
penance, but he had no power to enforce it. If the sinner refused to
perform the penance, all the soul-friend could do was to dismiss him
'gently and kindly'.[8] When persons 'older and more venerable' came
to confession the soul-friend was 'not to lay upon such persons strict
injunctions', but merely to read them the relevant passages from the
penitentials. The priest might, however, refuse to receive confession
from laymen who would not perform the penance he enjoined.

The Irish, like Evagrius and Cassian, recognised eight deadly sins:
gluttony, fornication, avarice, anger, *tristitia*, *accidie*, vainglory and
pride. Within the monasteries many of the rulings were aimed at the
control of the appetites. Sexual abstinence was to be complete for the
religious. Severity of diet varied from house to house. Two late eighth-
century reformers differed in their attitude to beer drinking. 'The
liquor that causes forgetfulness of God shall not be drunk here,' said
Máel-ruain; but his disciple Duiblitir answered, 'Well, my monks shall
drink it, and they will be in heaven along with yours.'[9] Even within
the same monastery dietary practices were not the same. The *Rule of
Carthage* reads: 'Different is the condition of everyone . . . different
the law by which food is diminished or increased.'[10] Within Máel-
ruain's community each monk was ordered to 'regulate his pittance
for himself . . . as much as suffices him and does not induce sickness'.[11]
Thus the final decision was left to the individual monk, though the
abbot could dismiss those who grossly contravened his standards.[12] In

---

[8] [*The Monastery of Tallaght*, edd E. J.] Gwynn and [W. J.] Purton, *PRIA* 29 (1911) C
pp 115–79.

[9] *Ibid* cap 6, pp 129–30.

[10] Ed Mac Eclaise, *IER*, 4 series, 27 (1910) p 510.

[11] Gwynn and Purton, cap 63, p 152.

[12] [*The Penitential of*] *Vinnian*, in [*The Irish Penitentials*, ed L.] Bieler (Dublin 1963)
pp 74–95.

fact we hear little of such dismissals: on the contrary, Máel-ruain refused to accept an anchorite whose standards of dietary asceticism were so severe that he would have been unable to do his share of the community's work. Regular, measured austerity was encouraged: 'Eat not till you are hungry', 'Eat your due portion of food', 'He does not praise fasting: he prefers moderate eating always' are typical phrases from the rules.[13]

Fornication and gluttony were straightforward subjects for legislation. But self-discipline was to be applied to the spirit as well as to the flesh. 'What is to be followed? No doubt. Staying at penitence . . . patience at tribulations.' The monk was to pursue 'silence and piety, good humour without moodiness, without murmuring, without envy'. Sins were to be cured by their contrary virtues, so the idler was to be taxed with extraordinary work and the man who harboured bitterness was to be healed *hilari vultu et leto corde*.[14] 'Patience must arise for anger, kindness and the love of God and one's neighbour for envy, for detraction restraint or heart and tongue, for dejection spiritual joy, for greed liberality.'[15]

This was the training in sanctity within the monastery, and, as we have seen, even here something depended on individual initiative. But the monk could withdraw to the solitude of the desert. Such anchorites were often supported by the monastery, but their degree of asceticism would be according to their own judgement. The ideals put forward in the hermit poetry vary considerably – one enjoying salmon, trout, eggs, honey, beer and strawberries, while another confined himself to an 'unpalatable meagre diet', of bread and water.[16] The sanctity of the hermits of the ninth century was closely linked with a delight in the natural world, for in it the hermits recognised the splendour of God. So we have poems like this joyous stanza:

> Let us adore the Lord,
> Maker of wondrous works,
> Great bright heaven with its angels,
> The white-waved sea on earth.[17]

There is considerable freedom and independence behind poetry of this kind.

[13] Columba's *Rule* in *Councils and Ecclesiastical Documents*, edd A. W. Haddan and W. Stubbs, II (Oxford 1878) p 120; J. Strachan, *Ériu* 1 (Dublin 1904) p 194; O. Bergin, *Ériu* 2 (1905) p 224.
[14] *Penitential of Cummean*, cap 5, Bieler p 120.
[15] *Vinnian*, cap 29, Bieler p 84.   [16] Murphy nos 8, 9.   [17] *Ibid* no 4.

The Irish regarded the hermit life as a kind of pilgrimage. 'All alone in my little cell . . . such a pilgrimage would be dear to my heart' sang one.[18] But a monk might leave his monastery to go on pilgrimage overseas. If a man left his country and his land, his wealth and worldly delight for the sake of the Lord of the Elements, this was the 'perfect pilgrimage'.[19] It meant abandoning the security of home, where the religious had a definite and well-recognised legal status with all the protection that this implied, and going forth as an exile. The pilgrim was a guest of the world, without stability, with only a travelling allowance. He might set out on the seas without oars or rudder like those Irishmen whose arrival on the coasts of Cornwall was reported in 891 by the Anglo-Saxon chronicler; men 'who had stolen away because they wished for the love of God to be on pilgrimage, they cared not whither'. This was another form of Irish ascetic discipline, of how a saint was to be made.

By the late eighth century the Irish were very conscious of their own saints. They were drawing up long lists of them. The earliest major text, compiled by the end of the eighth century, is the *Martyrology of Tallaght*.[20] It has daily lists of continental saints based on the Hieronymian martyrology, followed by lists of native saints. There are hundreds of Irish saints here (over two hundred for the month of January alone), some of whom are no more than names. The compiler must have consulted the records of a large number of churches and made lists of the obits of abbots, *sapientes*, and other people whom the churches remembered and probably prayed for. His work is very probably the culmination of a process, for the *Martyrology of Tallaght* seems too complete to be a first attempt.

The *Martyrology of Oengus*,[21] compiled between 797 and 805, is based on *Tallaght*. It is right up to date, for the latest saint mentioned in it died in 792. It is in Irish verse, and has many fewer names than *Tallaght*. The foreign saints form the core of the compilation – like those three who on 17 May unyoked their chariots upon the hill of heaven, thus taking possession – but there are almost as many Irish saints. The martyrology itself is full of clichés, but it has a splendid prologue and epilogue, and it tells us very clearly what the Irish thought about their own saints.

[18] *Ibid* no 9.
[19] K. Hughes, 'The changing theory and practice of Irish pilgrimage', *JEH* 11 (1960) pp 143–51.
[20] Edd R. I. Best and H. J. Lawlor, *HBS* 68 (1931).
[21] Ed W. Stokes, *HBS* 29 (1905).

The saints are people who have suffered the tribulation of martyrdom or who have sustained a life of asceticism. Now they are the 'king-folk' around the Lord of the Seven Heavens, the King of the Bright Sun. Visiting the tombs of king Donnchad of Meath (who died in 797) or Bran, king of Leinster (who died in 795) has brought the poet no comfort, but a visit to Máel-ruain's grave (he died in 792) heals the sigh of every heart. The saints are the champions of God, who have driven the old gods from the land:

> Old cities of the pagans to which length of occupation
> has been refused are deserts without worship. . . .
> The little places settled by twos and threes are sanctuaries
> with throngs, with hundreds, with thousands.
> Paganism has been destroyed though it was splendid and
> far-flung; the kingdom of God the father has filled
> heaven and earth and sea.[22]

The poet himself hoped to be counted among the saints: 'May I be for ever with thy kingfolk, in thy eternal, glorious kingdom.' He hopes to have the good luck of the saints he has commemorated, though they are but 'a sip from the ocean'. His poem is a buckler of piety to be recited to procure merit, for the saints are a convoy to paradise.

The vision literature, the poetry and monastic rules show us Irish sanctity in theory and practice. When we come to consider the cult of relics,[23] sanctity becomes mixed with secularity. From about 700 on, the Irish church was enshrining its relics. Armagh in the eighth century had relics of the holy blood, of Peter and Paul, Stephen and Laurence; but the relics we hear most about are those of native saints. They had useful social functions: they added to the binding properties of a sworn oath, they were constantly used for healing. They were also carried round on circuit when the abbot made a visitation, to exact his tax, and to promulgate his patron's law. They could be carried into battle. They were a church's most precious possessions, a source of prestige and income as well as spiritual power. When the vikings shook the bones of Comgall from their shrine with impunity in 824, it must have seemed to the Irish that the accepted sanctions of society had collapsed.

---

[22] Trans D. Greene and F. O'Connor, *A Golden Treasury of Irish Poetry* (London/Melbourne/Toronto 1967) p 65.

[23] For the archaeological evidence for the cult of relics see M. J. O'Kelly, 'The Belt-Shrine from Moylough', *JRSAI* 95 (1965) pp 149–88; F. Henry, *Irish Art in the Early Christian Period to AD 800* (London 1965) pp 99 ff; C. Thomas, *The Early Christian Archaeology of North Britain* (Glasgow 1971) pp 132-66.

The relics show the saints as protectors of the faithful, pursuers of the impious, and also as tax collectors.

The hagiography also shows the saint in popular guise. He was first and foremost a miracle worker, for his ascetic life was accompanied by extraordinary phenomena and gave him unusual power. Adamnán's *Life of Columcille*,[24] written between 688 and 704 is divided into three books: the saint's miracles, his prophetic revelations and his angelic visions. Cogitosus's *Life of Brigit*[25] has a series of miracles of plenty, and shows a saint in harmony with nature, who has wild animals doing her bidding, who can hang her cloak on a sunbeam.[26] It is probable that by the time Cogitosus wrote, perhaps nearly two centuries after the saint's life, stories of her powers had become confused with memories of the heathen goddess Bríg. Dr Bernard Wailes's excavations at Knockaulin, five miles from Kildare, are revealing a pagan sanctuary which seems to have been dismantled fairly late in the iron age.[27] One cannot help speculating as to whether the pagan goddess Bríg was worshipped here.

In Muirchú's *Life*,[28] St Patrick is the hero, who worsts the king's druids in a series of contests. The pagan fire dwindles and dies while Patrick's fire leaps higher and higher. The insolent druid Lochru, who blasphemes against the faith, is caught up in the air and has his brains dashed out on a rock. Darkness and confusion descend on king Lóegaire's host, who are utterly routed. Patrick and his companions escape by turning into eight stags and a fawn. The king's druid brings snow, but Patrick makes it disappear; the druid brings darkness but Patrick disperses it with sun; the druid burns to death in a house of green wood, while Patrick's lad is safe in a house of dry wood. Patrick always has the victory.

In the saint's *Life* his asceticism is nearly always stressed, but even as early as the seventh-century account of Muirchú, Patrick is treated as a hero performing competitive deeds of prowess, a very different figure from the Patrick of the fifth-century *Confession* who, according to his own account, was denigrated, imprisoned, often in fear of his life, *unus de minimis*. The worldly qualities of the *Lives* usually become much more emphasised after about 900. This was approximately the date

---

[24] [Adamnán, *Life of Columcille*, edd A. O. and M. O.] Anderson (Edinburgh/London 1961).
[25] *PL* 62 (1863) cols 777 ff.
[26] *Ibid* col 777D.
[27] *Journal of the County Kildare Archaeological Society*, 14 (Naas, Kildare 1970) pp 507–17.
[28] *Tripartite Life* [*of St Patrick*, ed W.] Stokes (London 1887) II pp 269–300.

when the *Tripartite Life of Patrick* was composed.[29] This text, meant to be preached for the entertainment and instruction of the public on the three days of the saint's festival, is concerned to establish the power of the patron and to claim the churches which come under his jurisdiction. One of its leading sequences tells how, on Croagh Patrick, the saint fasts in order to extract terms from a reluctant God. God's representative is an angel, who is gradually driven to make more and more concessions, until in the end the angel is worsted and Patrick gains his full demands. Two of these are conventional demands: rescue of souls from the pains of hell (seven persons for every hair on the saint's chasuble) and special benefits for saying Patrick's hymn. The other two have a surprisingly nationalistic sound: no Saxons to dwell in Ireland, and all Irishmen to be judged at doomsday by their own saint, Patrick. The emphasis of many popular *Lives* is on the power of the saint rather than the power of God.

The acquisitive element in much later Irish hagiography seems to me evidence of secularity. That acquisitiveness has peculiarly Irish features, for it is often accompanied by boasting and rivalry which may have been intended to amuse the audience. An encounter between two heroes in secular saga may be preceded by a boasting match. The account of the expulsion of Mochuda from Rahen by a group of northern saints is a story of demands and concessions, boasts, threats, curses and violence. The saints of many of these late *Lives* appear as selfish, arrogant, unprincipled, blood-thirsty and self-seeking, devastating cursers; the very opposite of the notion of sanctity provided in monastic legislation. This does not seem to matter as long as the saint can protect his followers and worst his opponents. An Irish audience was prepared to pay for a good story and did not require literal truth. The Elizabethan jesuit Edmund Campion in his *Historie of Ireland* shows that this was still true in the sixteenth century. 'So light are they in believing whatsoever is with any countenance of gravitie affirmed by their Superiours, whom they esteeme and honour, that a lewd Prelate within these few yeares needy of money, was able to perswade his parish: That S. Patricke in striving with S. Peter to let an Irish Galloglass into Heaven, had his head broken with the keyes, for whose reliefe he obtained a collection.'[30]

What was happening to the discipline of a church which was pre-

29 Ed and trans Stokes, *Tripartite Life*; ed K. Mulchrone, *Bethu Phátraic* (Dublin 1939).
30 *Ancient Irish Histories. The Works of Spencer, Campion, Hanmer and Marleburrough* (Dublin 1809) p 25.

pared to advertise its saints in such a fashion? First of all it should be appreciated that the Irish church never had a standard practice. There was no *Benedictine Rule*, no powerful king or emperor to impose it. It would be quite as untrue to term the earlier period spiritual as it is to regard the later period as purely secular. There was what gregorian reformers would have described as a secular element in Irish monasticism from the very start, or at least from almost the start. Let us examine it.

The church first established in Ireland was an episcopal church organised in dioceses.[31] But the clergy, including the priests, might be married. This is clear from the earliest Irish ecclesiastical legislation which we possess.[32] The position seems to have been the same in sixth-century Britain. At Llansadwrn in south-east Anglesey there is a grave slab to *beatus Saturninus . . . et sua sancta coniunx.*[33] To the sixth-century christians there seemed nothing strange in coupling a man described as *beatus* with a wife described as *sancta*. At Llantrisant in north-west Anglesey a *sanctissima mulier* is named as the most loving wife of a man who is *famulus Dei* and *sacerdos.*[34] This is perfectly consistent with Gildas's evidence. It can be argued that these husbands and wives formed a joint household, without cohabiting, but this seems to me extremely unlikely when one considers the physical conditions of life – small huts without privacy – and remembers that in Ireland pre-christian society was polygamous. It is surely much more likely that the celtic church was just old-fashioned. Before the fourth century a married priesthood had been common elsewhere. I think therefore that we should not regard these early Irish married clergy as evidence for 'secularisation', for a worldly as opposed to a spiritual manner of life. On the contrary the Welsh inscriptions use words like 'blessed' and 'holy', while the Irish canon imposes strict rules, telling the cleric to see that he and his wife are properly dressed: if they do not conform to Roman practice they are both to be held in contempt by the laity and separated from the church. So the early Irish married priesthood seems to me irrelevant to our argument.

What of the *manaig*? This word means 'monks' and is translated *monachi*. The *monachi* appear frequently in seventh-century legislation.[35]

[31] For evidence see Hughes cap 5.   [32] Bieler p 54.

[33] V. E. Nash-Williams, *The Early Christian Monuments of Wales* (Cardiff 1950) pp 61–3.

[34] *Ibid* p 63.

[35] There is a considerable amount. See H. Wasserschleben, *Die irische Kanonensammlung* (Leipzig 1885) for the volume of canons known as the *Collectio Canonum Hibernensis*; see also Bieler. There are also, usually later, monastic rules.

Some are what we should call choir monks, men who perform the *opus dei*, man the monastic *scriptoria* and normally provide the monastic officials. But others are married laymen, living on the monastic lands and rendering tithes on produce and cattle. The monastery offers educational facilities for the sons of *manaig*; and the *manaig*, though they are subject to the abbot as lord (*dominus*), also have some rights over the monastic property, for they can invalidate a contract made by an abbot without their knowledge if they act within ten days. There is also evidence that, under certain circumstances, the *manaig* may provide an abbot from among their own number. Moreover, they are under ecclesiastical discipline, men of one wife and following quite severe sexual restrictions.[36] At Armagh we hear that they attend church on Sundays.[37]

Thus the *manaig*, though they were married laymen, were part of the family of the church. How did they ever come into existence? They do not seem to be a secularised version of the choir monks, for they fulfill a different function. We do not really know how monastic *paruchiae* came into being, but there is some evidence that families were making over their lands to the church.[38] In early Irish society family land could not be alienated without the consent of the kin. The *Life of Samson* tells how the saint's father and mother, five brothers and sister, his father's brother with his wife and three sons all dedicate themselves to the monastic life, making over their family property to church foundations. Adamnán's *Life of Columcille* refers to what seems to be a family monastery.[39] It is called 'Clocher of the sons of Daimen', and the story it tells is about the daughter of Daimen who lived there as a holy virgin, presumably alongside her kinsmen. When a sizeable family property was converted into a monastery did everyone living on the land follow the same kind of ascetic life, sharing the work and worship equally; or did some men continue to live with their wives, supporting the rest with their labour and produce?[40] The *manaig* were

---

[36] I take it that they must have been the laymen for whom some of the penitentials legislate. It is difficult to see how the church could hope to impose these sexual restrictions on the lay population at large where, if we are to believe the secular laws, polygamy was still recognised.

[37] *Book of the Angel, Book of Armagh*, ed J. Gwynn (Dublin/London 1913) fol 21a 1. For translation see Hughes p 277.

[38] See Hughes cap 7, and [K. Hughes,] *Early Christian Ireland[: Introduction to the Sources]* (London 1972) pp 71–5.

[39] II.5, Anderson p 336.

[40] We also hear of grants of land made to the church with the dependants who inhabited the land.

certainly well entrenched by the seventh century. They are a part of the Irish monastic system, and I do not think that they, any more than the earlier married priests, are necessary evidence for worldly standards in the church.

Kin was very important in early Irish society, so it is not surprising to find that it plays a prominent part in monastic administration. At Iona all the early abbots were celibate, but Reeves's genealogical tree shows that the first, second, third, fourth, fifth, seventh, eighth, ninth, eleventh and twelfth abbots were all inter-related, though some only distantly. This takes us from Columba's day to 724. Such practice cannot properly be called secularisation. There is, however, evidence in the eighth century and later for married abbots, and for sons succeeding their fathers in office. At Lusk we can see the same family holding major monastic offices for three generations – father, three sons and four grandsons, between 736 and 805.[41] At Slane two families shared the succession for nearly a hundred years, one covering four generations, the other three.[42] At Clonmacnoise, though the abbatial succession until 799 was free from hereditary influence,[43] between 835 and 1134 nine generations of one family occupied important roles within the monastery, bishop, *erenagh*, confessor, anchorite, head of the schools.[44] At Armagh from 966 until the twelfth century seven generations of the same family held the abbacy as married men.[45] When Cellach, one of these Clann tSínaich abbots, was elected in 1105, he changed the pattern by having himself ordained and living as a celibate ascetic. It was an accepted principle of Irish society that a son should follow his father's calling, and the poet's advice 'Let the abbot's son enter the church' seems to have been adopted in a number of monasteries.

All this is evidence for what a European medievalist might well regard as secularisation. But how far did hereditary succession mean the secularisation of standards within the church? It did not mean the cessation of ascetic religion. In the second half of the eighth century there was an ascetic reform within the Irish church which continued vigorously for nearly a century. The reformers called themselves *céli dé*, anglicised culdees, 'clients of God', men who had entered into a contract of *célsine*, 'clientship', serving God as their lord. They stressed the

---

[41] Hughes p 162 for the family tree.
[42] *Ibid* p 163.
[43] See *Féil-sgríbhinn Eóin mic Néill*, ed J. Ryan (Dublin 1940) pp 490–507.
[44] See J. Kelleher, *Ériu* 22 (1971), genealogy opposite p 126.
[45] With two short and doubtful intervals. See [T.] Ó Fiaich, ['The Church of Armagh under Lay Control',] *Seanchas Ardmhacha* 5 (Armagh 1969) pp 75–127.

performance of the liturgy (here they are comparable to the slightly later movement in carolingian Gaul) and emphasised ascetic discipline within the monastery. Some new houses of culdees were set up, but many of the old houses supported anchorites, who might be living singly or as a reformed group. There was no administration to perpetuate the reform once the age of enthusiasm had passed, and some anchorites seem later to be married men. But ascetic religion did not completely die out. The later poets pray: 'May I attain perfect companionship with thee, O Christ; may we be together.' 'Grant this to me, O king of the seven heavens, thy love in my soul and in my heart', 'May our waking, our work and our activity be holy', 'May thy holy spirit be about us, in us and with us', 'May my soul, O Lord, be full of love for thee', 'O my love, my God, may thy blood flow in my heart'.[46] These are not the utterances of people who are spiritually dead, yet some are by a man who lived at Armagh during the period of the Clann tSínaich lay abbots.

Nor does family succession seem to have affected learning adversely. Monasteries had always been proud of their *scriptoria* and schools, as we can see in the high honour-price which the scribe held in seventh-century law. The late eighth and early ninth century anchorite reform, when hermits prayed alone with nature, provides a possible background for nature poetry, an unusual theme in European literature of this date, and written in new lyric metres.[47] The strong lay element in the church probably encouraged the development of vernacular literature in the monasteries of the viking age. The annals turn from a latin to a vernacular record early in the ninth century. Two literary genres, the *Voyages* and *Visions*, reach their flowering in the period after 800. The splendid *Vision of Adamnán*, from which I quoted at the beginning of this paper, dates from the tenth or perhaps the eleventh century. The *Voyage of Brendan*, the most popular of all the voyages, is in latin, but there are other voyages in the vernacular. The *Voyage of Brendan* is an ecclesiastical text which embodies the Irish ideal of pilgrimage and the contemplative idea of religious perfection; for Brendan and his crew, trusting themselves to the Lord of the Elements, set sail and, on one

---

[46] The poems from which these phrases are extracted may all be read in Murphy.

[47] This was Flower's view. See R. Flower, 'The Two Eyes of Ireland', *The Church in Ireland 432–1932*, edd Bell and Emerson (Dublin 1932) pp 66–74. It was accepted in its main features by K. Jackson, *Early Celtic Nature Poetry* (Cambridge 1935) and by Murphy. More recently, however, D. Greene has regarded nature poetry as a tenth-century development, while J. Carney wishes to date some of the poems considerably earlier.

island, find the hermit Paul, who is the ascetic par excellence, *sicut avis in ista petra*. This phrase is reminiscent of the Irish poem on St Brigit:

> Victorious Brigit loved not the world:
> She sat the seat of a bird on a cliff.

So must the ascetic take up only a narrow ledge in this world, trusting in God for his security. The laymen in the monasteries admired the ascetic ideal, though it was not for them, and the monasteries encouraged literary production. Our three great codices (*Lebor na Huidre*, Bodleian MS Rawlinson B 502 and the *Book of Leinster*), which contain collections of secular and ecclesiastical texts, were written during the period when major attempts were being made to bring Irish church organisation into line with the European norm. They show how strongly the pre-Norman church had supported and encouraged vernacular literature, both sacred and profane.

To reformers in Europe simony was one of the most prominent aspects of secularisation. Yet there is really very little evidence for simony in pre-Norman Ireland. Irish texts do speak very occasionally about the misappropriation of church property[48] and, more frequently, of unsuitable men in ecclesiastical orders.[49] The *Vision of Mac Conglinne* refers to 'an ex-laymen in the chair of a bishop', and the sense of the whole poem is that this is a preposterously unsuitable appointment.[50] The reformers of 1101 in the first canon of the synod of Cashel require that there shall be no 'making reward [or traffic] of the church of God to an ex-layman or to an ex-cleric till doom'.[51] This is usually understood as a reference to simony, but if this is the case, why are only these two classes of persons designated? It could be understood as a decree against unsuitable appointments. There is, however, a passage in the last paragraph of the *Rule of the Céli Dé*[52] about wicked, proud *erenaghs* and wicked, greedy kings who violate the church and sell or buy her; so simony was presumably known in the Irish church. Yet it must have been to some extent irrelevant to the situation,[53] for well-established

---

[48] The *erenaghs* who are in hell for this in the *Vision of Adamnán*.

[49] *Rule of Patrick*, ed J. G. O'Keefe, *Ériu* I (1904) p 218; compare the *Rule of the Céli Dé*, ed E. J. Gwynn, *Hermathena*, second suppl vol (Dublin 1927) p 80; *Adomnan's Life of Columba*, edd A. O. and M. O. Anderson (London 1961) p 280.

[50] Ed K. Meyer (London 1892) p 73.

[51] A. Gwynn, *IER*, 5 series, 66 (1945) p 82: 'Gan cennach egailse Dé do athlaochaib na do aithcleirchib go brath', where 'cennach' means bargain, transaction, reward, recompense.

[52] This is missing from the *Rule of Patrick*, which seems to be a different version of the *Rule of the Céli Dé*.

[53] This point has been made by Ó Fiaich.

kindreds often dominated ecclesiastical appointments in their own churches. These were, however, frequently related to kings and local nobility, so that passage from a secular to an ecclesiastical group of the same kin was not difficult. Political influence undoubtedly determined some appointments. Regulations against unsuitable ordinations and appointments must therefore have been far more frequently needed than regulations against the outright purchase of office.

Ireland had its own special evils of secularity. One was quarrelling and rivalry within the monastery.[54] Columbanus, in the year 610, says that he has been almost driven mad by disagreements among the brethren.[55] Writing to his successor he advises him to be very tactful, and wary even of his supporters: 'You must fear their very love.' Hatred and love are both dangerous, for 'peace perishes in hatred, integrity in love'. *In odio pax, in amore integritas perit*: it is a very columban phrase. Here are quarrels right at the very beginning of monastic life, among a most devout group of ascetic monks. We need not therefore be surprised that the annals later frequently record quarrelling within monasteries. In 783, for example, there was a battle between the abbot and the steward at Ferns, in 762 a bishop was killed by a priest in the oratory of Kildare, there was a battle at Emain Macha near Armagh in 759 'at the will of Airechtach priest of Armagh through discord with abbot Fer-dá-crích'. Sometimes there was rivalry between kin groups for control of monastic offices. We have especially full sources for Armagh, and here, at the turn of the eighth and ninth century, we can see two successive abbots who were members of the Clann tSínaich, one of the leading families of Airthir, opposed by three rival claimants, one of whom had help from the Uí Cremthainn. Airthir and Uí Cremthainn were neighbouring sub-kingdoms, both parts of Airgialla, the over kingdom in which Armagh lay.[56] It looks as if sometimes abbots joined in the battles of their secular relatives. The annals tell of a 'destructive battle among the Airthera themselves' in 800, in which the abbot of Daire-Eithnigh was slain. Physical violence does not seem to have worried eighth- and ninth-century Irish ecclesiastics.

Monasteries also sometimes went to war with each other. There was a pitched battle between the monasteries of Clonmacnoise and Birr in 760, and another in 764 between Clonmacnoise and Durrow, in

[54] See Ó Fiaich p 106; Hughes pp 169–72.
[55] G. S. M. Walker, *Sancti Columbani Opera* (Dublin 1957) p 28.
[56] This is best expounded by Ó Fiaich.

which two hundred Durrow men fell. Clonfert and Cork fought each other in 807, when the noblest of the family of Cork were killed. Taghmon and the king of south Leinster fought Ferns in 817, and when that king died two years later he was *secnap* (prior) of Ferns. Kildare plundered Tallaght in 824. It seems to me that this violence and quarrelling is genuine evidence of secularity in the Irish church, of worldly as opposed to spiritual standards. It has been suggested that the lay element in Irish monasticism encouraged violence, but it is a notable fact that reports of battles within and between monasteries drop off in the viking age, though the lay element in Irish monasticism increases. I think the evidence suggests that Irish churchmen rather enjoyed a good fight among themselves, until the fighting assumed the terrible proportions of the ninth century. In the tenth century and later, Irish princes, influenced by viking methods, were themselves attacking churches to an ever-increasing extent.[57]

The 'secularity' of Irish violence is deep-seated. In the epic literature the standard by which the hero is judged is his prowess, and he has to prove prowess in physical contests. Violence, therefore, is normal and proper. The stories may go back to the iron age, but they were being written down, revised and re-told throughout the early christian period, yet with remarkably little christian influence. Moreover, the annals, written by clerics in a foreign genre, at first in latin, show that kings (and there were scores of them in early Ireland) were continually engaged in battles. So were the nobility. Violent deaths are constantly reported.[58] The idea that an honourable man must immediately fight to prove superiority was entrenched in Irish society, and however much christian teachers might preach the contrary, it was inevitable that it should sometimes express itself. When we think of the values implied in the secular literature and the *Annals* it is natural that fighting should be a specifically Irish form of secularity in the church.

The twelfth-century reformers, influenced by the gregorian reform, legislated against married lay abbots. They wanted celibate men in orders.[59] They took the by now conventional gregorian view of what

---

[57] For the evidence see *Early Christian Ireland* pp 148–59. Compare D. Ó Corráin, *Ireland before the Normans* (Dublin/London 1972) pp 85–7 for an interpretation of the evidence which is rather different in emphasis.

[58] I have discussed this much more fully in a paper to be published in the *New History of Ireland*.

[59] A. Gwynn, 'The first synod of Cashel', *IER*, 5 series, 66 (1945) pp 81–92; 67 (1946) pp 109-22. Compare Hughes pp 263 ff.

constituted secularity. St Bernard, in his *Life of Malachy*, speaks of the Irish as a barbarous people, of the fewness of her priests, and even they living in idleness and ease among the laity; he calls the Clann tSínaich abbots of Armagh a 'damned race', a 'viperous brood', 'an evil and adulterous generation'. But even St Bernard implies that holy anchorites existed in Malachy's youth, and admits that the lay abbots were men of learning. Though Malachy's appointment to Armagh was resisted by the Clann tSínaich, with their entrenched interests, the ascetic was able to go about his pastoral work. Malachy longed to be a martyr, but, as Bernard says, there was none to stretch out a hand against him. To Bernard the spectacle of married abbots was abhorrent, whereas in fact the Irish church had functioned successfully with its ecclesiastical kindreds for centuries.

The papacy shared St Bernard's view of the Irish. Alexander III, praising his dearest son the invading king Henry II, who was to win himself an imperishable crown of eternal glory and bring the Irish race to salvation by his conquest, refers to 'this barbarous and uncouth race which is ignorant of the divine law'. Irish marriage customs were particularly objectionable to the pope, foul and abominable practices. The people, says Alexander, have 'wandered unbridled through the paths of vice and, abjuring the practices of the christian faith, has torn itself with internecine slaughter'. The charge of internecine slaughter seems quite well justified; but medieval historians have sometimes been too ready to accept all the accusations by which the papacy sought to justify Henry II's invasion.[60] The men who wrote the devotional poetry of the twelfth century had sought and experienced the presence of God.

Secular, as distinct from lay, control of appointments, and its attendant evil simony, seems to be less prominent in the Irish church than elsewhere in the early middle ages. Irish lay abbots were churchmen, and often interested in learning. Irish secularity lay in faction fights, in violence and in the physical and economic rivalry of individual churches. At the same time these worldly men were glad to support the ascetics and scholars who brought prestige to their monasteries. And though I have necessarily been concentrating in the last half of this paper on the bad features of Irish monasticism, the practice of sanctity went on throughout the whole period of the early Irish church; sometimes with splendid enthusiasm, sometimes limping along, but always sustained. Reformers tend to be inaccurate witnesses about the people and institutions they supplant; and St Bernard and pope Alexander, from

[60] For these letters see *EHD* II pp 776–80.

whom some people seem to derive their ideas of the pre-Norman church, seem to me especially prejudiced ones. Alongside their evidence we have put the witnesses for genuine religion: the poetry, the vision and some of the voyage literature, the existence of men like Cellach and Malachy whom the old system threw up, even the satire, which shows at least that the Irish were aware of evils in their own system. We might conclude by remembering that it is a twelfth-century poet, at the end of our period, reflecting as a contemplative religious, who tells us why he loves Derry:

This is why I love Derry, it is so calm and bright;
for it is all full of white angels from one end
to the other.[61]

[61] Murphy p 68.

ROYAL SAINTS AND EARLY MEDIEVAL KINGSHIP

by JANET NELSON

THE problem I want briefly to focus on concerns the significance of the saint-king in early medieval cosmology: what is his relationship to the sacral king of so many pre-industrial societies?[1] A commonly-accepted view has been that the sacral king was, quite simply, the immediate ancestor of the saint-king. To quote the recent but in some respects old-fashioned work of W. A. Chaney on Anglo-Saxon kingship: 'The sacral nature of kingship. . . . would lead the folk to expect God to honour the *stirps regia*. The recognised form of this in the new religion was sainthood.'[2] Christianity, so Chaney implies, simply makes a saint out of the sacral king: in essentials, nothing is changed.

This view has been rightly challenged. But we need, if possible to go further, and to substitute an alternative general interpretation of the phenomenon of the saint-king. The task has been made easier by recent research. Two contributions seem particularly important. First I would like to consider a paper by the Polish scholar K. Gorski on 'The birth of states and the saint-king', published in 1968 but originally delivered in 1965.[3] In this short but penetrating study, Gorski suggested that the appearance of saint-kings in certain kingdoms of Scandinavia and eastern Europe could be used analytically as an index of progress towards state-formation. Royal cults reflect 'the potential of the power of early

---

[1] Amid a vast literature the following works are especially helpful, and provide further bibliographical references: R. Folz, 'Zur Frage der heiligen Könige', in *Deutsches Archiv* 14 (Weimar 1958) pp 317 ff; O. Nachtigall, 'Das sakrale Königtum bei Naturvolkern', in *Zeitschrift für Ethnologie* 83 (Berlin 1958) pp 34 ff; *The Sacral Kingship. Contributions to the VIIIth International Congress of the History of Religions* (Leiden 1959); [H.] Wolfram, ['Methodische Fragen zur Kritik am "Sakralen" Königtum'], in *Festschrift O. Höfler* (Vienna 1968) pp 473 ff; L. Makarius, 'Du roi magique au roi divin', in *Annales* 25 (1970) pp 668 ff.

[2] *The Cult of Kingship in Anglo-Saxon England* (Manchester 1970) p 81. Compare the review by R. Brentano in *Speculum* 47 (1972) pp 754 f.

[3] 'La naissance des états et le "roi-saint" ', in *L'Europe au IXe au XIe Siècles*, edd T. Manteuffel and A. Gieysztor (Warsaw 1968) pp 425 ff. I have translated the passages quoted from the original French.

medieval state organisations – a potential which the Church might or might not reinforce'. Gorski offered as an explanation of the differential incidence of saint-kings in the various nascent states, the relative strength of political power already attained and the correspondingly variable attitude of the church: in brief, where political power was weak, the church sought to strengthen it by promoting the cults of royal saints. The one country where no saint-king appeared – Poland – was characterised by a uniquely strong kingship at a rather early date, so that 'the Church, considering monarchical power as not only consolidated but even excessive and disposed to tyranny, was not inclined to venerate a saint-king upon its altars'.

The great merit of Gorski's approach is its concentration on the relationship of religious authority to political power. Thus, following the time-honoured gelasian principle, we recognise that there are two equally necessary parties to this case. But the flaw in the argument also seems clear: its misinterpretation of the functional relationship of the 'feudal Church' to secular power. To Gorski, the whole question presents itself as 'a problem of feudal ideology'. But whatever its relevance to eastern Europe between the ninth and eleventh centuries, this way of viewing the problem is less helpful for the early medieval west – where, after all, saint-kings first appear. We can only hope to explain their incidence (why, for example, in seventh-century, rather than eighth-century Northumbria? and why not in late ninth-century Francia?) by exploring their significance to those who cultivated them.

Gorski lamented the absence of any structural study of early medieval sanctity. But even as he spoke, the gap was being largely filled by the Czech, F. Graus, whose important work, *Volk, Herrscher und Heiliger* was published also in 1965. Here are exposed the essential characteristics of the early medieval concept of sanctity, as revealed in merovingian hagiography. In brief, sainthood was defined by reference to monastic-ascetic values and it was virtually monopolised by representatives of the monastic and clerical orders of society. Graus went on to examine the specific case of the saint-king, taking into account evidence from western Europe as a whole. Saint-kings, he concluded, fell into two main categories: those who abandoned their kingdoms to become monks; and those who died as 'martyrs', innocent and often unresisting victims, either in battle or at the hands of traitors. They were not saints in virtue of their royalty, but in spite of it.[4] They qualified for sainthood

---

[4] [F.] Graus. [*Volk, Herrscher und Heiliger im Reich der Merowinger*] (Prague 1965) pp 390 ff.

either through the act of renouncing the world, most spectacular in their case because they had most to lose, or through self-subjection to defeat and death, in a conspicuous reversal of normal values showing themselves lacking in *felicitas* or in that martial valour which fights to the death.

In the hierarchy of early medieval values, sanctity was therefore not only superior to all other statuses including that of kingship, but it was available only to those who had withdrawn from the *ordo secularis*. Sanctity and secularity were, in effect, mutually exclusive. To bring about a rapprochement between them was one of the main conceptual tasks facing the early medieval church. By the tenth century, the saint-queen[5] and the saint-nobleman[6] were achieving recognition as acceptable models of *this*-worldly sanctity displayed in 'everyday life'. But the saint-king presented considerably more difficulties. Even in the eleventh century, he was still presented by clerical biographers as a 'crowned monk'.[7] How are we to account for this delay in bringing him, so to speak, down to earth?

Graus rejected the notion that sacral kingship had any widespread existence at all in pre-christian western Europe.[8] But it seems to me that it is precisely the recognition of sacral traits in early medieval kingship which can help answer our question. Gorski had already made the significant observation that there was never any 'saint-emperor' in Byzantium. The point has been taken up by a byzantinist scholar, who objects that there was a peristently 'sacral' element in byzantine imperial power.[9] But there is an obvious misunderstanding here, arising at least in part from confused terminology: English seems to be the only language which not only distinguishes *sacral* from *sacred*,[10] but (unlike Greek, Latin, French or German) also has two separate words for the

---

5 For the *Vita* of queen Matilda, wife of Henry the Fowler and mother of Otto I, see Graus pp 410 ff. I am also indebted to suggestions made in conversation by Mr Karl Leyser.

6 For the *Vita* of Gerald of Aurillac, see D. Baker, 'Vir Dei: secular sanctity in the early tenth century', in *SCH* 8 (1972) pp 41 ff.

7 J. T. Rosenthal, 'Edward the Confessor and Robert the Pious: 11th Century kingship and biography', in *Medieval Studies* 33 (Toronto 1971) pp 7 ff, at p 11. See also [F.] Barlow, [*Edward the Confessor*] (London 1970) pp 256 ff.

8 For this debate, and the views of Höfler, Baetke and others, see Wolfram; also K. Hauck, *Goldbrakteaten aus Sievern* (Munich 1970) and now the perceptive comments of [J. M.] Wallace-Hadrill, [*Early Germanic Kingship in England and on the Continent*] (Oxford 1971) cap I.

9 See the short notice of Gorski's paper in *BZ* 61 (1968) p 184.

10 The German *sakral* is a very recent borrowing from English, where the term 'sacral' was coined by the pioneer anthropologists of the later nineteenth century.

substantive 'saint' and the adjective 'holy' (or 'sacred'). Sacrality involves the transmission of otherworldly powers into this world, crosscutting the line between nature and supernature. Sacral rulership therefore transcends the distinction between clerical and secular (in societies where such a distinction is made at all). It constitutes an ascribed not an achieved status, for its bearer possesses magical powers by definition. Nothing has to be proved or approved: sacrality goes with the job, is carried in the blood. There was nothing here to attract, and much to repel, the christian churchman attempting to construct a model of royal sanctity. The riskiness of the enterprise was clear when there were always 'some people', as William of Malmesbury anxiously noted, who would claim that Edward the Confessor's healing powers flowed *non ex sanctitate sed ex regalis prosapiae hereditate*.[11]

In the end, the church was able to come to terms with a saint-king who was the exponent of specifically royal virtues in the world of men, yet posed no threat to the clergy's working monopoly of sacral powers.[12] In the first place, the church developed its own objective and differentiated idea of useful rulership, whose type was the *rex iustus*. Wallace-Hadrill has recently suggested that Bede's kings, notably the *sanctissimus* Oswald, were already sketches for the church's eventual full-scale portrait of christian kingship.[13] With the eighth- and ninth-century development of the practice of royal anointing, along with its accompanying ideology, clerical theorists could present kingship as an office within the *ecclesia*, clerically-conferred (*per officium nostrae benedictionis*) and clerically-conditioned in content and exercise.[14] In principle, the suitable candidate required the approval of both clergy and people, and he could achieve his kingly status only through the

---

11 *Historia Regum* ed W. Stubbs, RS 90 (1887) II, i, p 273. See M. Bloch, *Les Rois Thaumaturges* (Strasbourg 1924).

12 We must take into account that strain in christian tradition which always regarded earthly power with misgivings. Compare Graus, p 432: 'Der heilige König ist in der Hagiographie nicht Garant des Wohlergehens, sondern zu seiner Schilderung wird ... nur der Topos vom goldenen Zeitalter verwendet. Diese "gehemmte" Entwicklung hat ihren letzten Grund wohl in der Erkenntnis kirchlicher Kreise, dass selbst ein "guter König" nur bedingt den "christlichen Idealen" entsprechen konnte.' Even in the eleventh century, Gregory VII repeated (*Reg* VIII, 21) the idea that royal dominion was the work of the devil – by that date, not such a common view. The origins of this specifically western line of christian political thought were clearly traced by W. H. C. Frend, *Martyrdom and Persecution in the Early Church* (London 1965).

13 Wallace-Hadrill, cap IV. Compare Graus, pp 416 ff, where too little account is taken of the positive and 'useful' aspect of Bede's image of kingship.

14 See W. Ullmann, *The Carolingian Renaissance and the Idea of Kingship* (London 1969). The quotation is from the crowning-prayer of Hincmar's *Ordo* for Louis the Stammerer, 877 (*MGH Capit*, II, 461) which reappeared in many subsequent *Ordines*.

sacral ministrations of the clergy. The anointing rite was the means whereby the *electus* was made, not replete with magical powers, but capable, through grace, of fulfilling his this-worldly royal function.[15] Once 'useful' qualifications were clear, the notion of 'useless' kingship too could acquire juristic definition;[16] and the so-called coronation-oath could become a constitutional check.[17] Thus the consecrated king was the church's model of desacralised rulership.

In the second place, the concept of sanctity itself[18] could be not only sharply differentiated from sacrality but turned against it. For what distinguishes a saint from a sacral or holy person is the very obvious, but crucial, fact that a saint is dead: it is his bones (real or believed) which are the object of a cult. The living determine the criteria of sanctity and establish the qualifications of the prospective saint. His life and/or death must be adjudged worthy, and his relics must be believed to work wonders. As the subject of a critical assessment, therefore, the saint must achieve and be assigned his status. However positively king-ship may be valued, if sanctity has to be earned and recognised there can be no sanctification of royalty *per se*. I cannot see the church's *auctoritas*, operated increasingly from the eleventh century as a papal monopoly,[19] functioning here as a simple adjunct of 'feudal' political institutions. Even if the initiative in promoting a saint's cult was usually clerical, popular acceptance was essential to its success. Cowdrey has shown in relation to the peace movement of the eleventh century how saints were summoned into cooperative action by clergy and people.[20] The general point is no less valid for royal saints in particular. It is significant that all but a few of these cults remained obscure and localised, while some, for example that of Edgar at Glastonbury, never got off the ground. Family interest and clerical support were not enough to guarantee long-term or widespread recognition:[21] a more public utility had to be demonstrated.

For royal saints, manipulated by the living, provided not just a model

---

[15] Compare my paper, 'National synods, kingship as office, and royal anointing', in *SCH* 7 (1971) pp 41 ff.

[16] See E. Peters, *The Shadow King* (New Haven 1970).

[17] See W. Ullmann, *Principles of Government and Politics in the Middle Ages* (London 1961) pp 143 ff, 186 ff.

[18] On the origins of the christian idea of the saint, see Graus, part III; A.-J. Festugière, *La Sainteté* (Paris 1949); and the penetrating remarks of P. Brown, *Religion and Society in the Age of St Augustine* (London 1972) p 142.

[19] See E. W. Kemp, *Canonisation and Authority in the Western Church* (Oxford 1948).

[20] 'The Peace and Truce of God in the Eleventh Century', in *PP* 46 (1970) pp 42 ff.

[21] Graus pp 390 ff; Wallace-Hadrill pp 81 ff.

but a yardstick of kingly conduct and performance in office. Such a tool was useful to other workmen than clerics and princes. Thus St Edward the Confessor was a potent figure in twelfth-century England less for propagandisers of beneficent royalty than for those who, in order to put limits on royalty's operations, were already making what Jolliffe so aptly termed the advance 'from law to politics'.[22] Even from the arch-example of a dynastic saint-king, Joinville points the following moral: Louis IX's canonisation 'has brought great honour to those of the good king's line who are like him in doing well, and equally dishonour to those descendants of his who will not follow him in good works. Great dishonour, I repeat [Joinville's emphasis is significant] to those of his line who choose to do evil. For men will point a finger at them and say that the saintly king from whom they have sprung would have shrunk from doing such wrong.'[23] The prediction was accurate: in 1314, Philip IV was forced by his subjects to confirm the liberties his saint-grandfather had allowed, just as in England a century earlier, Edward the Confessor's sanctity which 'was known to include the remission of taxes[24] was held up against the tyrannous king John. There is more than coincidence here: it was because the saint-king's past was *not* that of sacral kingship that he had at least a potential future as a symbol of constitutional monarchy.

22 J. E. A. Jolliffe, *Angevin Kingship* (London 1963). On St Edward, see [J. C.] Holt, [*Magna Carta*] (Cambridge 1965). J. C. Russell, 'The Canonization of opposition to the king in Angevin England', in *C. H. Haskins Anniversary Essays* (Boston 1929) pp 279 ff, comments interestingly on the implications for English royalty of the popular 'sanctification' of anti-royal leaders, without, however, noting that a saint-king could play a similar role.

23 *Chronicle of the Crusade of St Louis*, trans M. R. B. Shaw (London 1963).

24 Holt p 96. Compare Barlow pp 265 ff.

'THE SUREST ROAD TO HEAVEN': ASCETIC SPIRITUALITIES IN ENGLISH POST-CONQUEST RELIGIOUS LIFE

by DEREK BAKER

THAT the changes which occurred in the conduct of the regular and ascetic life in the eleventh century were deep seated has long been accepted, and their dependence on a fundamental reappraisal of the principles and practice of that life is clearly demonstrated by contemporaries. This 'crisis', as it has become normal to term it, was characterised by a rejection of the world and worldly values. In a general social context it can be seen in 'gregorian' ideas and attitudes on the relations between church and state, on the status and attributes of the clergy, and on the position and authority of the popes as individuals and the papacy as an institution. In the context of the regular life it is evident in a rejection of the formal round and ritual over-elaboration of monastic observance, and in an abhorrence of the complex inter-relationship and inter-dependence of monastic communities and the secular society in which they were set. When the papal legate Hugh, archbishop of Lyons, wrote to Robert of Molesme[1] accepting and authorising the abbot's proposed initiative he indicated where the issues and problems lay

> you and your sons, brethren of the community of Molesme, appeared before us at Lyons and pledged yourselves to follow from now on more strictly and more perfectly the rule of the most holy Benedict, which so far in that monastery you have observed poorly and neglectfully. Since it has been proven that because of many hindering circumstances you could not accomplish your aim in the aforementioned place, we . . . consider that it would be expedient for you to retire to another place which the divine munificence will point out to you and there serve the Lord undisturbedly in a more wholesome manner.[2]

[1] Trans [L. J.] Lekai, [*The White Monks*] (Okauchee 1953) pp 252–3.
[2] *Ibid.*

So it was, as the *Exordium* recalls, that some twenty-one monks, 'devoted to the rule', left Molesme and

> happily started on their way to the hermitage (*heremum*) which was named Cîteaux. This area ... was inhabited only by wild animals, since it was a wilderness of dense woods and thorny thickets, impenetrable for humans. Here then came the men of God and the more they discovered it to be depised and unapproachable by worldly men the more they found this place suited for their religious life as they had first intended and for which reason they had come there. After they had cut down the woods and removed the dense thorny thickets they began to build a monastery there under the approval of the bishop of Châlons and with the permission of the landlord. These men, while still living in Molesme and inspired by divine grace, often spoke, complained and lamented among themselves over the transgression of the rule of St Benedict, the father of monks. They realised that they themselves and the other monks had not at all observed it, even though they had promised by solemn vow to follow the rule. That was the reason why they came into this solitude by the authority of the legate of the apostolic see, namely to fulfil their vows through the observation of the holy rule.[3]

The aim of these first cistercians was, as Paschal II noted,[4] to leave not simply 'the broad paths of the world', but also 'the less strict paths of a laxer monastery'. Like St Benedict they proposed to establish themselves 'in places remote from the traffic of men',[5] staying aloof from the doings of the world 'which should not have any place in the actions or in the hearts of monks, who, in fleeing the world, ought to live up to the etymology of their name'.[6] In all this the primitive community of Cîteaux was characteristic of the ascetic experiments of the time, and for all that the *Exordium* lays dramatic stress upon the failure of the New Monastery to attract recruits the 'unprecedented rigour'[7] of the life at Cîteaux and elsewhere was to make a powerful appeal to all classes of society, to 'literate clerics as well as laymen who were in the world as powerful as they were distinguished',[8] and to the rank and file who constituted the army of lay brethren.

In considering this development, and in evaluating these phenomena,

---

[3] *Ibid* p 253.   [4] *Ibid* p 261.   [5] *Ibid* p 264.
[6] *Ibid* p 263.   [7] *Ibid* p 264.   [8] *Ibid* p 265.

it is all too easy to over-simplify and, in consequence, to distort. However austere and uncompromising the ideals of these new desert fathers, however general the flight to the desert, there could be no total rejection of the world. As one author has recently emphasised, 'when historians write of the church as if it could be separated from secular history they are simply repeating the mistake made by medieval ecclesiastical reformers, who were never more clearly the captives of their environment than when they spoke of their freedom from it'.[9] Wherever we look in this period of spiritual experiment and ecclesiastical renewal the world intrudes. If it is most immediately evident in the creation of a papal monarchy, it is none the less clearly to be seen in the formation of the microcosmic elements of christian society. The influence of professional, ecclesiastical and family relationships on the administration of patronage and the incidence of benefaction is plain not simply with older black monk communities, but with the newer orders of canons and monks.[10] In similar fashion such relationships infiltrate and condition the conduct of more strictly ecclesiastical matters. Promotion and advancement even amongst the new orders, are not entirely unconnected with birth and family connections,[11] and in the dispute at York over the election of a successor to archbishop Thurstan, one of the great ecclesiastical issues of the first half of the twelfth century, the attitudes and actions of the representatives of the new elements in the religious life of the north of England were not unaffected by what may fairly be termed the 'secular' issues of capitular rivalry, personal and community interest and family influence.[12] The most obvious demonstration of the conjunction of spiritual and secular, however, is to be found in the phenomenal success of all the new orders. 'Great success depended on great benefactors with the right kind of property',[13] and to potential benefactors the new orders offered considerable returns on investment. The suitability and economic usefulness of these communities on the expanding frontiers, and in the wastelands, of christendom, the pastoral utility of the canonical way of life and, above all, the spiritual prestige, and consequential powers of intercession, of the reformed way of life commended the new orders to patrons and benefactors all over Europe. Of Cîteaux William of

---

9 [R. W.] Southern, *Western Society [and the Church in the Middle Ages]* (London 1970) pp 1–2.

10 See, for example, J. C. Dickinson, *The Origins of the Austin Canons* (London 1950).

11 See Jocelin of Furness, *Vita Sancti Waldeni*, and [Derek Baker], '*Viri religiosi* [and the York election dispute]', *SCH* 7 (1971) pp 90–4.

12 See *Viri religiosi*.   13 Southern, *Western Society* p 261.

Malmesbury remarked[14] that it was 'so translucent from the abundant piety of its monks that it is not undeservedly esteemed to know God himself'. Cistercians were 'a model for all monks, a mirror for the diligent, a spur to the indolent'. The cistercian order was 'the surest road to heaven'.[15] It is small wonder that St Bernard saw no need to justify his description of Clairvaux as the new Jerusalem, and the monks left behind at Molesme are witnesses to the striking impression made by the new way of life even at its very inception – 'they had no hope that peace and quiet could return to the community of Molesme'[16] unless their former abbot was returned to them. They complained of 'the sad conditions and the ruin' of Molesme, and stressed that 'the regular life in their monastery has declined and that they have become hated by the princes and other neighbours'.[17] The evidence for the early patronage of Cîteaux by Odo, duke of Burgundy,[18] lends point to their complaint and gives substance to their fears: it also indicates how difficult it was for men like the first cistercians to escape the world, however much they might want to. Patrons, benefactors and disciples sought them out, and in so doing forced change and development upon them.

The extraordinary success of the new orders is unmistakable, but it is questionable whether their founders would have regarded such phenomenal expansion as the necessary and natural outcome of their aspirations, or even as desirable. In about 1080 the future founder of the Chartreuse discussed with some friends their plans to leave 'the false lures and perishable riches of this world'. Bruno alone, in fact, persevered in his resolve, and twenty-five years later wrote from his ascetic retreat in Calabria 'I live the life of a hermit far from the haunts of men . . . [and] await the Lord's return in holy watching, that, when He knocketh, [I] may open to Him immediately . . . only they who have experienced the solitude and silence of a hermitage know what profit and holy joy it confers on those who love to dwell there'.[19] The ideal, as in the Egyptian deserts of St Antony's day, or in the practice of the early Irish church,[20] was one of renunciation of all social and family ties, and dedication to the service and worship of God. Everything was determined by the divine will. Irish saints embarked on their *peregrinatio*, on their 'voyages', trusting solely to the divine providence to direct

---

[14] Trans *EHD* II p 695. [15] *Ibid* p 697. [16] Lekai p 255.
[17] *Ibid* pp 254–5. [18] *Ibid* pp 253–4.
[19] Trans R. W. Southern, *The Making of the Middle Ages* (London 1953) pp 167–8.
[20] See above pp 21–37.

48

their wanderings. The trials which the hermit endured, the relief and miraculous sustenance he was granted, derived from an inscrutable providence to which he had totally abdicated all personal choice and individual freewill.[21] In St Benedict's phrase, the hermit went out 'to the solitary combat of the desert ... able now to live without the help of others, and by [his] own strength and God's assistance to fight against the temptations of mind and body'.[22] For those who embraced the desert life of austerity and asceticism, whether in total seclusion or in company with others – in the forest of Craon, at the Chartreuse, at Cîteaux – social or institutional success was not simply irrelevant, it was abhorrent: inimical to the existence of the ideal itself. The Norman knight Reinfrid, one of the trio who restored regular life in the north of England, went north 'to lead the solitary life'.[23] His companion Aldwin 'placed voluntary poverty and contempt of the world above all worldly honours and riches' and both men left Jarrow when it attracted recruits and patrons. At Whitby, where Reinfrid next settled, he was found by Stephen of Whitby with a few disciples 'leading the life of hermits', but once again success caught up with him, and he sought obscurity in the abdication of any responsibility for the growing community. Such examples could be multiplied – Adam, whose abbacy at Meaux was a disaster for the community, resigned his charge and established himself as an anchorite under the church at Watton; Gervase, abbot of Louth Park, who resigned in 1149 lamenting his lack of ability, was described as a man 'unwilling to undertake any extraneous responsibility, desirous always of serving rather than ruling'. It was not, however, that such a man was simply incompetent – his career gives the lie to that view – rather, like abbot Richard II of Fountains, *tota aviditate suspiratur ad heremum*, and there could be little desert stillness for men who administered these struggling communities. The example of their ascetic life, the emulation it inspired, the disciples it attracted, placed men like Reinfrid and Gervase in an intolerable position: there could be no satisfactory reconciliation of the individual life of devotion to which their consciences directed them and the burden of responsibility, spiritual no less than administrative, which the growth of communities created, and the patronage of spiritually minded bishops and pious laymen aggravated. Richard II of Fountains was forced, so the historian of the abbey

[21] *Ibid.*
[22] *The Rule of St Benedict*, ed and trans J. McCann (London 1952) I, p 15.
[23] For Reinfrid, and discussion of the ascetic impulses of the northern revival see [Derek Baker,] 'The desert in the north', *NH* 5 (1970) pp 1–11.

tells us, to adopt the role of Martha when all he really wanted was to sit at Christ's feet like Mary: in company with many of his contemporaries *spiritualibus siquidem deliciis deditus, occupationes moleste admisit.*

It is impossible not to sympathise with this predicament, and, in consequence, to tend to view this period in the development of the religious life as one in which the dynamic individual asceticism of the eleventh century is increasingly debased and formalised within the new religious institutions of the twelfth century. There is, of course, much truth in this view – it is difficult to imagine how the observance of primitive Cîteaux could have been maintained in the enormous community at Rievaulx in Ailred's day, and the serious problems he inherited when he became abbot come as no surprise – but it is altogether too simple an analysis, and one that does little justice to the spiritual diversity of the time.

Alexander, first abbot of Kirkstall (1147), ruled his community on its first, unsatisfactory site at Barnoldswick for six years before a chance meeting with a group of hermits established at Kirkstall enabled him to gain both a better site for his own community and recruits to the cistercian way of life. The historian of Kirkstall gives a circumstantial account of the arguments by which Alexander was able to win over Seleth and his companions – 'he began therefore to admonish them gently about the salvation and advantage of their souls, pointing out to them the dangers inherent in self-will and lack of numbers, the perils of being disciples without a master, laymen without a priest, persuading them to a greater perfection and better form of religion'.[24] What is of interest here is not Alexander's business sense, but his view of what constituted the *maiorem perfectionem et meliorem formam religionis.* He is not, as might seem at first sight, denying the merits of the eremitical vocation. He is suggesting that it can be better followed in his small austere community where self-will can be given direction by men trained and instructed in the ascetic life, by spiritual masters. This is a spiritual attitude which is concerned for order and orthodoxy within the ascetic life, and prepared to accept responsibility for it. It may be far removed from the exclusive isolation of an Antony in his inner mountain, but it is no less spiritual for that, and it is wholly Benedictine. It is perhaps worth emphasising that the desert has its place in St Benedict's rule, while stressing that the spirituality which Alexander exemplifies is an ascetic, eremitical spirituality of the world, outward as well as

[24] *Fundacio Abbathie de Kyrkestall,* ed E. K. Clark, *Thoresby Society* 4 (Leeds 1895).

inward looking, purposeful, and shaped and conditioned by the world
it rejected.

Symeon of Durham is clear that Aldwin, Reinfrid and Aelfwig left
Evesham in order to seek a life of poverty and seclusion in the wastes of
Northumbria, but it is worth examining the background to their
expedition, and the assumptions on which it rested, further. Reinfrid,
we are told, was influenced towards a religious life by his visit to the
deserted ruins of Whitby in 1069, but his monastic vocation was not
realised until he entered Evesham in 1070[25]. The background to the
revival is, in fact, to be found in the vigorous life of the communities
ruled by Wulfstan of Worcester and Aethelwig of Evesham. They
were 'the last representatives of the old monastic life, peculiarly national
in character',[26] and it was not unnatural that in them the traditions of
the great age of Anglo-Saxon christianity should be cherished and
studied, and that from them should come the initiative to restore the
religious life of Bede's Northumbria. With Aldwin, the prior of
Winchcombe, we are told that it was his reading of Bede which directed
him to the deserted northern shrines, and though Reinfrid's first-hand
experience of northern conditions, and his previous connection with
the Percy family, made him a useful and natural recruit for such a
venture there can be little doubt that his participation was inspired by
what he had learnt at Evesham. This historical conditioning was decisive, for it directed the party, and their disciples, to particular sites –
Monkchester, Jarrow, Melrose, Wearmouth, Whitby – and though the
northern revival has been compared to the eremitical movements which
produced Camaldoli, the Chartreuse or Cîteaux,[27] it stands in fact in
sharp contrast to them. The northern revival was not the result of
random ascetic inspiration, but was shaped by history and tradition.
Its sites were not remote, like Cîteaux inaccessible to men, but associated with local communities and their lords. Nor was the life itself
strictly eremitical. Aldwin and Reinfrid might wish to lead a poor and
solitary life, but amongst the very little which they took with them from
Evesham were vestments and liturgical books. They sought to re-
establish regular communities, and from the first they accepted recruits
and instructed them: Aldwin, as Symeon of Durham records, was
'always yearning towards heavenly things, and taking thither such as
would follow him'. Their poverty and seclusion were relative. If they

25 See 'The desert in the north'.
26 [David Knowles, *The*]M[*onastic*] O[*rder in England*] (2 ed Cambridge 1963) p 193.
27 *Ibid* p 167.

fled from the commitments and burdens inherent in the rule of rapidly
developing communities like Jarrow or Whitby there can be no doubt
that they accepted unquestionably a form of communal poverty and
asceticism in accordance with the English benedictine tradition in
which they were trained, and centred on the historic sites of the Anglo-
Saxon church.

It was the actual business of leadership, the administration and
mundane responsibility, which men like Aldwin rejected: spiritual
direction, if only it could have been exercised in isolation, was not
anathema to them. For other men, however, there was little or no
conflict. To them the regulation of a community in all its aspects was
both natural and necessary. There was a natural acceptance by such
men of the principles and essential forms of the life which they had
chosen, to which they were accustomed and in which they had been
trained, and there was a positive sense of duty and obligation which
made the assumption of responsibility instinctive. The ablest amongst
them were able to control, shape and direct all the demands made upon
them: the less able were not infrequently driven to despair. Alexander
of Kirkstall, brother of the sacrist of St Mary's, York, was prior of
Fountains before he became abbot of Kirkstall. His competence, his
ability to cope, are his most striking characteristics and, as we have seen,
he had a clear understanding of the necessity for instruction and direction in the endeavour to achieve the 'better and more perfect life'.
Richard, first abbot of Fountains, had been prior of St Mary's, York, *in
quo tota pene monasterii cura pendebat.* He was *prudens in exterioribus,
amicus potentium.* His abilities marked him out. He attended the legate
Alberic of Ostia in 1138, and accompanied him back to Rome in 1139,
charged with important business at the papal curia by archbishop
Thurstan. Yet, as the historian of Fountains records, he was a man of
real spiritual example – *homo religiosus et timens Deum.* Like archbishop
Bardo of Mainz, 'although . . . accustomed to a life of contemplation
at the feet of God, yet he showed himself to have experience in practical
affairs, imitating Him Who . . . assumed the veil of the flesh and was
manifest in human form.'[28] Godric of Finchale testified to the sanctity
of Robert, first abbot of Newminster, but the ability of the saint to
repair the devastation of his house within six weeks of its foundation,

[28] See Derek Baker, 'The Foundation of Fountains Abbey' *NH* 4 (1969) pp 29–43; 'The
desert in the north' pp 6–11; *Vita Bardonis,* cap 6, *MGH, SS* 11, p 325, trans in [G.]
Tellenbach, [*Church, State and Christian Society at the Time of the Investiture Contest*],
trans R. F. Bennett (Oxford 1940) p 51.

and to establish three daughter houses by 1148 demonstrates a happy conjunction of spiritual and practical qualities.

Nor is it only in men like Alexander, Richard and Robert, on whom the cares of abbacy sat lightly, that spiritual impulse and practical concern cohabit. Adam of Meaux, a veteran of the northern revival, had supervised the building of Kirkstead, Woburn and Vaudey before accepting election as abbot of Meaux in 1150. Gervase, first abbot of Louth Park, had been sub-prior of St Mary's, York, Richard, second abbot of Fountains, sacrist of the same house and the first leader of the reforming group there. Men like these, who all protested or demonstrated their insufficiency, and resigned or sought to resign their responsibilities, were not so much crushed by the encroaching cares of an intrusive world as overcome by the day-to-day demands of their way of life. The burdens which overwhelmed them were of their own making. They arose from an ordering of the regular life which was not questioned, and which automatically accompanied the move from the old to the new, from St Mary's to Fountains. Like Aldwin, Gervase, Adam and Richard II accepted the structure they knew, and like him were prepared to accept responsibility within it – but a limited responsibility, giving priority to the spiritual life and the individual vocation. It was unfortunate for them that they were called upon to direct poor, struggling communities, on difficult sites, and established in the uncomfortable years of anarchy and dispute in church and state: when Richard II's abbacy is set against the complexities of the York election dispute it is scarcely surprising that he tried so hard to resign his charge. Yet for all his protestations, and those of Gervase, it must be emphasised that they are community ascetics: they are not cast in the same mould as Seleth and his companions, or as those whom Bernold of St Blasien condemned – 'those who believe that they are excepted from the pains of excommunication because, being monks and religious and having fled the world, they are not subject to the spiritual shepherds'.[29]

Not all those numbered amongst the first leaders of the new orders had derived their basic social and spiritual standards from a training and education in a religious community. Some entered the religious life trained and experienced in the outside world, and amongst these the most outstanding was the future abbot of Rievaulx, Ailred.[30] Ailred's

---

[29] See Tellenbach p 46.
[30] See Walter Daniel, *Life of Ailred*, ed and trans F. M. Powicke (Edinburgh 1950); R. L. G. Ritchie, *The Normans in Scotland* (Edinburgh 1954) pp 246–55; Ailred,

spiritual qualities and his deep spiritual concern are amply chronicled in
the pages of his biographer, and in those of his own works. From the
moment of his decisive and by no means tranquil conversion his delight
in the primitive cistercian life is self-evident – 'Self-will has no scope;
there is no moment for idleness or dissipation. . . . Everywhere peace,
everywhere serenity, and a marvellous freedom from the tumult of the
world . . . no perfection expressed in the words of the gospel or of the
apostles, or in the writings of the fathers, or in the sayings of the monks
of old, is wanting to our order and our way of life.'[31] But this is no
desert solitude. Ailred's Rievaulx is a community of saints, allowing
scope for the individual vocation but only within a well-ordered and
strongly disciplined framework of life. There might be 'a marvellous
freedom from the tumult of the world' but Rievaulx was a world of its
own, and it was the disciplined fervour and example of the community
which attracted Ailred to it. For all Ailred's own ascetic practices, and
his friendship with hermits, he never sought to adopt the hermit life
himself. Communal life was natural to him, and he was a man of the
world in a way which his friend Waldef was not. There is no need to
rehearse Ailred's career here, but it may be noted, in spite of Walter
Daniel's hagiographical account, that up until he entered Rievaulx he
exhibited little more than conventional piety. His family background,
his education at the Scottish court, his familiarity with the royal house,
and his preferment and employment in the royal service foreshadow a
distinguished secular career and testify to his abilities and character. He
was a man to be trusted, capable, used to responsibility, familiar with
the processes of contemporary government at its highest level. These
were qualities which he took into Rievaulx with him, and they were
soon recognised and employed, both by his own community and
within the wider concerns of his order. There can be no doubt as to his
spiritual vocation, or to the quality of his own life in religion, but his
background and training made social involvement natural for him. He
had been trained for leadership and responsibility, he expected to
exercise it, and there can be little doubt that the community, not the
hermitage, was his proper environment.

Ailred is, of course, exceptional in the qualities he combined and the
example he demonstrated. His friend Waldef, with his uncertainties and
irresolution, is probably a more typical example of the spirituality

De Anima, ed C. H. Talbot, Medieval and Renaissance Studies, Suppl 1 (London 1952).
[31] Trans MO pp 220-1.

54

of the time, though he too was reckoned a saint. Even with an Ailred, however, there is a tendency to place this communal asceticism and spirituality at a lower level than that of the hermit. Some contemporaries might mock the hermit for his arrogance –

> John to an angel turned him,
> He contemplates the doors of Heaven,
> And men no more concern him.[32]

– but Hugh of Flavigny placed hermits immediately after the apostles in the order of precedence at the last judgement, while for William of St Benigne 'the contemplation of God is the only thing to which all works of justification and all striving after virtue are inferior'.[33] Once lesser men than Ailred are considered the tendency to classify in this way is strengthened. Ralph Haget's discourses might be edifying for the monks he ruled at Fountains, but they were scarcely gems of spiritual counsel, or evidence of any deep and extended thought. If the formal and fully developed treatment of the 'Joys of the Virgin Mary' by another English cistercian abbot is considered the picture is not really changed. Stephen of Easton,[34] a monk of Fountains, is first seen as cellarer of his house, then successively as abbot of Sawley, Newminster and, finally, Fountains, dying in 1252. He had a certain reputation for holiness – miracles were associated with his tomb – and his preferment indicates his practical qualities. Otherwise he is unremarkable. He was not notable either as a scholar or as a theologian, and seems to have received only the normal monastic education within his community. His fifteen *Meditations on the Joys of the Virgin Mary*, with their subdivision into three groups of five, and the tripartite arrangement of each meditation into *meditatio, gaudium* and *peticio*, have nothing of any profundity to say. As his editor remarked 'our author cannot be counted amongst the writers of note',[35] and it is difficult to see what sort of benefit could have been derived from his *Meditations*. If Stephen of Sawley can be taken to stand for the norm of cistercian ascetic spirituality then it is difficult to deny that it, and the life it represents, is inferior to the eremitical example, and a sad demonstration of what follows from allowing the world to intrude into the realms of the spirit. Yet for all the formal banality of the *Meditations* there is a quality of

---

[32] Trans H. Waddell, *The Wandering Scholars* p 90.
[33] See Tellenbach p 44.
[34] See [A.] Wilmart, [*Auteurs spirituels et textes dévôts du moyen âge latin*] (Paris 1971) pp 317–60, 'Les méditations d'Étienne de Salley sur les Joies de la Vierge Marie',
[35] *Ibid* p 323.

human concern and involvement which commends them, and which contrasts favourably with the intensely self-centred asceticism of the hermit. Stephen of Sawley writes, he says, because he has been asked to by one of his monks. Such an attribution is, our course, conventional, and collections of similar meditations were not uncommon. There is, however, sufficient indication in the *Meditations* to suggest that this was in fact the case, and to suggest why he should have been asked to write. Stephen of Sawley's interest in the circumstances of Christ's life is an intensely human one, and displays a sensitive personal awareness of the relations of mother and son – 'Mary is honoured, exalted, invoked not for herself but because of her privileged, and special relationship with the Son of God made man'.[36] In emphasising the human aspects of this relationship Stephen of Sawley made it intelligible and accessible to his monks, and it is likely that in their first form his *Meditations* were the substance of spiritual instruction given by him to his monks verbatim, and sufficiently striking for him to be asked to give them a more permanent, literary form.

Stephen of Sawley may be 'a man of the second rank', simply 'a convinced and modest religious', but at that level he is representative of spiritual qualities which find more striking expression in the *Pastoral Prayer* of Ailred.[37] No paraphrase can do justice to the eloquence and fervour of the language in which Ailred seeks divine assistance and forgiveness. He asks for his faults to be rectified, his wounds healed, for the gift of the holy spirit, for strength in his labours and his vigils. In all this, however, he speaks as the poor and useless shepherd, concerned not simply for himself but for the sheep entrusted to him, and the prayer reaches its climax in a great and extended plea for God's assistance and direction in all the manifold tasks he must undertake –

> Doce me itaque dulcis domine corripere inquietos, consolari pusillanimes, suscipere infirmos, et unicuique pro natura, pro moribus, pro affectione, pro capacitate, pro simplicitate, pro loco et tempore, sicut tu videris expedire, memetipsum conformare. . . .

It is impossible to read the whole prayer without feeling that there is a different dimension to the spirituality it embodies. Ailred is too remarkable a figure to be wholly representative, but his prayer may speak for a spiritual attitude which finds more normal expression in men like Richard of Fountains or Stephen of Sawley.

[36] See [A.] Wilmart p 330.
[37] Wilmart pp 287–98, 'L'oraison pastorale de l'abbé Aelred'.

The surest road to heaven

There were, essentially, two ascetic spiritualities to be found in the revived religious life of the post-conquest north of England. One, the true life of the desert, without rule or support, and centred on the individual search for and devotion to God is represented by men like Seleth. Others, like Reinfrid or Gervase of Louth Park who were drawn to that ideal found themselves frustrated and hindered in its pursuit and practice by their acceptance of the conventions and forms of the life in which they had been trained, and by the forces of tradition. The other was an ideal which did not seek to achieve total seclusion for the individual, but recognised a need and a duty for spiritual instruction and leadership. Within the structures of the reformed ascetic monasticism of the twelfth century men like Ailred sought the spiritual salvation of the many. Such an ideal is likely to seem more attractive and more 'useful', in the context of christian society as a whole, but it could also seem less exalted – 'sanctity . . . was available only to those who had withdrawn from the *ordo secularis*. Sanctity and secularity were, in effect, mutually exclusive'.[38] This is the crux of the matter. Can sanctity be achieved, the divine will obeyed, only by the individual's flight from the world? Or was it possible to transform, to spiritualise the world itself by ascetic endeavour and example within it? In the ascetic spirituality which Ailred represents there was a dynamism and potential lacking in the desert withdrawal of an Antony. There may be little that is remarkable in the *Meditations* of Stephen of Sawley, but in their attempt to make Christ accessible to the ordinary religious through His humanity, and His filial relationship to Mary they contributed to the creation of a general holy family of all christians, and indicated 'the surest road to heaven'.

[38] See above p 41.

THE BLESSINGS OF WORK:
THE CISTERCIAN VIEW

by CHRISTOPHER J. HOLDSWORTH

AROUND 1180 Conrad of Eberbach writing about the history of his own order, the cistercian, noticed that it had been founded the year before Jerusalem was freed from the saracens and close to the beginning of the carthusian and premonstratensian orders.[1] This seemed to him a significant cluster of events, for as the holy city was restored to the christians, so the orders of monks, hermits and canons were being brought back to their old and proper ways of life by the new orders. Whilst today we may find Conrad's chronology a little puzzling (La Grande Chartreuse and Prémontré were founded in 1084 and 1120, Cîteaux in 1098, whilst Jerusalem was freed in 1099), we can recognise that the first cistercians were aware that they were attempting a new thing; they called their first home at Cîteaux the New Monastery, thus distinguishing it from Molesmes, the old monastery from which they had come, and from the monastic world at large.[2]

The degree to which the first white monks had a programme in the first two decades of their experiment has been debated all over Europe in a plethora of periodicals during the past twenty years.[3] I must, therefore, make clear at the outset that I do not intend to wade far into what at times appears as bottomless and depressing a pit as the Slough of Despond. What, I would suggest, has emerged from the debate is that the new monks did not spring like Minervas from the head of their Zeus, Molesmes, clad in the whole armour of the discipline and customs with which they were armed by the middle of the twelfth century. Instead, these things were assumed in response to the opportunities and difficulties which they met over the years. Such a general

---

[1] *Exordium Parvum*, ed B. Griesser, *Series Scriptorum S. Ordinis Cisterciensis* II (Rome 1961) bk I, cap 19, p 73.

[2] J. Marilier, *Chartes et Documents concernant l'abbaye de Cîteaux, 1098–1182, Bibliotheca Cistercienses* I (Rome 1961) pp 22–7.

[3] For a clear summary to 1963 see M. D. Knowles, *Great Historical Enterprises* (London 1962) pp 197–224, and [The] *Monastic Order* [*in England*] (2 ed Cambridge 1963) pp 752–3. Subsequent contributions are noticed in *ASOC*, *RB*, and *SM*.

picture of the way a religious institution develops seems to me much more inherently likely than the old picture which had Stephen Harding, almost as a latter-day Moses, handing tablets with the *Carta Caritatis*, *Instituta* and *Consuetudines* upon them, down to his flock almost overnight. Perhaps, one may conjecture, without being discourteous to continental scholars, that some of the misunderstandings created, and oddly rigid claims made, in the last years have sprung from the innate preconceptions of individuals who themselves live in societies which have fundamental laws and constitutions produced within very short times. Perhaps on this side of the channel historians, who have lived for a long time with the idea that the original English constitution was a *chimera*, have not been so surprised to contemplate the possibility of there not being much to the original cistercian constitution. But all this is not to say that those first voluntary exiles from Molesmes had no aim at all and all scholars would, I believe, accept that a letter of Hugh, archbishop of Lyons, written probably in 1097, gives an authentic account of its essence.[4] The letter is addressed to Robert abbot of Molesmes and to 'those brothers who desire with him to serve God according to the rule of St Benedict'. It goes on to say that Hugh understood that the group wished to cleave to the rule more strenuously and more perfectly, not it should be underlined to follow the rule *au pied de la lettre*: later this note does sound sometimes in cistercian circles, but it was not there at first. Here in the first two sentences of a letter written by a sympathetic outsider we may see the kernel of a new way of life, from which indeed some things followed over the years which could not be found in the rule to which these pioneers wished to cleave.

It cannot be doubted, however, that they read the rule to mean that manual work was a proper activity for a monk and that a monastery should attempt to live by the fruit of its own labour. Fairly quickly the New Monastery found that the other demands of monastic life, the *opus Dei* and giving opportunity for private prayer and reading, could not be fulfilled if the monks were to provide for themselves without any assistance. It was to meet this need that they made use of an institution, the lay brotherhood, which was not without precedents among other groups, but which received its greatest development among them.[5] At the same time they also used lay paid servants.

[4] P. Claudius Noschitzka, 'Codex manuscriptus 31 Bibliothecae Universitatis Labacensis', *ASOC* (1950) pp 7–8.
[5] Jacques Dubois, 'L'Institution des Convers au XIIe siècle. Forme de vie monastique propre aux laics', in *I Laici* [*Nella 'Societas Christiana' dei Secoli XI e XII*] (Univ del

The blessings of work: the cistercian view

Everyone knows how successful this new work-force was in enabling the white monks to bring into cultivation land on the edges of cultivation, which suited their desire to live far from the temptations and disturbances of centres of population.[6] The desert which they had sought for spiritual reasons often contained places which could be made extremely fertile, so that their barns and store houses filled up with corn and wool. The purpose of this paper is not to go over this well-tilled ground again but to plough a differently angled furrow: whether work with their hands had any effects upon their spirituality, and whether this in turn had any significance in changing attitudes in wider circles. This is a question which as far as I can see, has not been much explored by English scholars, although I am very conscious that on the continent it has.[7] I cannot claim a high degree of originality therefore for my approach, but I hope it may contribute to the theme of 'secularity and sanctity' which the Society is exploring this year.

In a recent survey one of the best-read scholars in the field, Jean Leclercq, has stated that manual work was one of the most important features of cistercian ascetic practise and that it was in writing of manual work that cistercian authors spoke with characteristic vehemence and regularity.[8] This opinion might lead one to believe that white monks devoted specific books to the discussion of manual work, which is not the case; the lineaments of their teaching have to be drawn normally from writings whose general aim was wider. Nonetheless it is possible to reconstruct the main contours of this teaching with a fair degree of confidence from the testimony of a number of writers, all at work between *c.* 1120 and the end of the twelfth century, who reinforce each other.

In the first place manual work appeared to them as an intrinsic part of the life of poverty which they had freely embraced, since having given up all their own possessions they had to work if they were not to

---

Sacro Cuore, Milan 1968, being *Miscellanea del Centro di Studi Medioevali* 5) pp 183–261. There is a useful summary of the literature about origins in Knowles, *Monastic Order* pp 754–5.

[6] Colin Platt, *The Monastic Grange in Medieval England* (London 1969) *passim*.

[7] I owe most to J. Leclercq, 'Comment vivaient les frères convers', in *I Laici* pp 152–76. It also appears in *ASOC* 21 (1965) pp 239–58 which itself depends on E. Mikkers, 'L'idéal religieux des frères convers dans l'Ordre de Cîteaux aux XIIe et XIIIe siècle', *COCR*, 24 (1962) pp 113–29, and Dom Othon (Ducourneau). 'De l'Institution et des Us des convers dans l'Ordre de Cîteaux', in *St Bernard et son temps* II, Assoc. bourguignonne des sociétés savantes, Congres de 1927 (Dijon 1928) pp 139–201.

[8] J. Leclercq, F. Vandenbrouke, Louis Bouyer, *La Spiritualité du Moyen Age* (Paris 1961) pp 270–1.

be a charge on others. The model for them was Christ who, as St Bernard put it, had given up everything for them, and so they had put aside all their own possessions to be free to follow him wherever he led.[9] The unknown author of the *Exordium Parvum*, using a phrase which echoes St Paul, the rule and St Jerome, said that they were 'new soldiers of Christ, poor like Christ himself'.[10] Taking a wider setting, that of sinful humanity, Isaac of Stella showed that work was a part of the lot of mankind since God had said to Adam 'In the sweat of thy face shalt thou eat bread' (Genesis 3: 19) and so by working the cistercian expressed his solidarity with all men who, like Adam, were outside paradise.[11] Isaac went on to develop this theme by saying that their manual work was modelled on that of the penitent Adam, whilst for the fact that they had servants and flocks they had a model in the life of the patriarchs of the Old Testament: 'Our fathers, as someone said, were shepherds of sheep.'[12] This appeal to biblical precedent, which may not strike us today as peculiar, may, I would suggest, have sounded odd in an age which tended to spiritualise the people of the Old Testament, and even the New too, into types and figures of spiritual truths,[13] but clearly for Isaac, who here speaks for many other cistercians, Adam, Isaac the patriarch, and Jacob gave the mark of authenticity to their own experiment with the apostolic life. Isaac also pointed out in this same sermon that he and his fellows worked hard so that they could give to others the more fully, so following that monition of Jesus only recorded by Paul 'It is more blessed to give, than to receive' (Acts 20: 35).[14] Their predecessors indeed practised hospitality, he said, and were rewarded with the visit of angels – an allusion, one may hazard, not only to Lot or Tobias but also to the classical story of Philemon and Baucis.[15] What was the purpose of this daily work, which weakened the body and also provided for it, asked Gilbert

---

9 *S. Bernardi Opera*, [edd J. Leclercq, H. Rochais,] V (Rome 1968) *Sermo in Feria IV Hebdomodae Sanctae* 12, p 65.

10 *Exordium Parvum*, cap XV, ed C. Noschitzka, *ASOC* 6 (1950) p 14.

11 *Sermo L in Nativitate Petri et Pauli*, PL 194 (1855) col 1858. The whole sermon is analysed by Leclercq 'Le travail: ascèse sociale d'après Isaac de l'Etoile', *COCR* 33 (1971) pp 159–66.

12 Col 1860.

13 Beryl Smalley, *The Study of the Bible in the Middle Ages* (2 ed Oxford 1952) pp 242–63, and see the essay by C. S. Lewis, 'The Literary Impact of the Authorised Version' in *They Asked for a Paper* (London 1962) pp 26–50, esp pp 28–30.

14 *PL* 194 (1855) col 1861.

15 Gen. 19:1 ff; Tobit 5:5 ff; *Metamorphoses* VIII, 611 ff. There is a nice version from Melrose in Jocelyn of Furness, *Vita Waldeni*, ASB, August, I, pp 262–3.

of Hoyland? 'The fruits of their hands not only feed the workers, but the little there is is shared with the needy, so that their labour may to some degree provide for others.'[16] Manual work was therefore a proper activity for those who had freely embraced a life which included a place for it, and were not labouring under what Ailred of Rievaulx called 'the curse of the peasants', that is to say who had not been forced to work willy-nilly.[17] One may note, incidentally, how Ailred brought out in his lives of two noble christians who lived in the world, David of Scotland and Edward the Confessor, that whilst one made a place in his life for gardening, the other's elderly widow, Edith, besides occupying herself with reading, also worked with her hands.[18] Gardening and needlework perhaps could just pass as gentle acts in the twelfth century; ploughing, typically in Conquest England the work of slaves, and stock-rearing could not.[19] One may note, incidentally, that those of noble birth did not always find agricultural work easy. St Bernard's first biographer tells of him weeping because he did not know how to cut corn, a scene which to the modern reader irresistibly summons up Tolstoy's picture of Levin trying to scythe hay.[20] But the author of the famous *Dialogue of a Cluniac and a Cistercian* in typically aggressive mood wrote 'We give ourselves to rustic work which God himself created and instituted.'[21]

But what did the cistercians say to those who protested that the first duty of a monk was to pray and to move into that state of calm in which they could attend to God? In the first place, they claimed that just because someone was working with their hands it did not mean that they could not be praying or intent on God at the same time. In the *Dialogue* just referred to, for example, the cistercian claims that as he and his fellows work they sing psalms, feel compunction and weep, the last a very traditional function of the monastic order.[22] Arnulf of Bohéries writing around the turn of the twelfth and thirteenth centuries said that the monk had to think not about *what* he was doing when he worked, but why he was doing it – dangerous advice one might think if followed literally when herding cattle.[23] 'Happy is the

[16] *Sermo 33 in C[antica] C[anticorum]*, 3 : PL 184 (1854) col 120.
[17] *Speculum Caritatis ii*, 15, *Aelredi Rievallensis Opera Omnia*, edd A. Hoste and C. H. Talbot, I, *Corpus Christianorum Continuatio Mediaevalis*, I (Turnholt 1971) p 83.
[18] Aelred Squire, *Aelred [of Rievaulx A Study]* (London 1969) pp 86, 97.
[19] H. R. Loyn, *Anglo-Saxon England and the Norman Conquest* (London 1962) p 349.
[20] William of St. Thierry, *Vita Prima S. Bernardi*, PL 185 (1855) cols 240–1.
[21] *Dialogus [inter Cluniacensem monachum et Cisterciensem]*, edd E. Martène and U. Durand, *Thesaurus novus anecdotorum*, V (Paris 1717) col 1623.
[22] *Dialogus*, col 1624. [23] *Speculum Monachorum*, PL 184 (1854) col 1175.

man', exclaimed Guerric of Igny, 'who in all his labour and travels seeks the blessed rest' and who draws his mind back to the peace and quiet of the Spirit from the many distractions of business.[24] Perhaps more realistically Gilbert of Hoyland said that it was in the intervals of work that the feelings of the spirit would take wing, so that among the weary-bodied workers there would be those who wept silently, while others would sigh or groan and those who felt no urge to spiritual things would find themselves stimulated by the example of others.[25] It is difficult, of course, to know how often such an exercise, reminiscent of the sighs and exclamations of the very different pentecostal groups, or of the camp meetings of revivalist churches, ever actually took place, but that this kind of thing was expected cannot be doubted from both cistercian sources themselves and from some testimony produced outside the order.

In particular, again and again, cistercian writers spoke of the positive value of the alternance of work and contemplation, as a kind of rhythm which would enable the soul to come closer to God. St Bernard, for example, taking as his starting point the words of Job (7: 4) 'When I lie down, I say, When shall I arise, and the night be gone? and I am full of tossings to and fro unto the dawning of the day', wrote 'Resting in the evening of contemplation he longs for the morning when he will rise to action, whilst on the other hand, exhausted with his labours he longs for the evening, willingly turning again to the calm of contemplation.'[26] Elsewhere in one of his sermons on the *Song of Songs* he suggested that man, whilst in the body, could only bear the strain of contemplation briefly, whilst his continuator, Gilbert of Hoyland, suggested that the alternance of work and contemplation served to make the presence of Christ known more fully.[27] 'You will preserve your mind more fruitfully when Christ has withdrawn, by the merits of good works. . . . Fastings are varied with food, work by rests, vigils by sleep. This alternation assists the refreshment [of the soul], not its collapse.' *Vicissitudo refectionem affert, non defectum.*

A great deal of the cistercian discussion of the relationship between manual work and the contemplative life takes place in the form of a discussion of the roles of Martha and Mary, the sisters of Lazarus. Traditionally, at least since the time of St Augustine, they had been taken as

---

[24] *Sermo III in Assumptione B. Mariae* 2, PL 185 (1855) col 194.
[25] *Sermo 23 in CC* 3, PL 184 (1854) cols 120–1.
[26] *S. Bernardi Opera* VI pt 1, *De Diversis* III, 4, p 89.
[27] *Ibid* II, *Sermo 51 in CC* I, 2, p 85; Gilbert, *Sermo 43 in CC* 9, PL 184 (1854) col 230.

types of the active and contemplative lives.[28] Usually until the twelfth century Martha stood for the active life concerned with the pastoral functions of preaching and the care of souls, whilst Mary stood for the people who had devoted themselves entirely to the life of prayer and waiting on God. In monastic circles it was assumed that monks had chosen Mary's part and there was, therefore, little discussion of the relationship between the roles of action and contemplation as far as monks were concerned.[29] But for the white monks the problem was a real one, and the group at Bethany often appear in their writings, sometimes in close association with Laban's daughters, Leah and Rachel the wives of Jacob; Leah being paired with Martha, the fruitful actives, whilst Rachel is paired with Mary, the sterile contemplatives.[30] Sometimes the group are discussed in the traditional context, that is to say in the relationship between pastoral responsibility and the life of prayer, a divided pull which cistercian abbots felt with as much anguish as had St Gregory, for example; sometimes they come into the discussion of the problems facing monks who are called to other offices within the monastery. Here we are merely concerned with the relationship between work and contemplation.

In the first place cistercian writers pointed out that Mary's life depended upon the work of Martha, someone had to sweep the house and clean the dishes if Mary and Jesus were to talk together uninterruptedly.[31] Action indeed was the thing which came first, before contemplation, in the growth of the soul, and St Bernard found symbolic justification for this idea in the fact that it was Martha, not Mary, who received Jesus in the house.[32] The sisters should be like good companions, *contubernales*, he said elsewhere.[33] This idea is developed further by Ailred who places the sisters within each soul and linked this association with the whole meaning of the life which St Benedict prescribed for his followers:

> Realise, brethren, that never in this life should these two women be separated. When the time comes that Jesus is no longer poor,

[28] Cuthbert Butler, *Western Mysticism* (2 ed London 1926) pp 159-60. Compare the *Glossa Ordinaria*, PL 114 (1879) col 287.

[29] J. Leclercq, 'Contemplation et Vie Contemplative du VIe au XIIe siècle' in DS II.2 (1950), cols 1929-48; the article by J-M. Déchanet, 'La Contemplation au XIIe siècle', cols 1948-66 is also useful. M. L. Merton, 'Action and Contemplation in St Bernard', COCR, 15 (1953) pp 26-31, 203-16; 16 (1954) pp 105-21 is suggestive.

[30] Compare Luke 10: 38-42, Gen. 29: 16 ff.

[31] Guerric of Igny, *Sermo III in Assumptione*, 2 PL 185 (1855) col 194.

[32] *S. Bernardi Opera*, V, *In Assumptione B. Mariae, Sermo III*, 1, pp 238-9.

[33] *S. Bernardi Opera*, II, *Sermo 51 in CC I*, 2, p 85.

or hungry, or thirsty, and can no longer be tempted, then Mary alone, that is, spiritual activity, will take over the whole house of the soul. This St Benedict, or rather the Holy Spirit in St Benedict, saw. This is why he did not confine himself to saying and laying it down that we should be occupied with reading like Mary, while passing over work such as Martha does; but recommended both to us, and set aside definite times for the work of Martha, and definite times for that of Mary.[34]

Aelred Squire, whose translation I have just used, points out that in this passage Ailred was claiming that St Benedict had quite deliberately provided for that alternation, or balance, which was so constructive for the soul. The same point was made by a man who probably joined the community at Rievaulx under abbot Silvanus, Ailred's successor. Writing to a friend still in the world, Matthew the precentor commended the cistercian way of life because it imitated both Mary and Martha: like the former they contemplated and like Martha they worked. 'And so', he said, 'at certain regular times work gives place to contemplation and contemplation to work, so that contemplation does not impede work, nor work disrupt contemplation.'[35]

Thus far I have spoken primarily of the ideas which cistercian monks had about the spiritual value of work and before turning to some discussion of the effects this attitude may have had on others, I must turn to the lay brothers. It must be admitted at the outset that direct evidence of the thoughts and feelings of lay brothers is lacking. Nearly all of them were illiterate and as time went on recruits who had sufficient letters to follow services in choir, or were not thought too old to learn, passed into the ranks of the monks. We have, therefore, to depend on what monks wrote about lay brothers, and it must be admitted that the reporting process could have distorted things. A second difficulty has been raised by a recent critic, Van Dijk, who has expressed fundamental scepticism about the possibility that many lay brothers could have had any positive attitude about the work which dominated their lives. He seems to have reached his view because he holds that most of those who might have taught the lay brothers would not have been concerned to give any positive value to earthly activity.[36]

34 *Sermo XVIII in Assumptione B. Mariae*, PL 195 (1855) col 306, as translated by Aelred Squire, *Aelred* p 56.
35 [A.] Wilmart, 'Les Mélanges [de Mathieu Préchantre de Rievaulx au début du XIIIe siècle',] *RB* 52 (1940) p 74.
36 Clemens Van Dijk, 'L'instruction et la culture des frères convers dans les premiers siècles de l'Ordre de Cîteaux', *COCR* 24 (1964) p 254.

Such a conclusion does not seem to me to tally with the views about manual work which I have just described, and although St Bernard and Ailred may not have been typical of abbots in the grace of their lives and the interest of their ideas, they were moulded by the same monastic discipline as their fellows. Van Dijk's scepticism need not, therefore, command our assent, but one certainly has to be aware that what we know of the lay brothers comes through a monkish filter. Most material comes indeed from two great collections of stories about the order: the *Exordium Magnum* by Conrad of Eberbach already referred to and the *Dialogus Miraculorum* by Caesarius of Heisterbach.[37]

One of the most striking stories told by Conrad is of a lay brother, a ploughman at Clairvaux, who dreamt one night that Christ was with him in the field holding the goad with which the oxen were urged on as they pulled the plough.[38] To an English reader the prefiguration of Piers is extremely striking, and it is scarcely necessary to draw out the way the story expresses part of the truth about the value of work in terms accessible to a layman. Caesarius, for his part, has a series of stories about Simon a lay brother at Aulne who was blessed with the gift of seeing into the condition of others, which Caesarius called prophetic.[39] The significant thing for the present is to remark that he commented Simon had this spiritual gift because he had administered earthly things in his care, he was master of a grange, with prudence.[40] One could mention many stories which, while not arising so obviously out of manual work, make the point that lay brothers saw visions or received various types of blessing in the intervals of their busy life.[41] These seem to me to carry the general message that a life which was after all almost entirely spent toiling in the fields was acceptable to God. Their work had its significance and reward. Admittedly this sort of evidence cannot be used in a fashionable manner to quantify the number of lay brothers there were say around 1200 who did see things so clearly, but I would suggest that those who doubt whether many lay brothers could have regarded their labours in a spiritual light have to take a very cynical view of the motives which led people to become lay brothers. Undoubtedly some joined because they were in need, hoping to be fed, clothed and housed in a relatively easy environment,

[37] Ed J. Strange (Cologne 1851) 2 vols. There is an English translation by H. von E. Scott and C. C. Swinton Bland, 2 vols (London 1929).
[38] *Exordium Magnum*, dist IV, cap 18, pp 243–4.
[39] *Dialogus Miraculorum*, dist 3, cap xxxiii, ed Strange i, pp 150–6.
[40] *Ibid* i, p 151.
[41] For example *Dialogus Miraculorum*, dist 7, caps xii, xiii, lii, ed Strange ii, pp 151, 6, 73.

and it was presumably among this group that the leaders of riots were found,[42] but to deny to most lay brothers a positive view of the principle activity of their own life seems to me to remove what must have been the one motive which could have kept them going.

The originality of the cistercian attitude to manual work becomes clear if it is set against the attitude prevailing in monastic circles in the twelfth century. This attitude was affected by three things, the type of work monks did, the demands of the monastic life, and the literary tradition about manual work. Broadly speaking after the time of Benedict of Aniane it was very rare for monks to work in the fields, less rarely they were occupied for some period in domestic work, or at producing say metal work or some other craft work.[43] Increasingly, however, from the foundation of Cluny onwards, the only work shared in by monks was the *opus Dei*, which came to fill more and more of the hours of darkness as well as those of light. Anything else became exceptional and distinctly secondary in importance, so that it does not surprise one to find not a single reference to field or garden work being a 'common exercise' among English black monks in the twelfth century.[44] The literary tradition provided ample reinforcement for the disappearance of manual work from the monk's life since it conveyed the idea that it was not fit for free men because contact with matter was soiling. The liberal arts on the contrary were the proper field of action for the free man: agriculture, one of the *opera servile*, was only for the serf. It was because manual work was degrading that it was supposed to stop on Sundays and holy days, lest they were defamed.[45] This, if taken to extremes, is obviously nonsensical: certain animals have to be cared for whatever the day of the week, but this is merely to underline how remote from life some theorists of the liberal arts could be. We find a good reflection of this attitude in a dialogue written by Adam of Dryburgh, where the soul and reason argue over the usefulness of manual work for those who have adopted a rule of life, the religious men.[46] The soul protests that such are not serfs who can properly engage in servile and coarse tasks (*operibus vilibus et servilibus*). Even in cistercian circles there were those whose upbringing had made them not merely, like Bernard, unskilled when faced with certain jobs, but unwilling to do them. There was, for example, the lay

42 Knowles, *Monastic Order* p 660.
43 *Ibid* p 27.   44 *Ibid* p 467.
45 M-D. Chenu, 'Arts "mécaniques" et œuvres serviles', *Revue des sciences philosophiques et théologiques*, 29 (Paris 1940) pp 313–15.
46 *Soliloquium de Instructione Anime*, bk 1, cap 8, PL 198 (1855) cols 855–6.

brother, who seems to have joined the order in his old age, who was put in charge of the pigs and complained that he was well-born yet because of the vile task he had been given was despised by all his friends.[47] Also revealing, but in another way, is the story of the man who had been a benedictine for twenty years and then moved to Clairvaux, where he was astonished to see 'so many wise, noble and gently raised men' exerting themselves through the heat of the day to get the harvest gathered.[48]

A good deal of the traditional attitude to manual work emerges in the responses of the black monks to the challenge presented to them by the whole cistercian way of life and by the polemics of the white monks, of which St Bernard's *Apologia* is the most famous. Peter the Venerable, for example, argued that as long as monks were occupied in good works, which he pointed out did not just mean manual work, and so avoided that laziness which St Benedict had said was a danger to the soul, all was well.[49] No one could claim that the rule was broken as long as *otiositas* had been put to flight. Another form of special pleading is offered by Rupert of Deutz who tries to deduce that Benedict did not actually prescribe manual work from the fact that when regulating the hours of meals and fasts St Benedict allows for the contingency that they may not have field work to do: *si labores agrorum non habent monachi . . .*[50] According to him Benedict only allowed manual work where the monks did not have other means of livelihood available; where such resources existed there was no need for monks to work. The battle is carried into the enemy's camp with characteristic verve by Hugh of Amiens, sometime prior of Lewes and abbot of Reading.[51] He paints an ironic picture of the cistercians going out into the fields where they are refreshed by the delightful scenery, 'now by the fields richly coloured with wild flowers, now by green woods planted with beautiful shrubs', in the midst of which their ears are ravished by the choirs of birds *delectabilem efficiens armoniam*. 'O what a hard and

---

47 *Dialogus Miraculorum*, dist 4, cap iv, ed Strange i, p 205.
48 *Exordium Magnum*, dist iv, cap 13, pp 176–7.
49 *Epistola*, bk I, no xxviii, *PL* 189 (1890) col 128. The reference is to [*S. Benedicti*] *Regula*, cap XLVIII. Peter's view is discussed by David Knowles, in 'Cistercians and Cluniacs', in *The Historian and Character* (Cambridge 1963) pp 50–75.
50 *Regula*, cap XLI; Rupert of Deutz, *In Regulam S. Benedicti*, bk 3, cap IV, *PL* 170 (1894) col 513.
51 [A. Wilmart,] 'Une riposte [de l'ancien monachisme au manifeste de S. Bernard'], *RB* 46 (1934) p 335. Compare J. Leclercq, 'Une nouvelle réponse de l'ancien monachisme aux critiques des Cisterciens', *RB* 57 (1957) pp 77–94 for another reply probably produced in the mid-twelfth century in England.

unbearable Order it is,' he exclaims. The Canterbury monk, Nigel Wireker, surveying the different forms of religious life through the eyes of his ass, Burnellus, reached an opposite estimate.[52] The cistercian life is not for him because there is no calm, *otium*, there: he would have to work all the time. *Otium*, or its plural *otia*, was one of the favourite words used for the opportunity which the monastic life should provide to be open to God.[53] In the *Dialogue*, the Cluniac is made to say, by a cistercian author admittedly, but here he truthfully reflects the situation, that he has chosen *sanctum otium* with Mary and is dedicated to the contemplative life.[54]

Among the premonstratensians, the order of canons founded not so very long after the cistercians, a slightly more positive view was taken of manual work. Their way of life, was after all, very much influenced by Cîteaux and the canons were expected to do some manual work.[55] Adam of Dryburgh in the work already referred to comes down in favour of manual work having value for religious men but on the traditional ground, admitted by Peter the Venerable for example, that it keeps idleness at bay and so prevents the devil finding work for idle hands to do.[56] He adds a vague statement that some holy men have also commended work because it satisfies the needs of the body and helps the soul achieve purity, but there is not much of a spirituality of work here.[57] One should note, however, that like the cistercians, though not for entirely the same reasons, the white canons associated lay brothers with them. One of the most famous canons, Anselm of Havelberg, described their life as a bearing the yoke of Christ and a 'labouring with their hands and in penitential habit crucifying their flesh with its vices and fleshly desires'.[58] As far as I know not much has yet been discovered which would give one any idea about how the premonstratensian lay brothers regarded their own life, but they should not be excluded from having a place alongside the cistercians in changing attitudes to work.

At this point I move on to the other side of the furrow which I hope

---

52 *Nigel de Longchamps Speculum Stultorum*, edd John H. Mozley and Robert R. Raymo (Berkeley Calif 1960) p 78.
53 J. Leclercq, *Otia Monastica. Etudes sur le vocabulaire de la contemplation au moyen âge, SA*, 51 (1963).
54 *Dialogus*, col 1574.
55 [H. M.] Colvin, [*The White Canons in England*] (Oxford 1951) pp 360–2.
56 *PL* 198 (1855) col 856, compare *PL* 189 (1890) col 128.
57 Compare F. Petit. *La Spiritualité des Prémontrés au XIIᵉ et XIIIᵉ siècles* (Paris 1947) where manual work is scarcely mentioned.
58 Cited by Colvin p 360.

to plough: did the cistercian attitude to manual work have an effect on ideas beyond the confines of the order? I have just drawn attention to cistercian influence on another group of religious, the regular canons of Prémontré, and to these one can add the purely English order of the Gilbertines whose lay brothers followed a way of life modelled upon that of the cistercians.[59] It is well known, also, that within the cluniac family changes were made during the life of Peter the Venerable which gave some place to manual work.[60] The practice, therefore, did spread, but a spirituality of work was not much developed in monastic circles, except by the cistercians. But if we turn outside monastic circles we certainly find signs of what that pioneering French art historian Emile Mâle called the 'Glorification of Manual Labour'.[61] He drew attention to the labours of the months which are found over the portals of churches like Chartres, Paris and Rheims, in the thirteenth century, where the typical tasks of the rural community are, as it were, hallowed, along with the signs of the zodiac which represent the months. It seems to me interesting that before the twelfth century these labours only appear in books, they do not enter into the physical church. This negative argument should perhaps not be pushed too far, but I think one can hardly doubt that with an object like the font at Brooklands church in Kent everyday work has been truly consecrated.[62] This lead font, probably cast in Normandy, in the last quarter of the twelfth century, has a fine complete set of the labours with the signs of the zodiac upon it providing 'some of the earliest introductions to the twelfth century sculptor of genre scenes taken from contemporary life'.[63]

The literary evidence for England was explored by another great pioneer, professor Owst, in a book first published forty years ago: *Literature and Pulpit in Medieval England*.[64] He showed quite conclusively that the view which Huizinga put forward in his *Waning of the Middle Ages* that 'England gave towards the end of the fourteenth century, the first expression of the sentiment of the sanctity of productive labour' in *Piers Plowman* was quite false. In this respect, as in

---

[59] Knowles, *Monastic Order* p 206.

[60] *Statuta Congregationis Cluniacensis*, cap xxxix, PL 189 (1890) cols 1036–7.

[61] Emile Mâle, *L'Art Réligieux du XIIIᵉ siècle en France* (Paris 1910) p 84.

[62] G. Zarnecki, *English Romanesque Lead Sculpture* (London 1957) pp 17–18 and plates 56, 59, 60, 65, 68–70. The recent survey by Mlle Yvonne Labande Mailfert, 'L'iconographie des laics dans la société religieuse aux XIᵉ et XIIᵉ siècles', *I Laici*, pp 488–522 does not consider calendars and representations of the labours.

[63] L. Stone, '*Sculpture in Britain: the Middle Ages*' (London 1955) p 89, and plate 66B.

[64] First published Oxford 1933.

many others, Langland proclaimed views very commonly found earlier; admittedly, rarely expressed so skilfully.[65]

As far as I know professor Owst did not comment upon the sources which may have inspired, for example, the English author of the late thirteenth century *Speculum Laicorum*, or John Bromyard the dominican writing in the next century, to take such a positive view of manual work. My own suggestion would be that the cistercian contribution should not be forgotten. Take, for example, the phrase which Bromyard has against the word blessedness, *beatitudo* in his *Summa Predicantium: Per viam laboris pervenit ad mercedem consolationis.*[66] Coming upon this after reading Guerric of Igny, I was struck with the similarity with one of his phrases *Labor in actione, fructus seu merces in contemplatione.*[67] Let me make myself clear; I am not suggesting that Bromyard depends upon Guerric, but that he does have a very similar idea, that labour, work, merits a reward from God. Piers the Plowman, himself comes out of a climate which has absorbed the message of the vision of Christ appearing to the cistercian lay brother.[68] But fourteenth-century literature also makes it clear that other influences were at work.

Recently, by a happy chance, I was re-reading the poem written by the Welsh poet Iolo Goch called *The Ploughman*, which suggests two other directions from which the consecration of labour may have come.[69] The poem, written in the second half of the fourteenth century praises the work of the ploughman, 'the plodder of fields', 'the best of men'. To strengthen his case the poet appeals to the useful old *Elucidarium*, the wise old book which

> put it thus happily,
> 'Blessed is he who through his youth
> holds in his hands the plough'.

This is a clear reminiscence of the work written by the still shadowy figure Honorius Augustodensis, who devotes one chapter of his *Elucidarium* to the hope of salvation for various kinds of laymen.[70] For most

[65] *Ibid* (2 ed 1961) p 568. The quotation from Huizinga is on p 162 of the 1924 English ed of *The Waning of the Middle Ages*.

[66] Owst p 555.

[67] *Sermo IV in Assumptione B. Mariae*, 3 *PL* 185 (1855) col 199.

[68] Compare Helmut Maisack, *William Langlands Verhältnis zum Zisterziensischen Mönchtum* (Balingen 1953) tried to argue that Langland depended almost exclusively on cistercian ideas which goes too far. Maisack does not refer to Owst.

[69] [Gwyn] Williams, [*The Burning Tree*] (London 1956) pp 106–11.

[70] *Elucidarium* bk II, cap 18, *PL* 172 (1895) col 1149. The passage occurs on p 429 of the ed by Yves Lefèvre, *L'Elucidarium et les Lucidaires*, Bibl des Ecoles Francaises d'

he is extremely sceptical, but for the farmer, *agricoli*, he says 'most of them will be saved, because they live humbly, feeding the people of God through their sweat as it is said "Blessed are those who eat the labour of their hands" ' (a reminiscence of Psalm 128: 2). Here is evidence of a more positive tradition, which might well repay exploration. It would be interesting to see, incidentally, how strongly this tradition comes through the latin sermon literature of the eleventh and twelfth centuries which is now becoming accessible to scholars.

Iolo also draws on another tradition, that of the vernacular *chanson de geste* for he appeals to the example of Huw Gadarn who

> after defeat took up,
> the nimble, fine-beamed plough,
> for this hale, host-scattering lord,
> this great leader never sought bread
> but, so well instructed was he,
> by his own labour.

This great commander had wished to show 'one craft was best, a sign of triumph, that ploughing is a scholarship'. Huw was known to Iolo probably through a still extant fourteenth-century Welsh translation of the *Pélerinage de Charlemagne* which itself originates in the mid-twelfth century.[71] In the original, Hugh li Forz is found by the emperor and his knights behind a golden plough. The fantastic details need not detain us, but it will not escape attention that the episode shows another delicately reared man performing, voluntarily, a servile task, the type of sight which shocked some contemporaries of the first cistercians.

To these two traditions which may have created a climate along with the cistercian we may add a third, which in some sense brings us back to the white monks, the tradition from the desert. The *Vitae Patrum*, the *Collations* of Cassian, the *Life of St Antony*, to mention but three of the works through which the life of the desert lived on in men's minds, all show austere lives of prayer being combined with manual labour. The former contains a story of the practical way a certain abbot Silvanus showed a brother that Mary and Martha each need one another, which might have come from Rievaulx many centuries later,

---

Athènes et de Rome 180 (Paris 1954). For Honorius see R. W. Southern, *St Anselm and his Biographer* (Cambridge 1963) pp 209–17.

71 Eduard Koschwitz: *Sechs Bearbeitungen des altfranzosischen Gedichts von Karls des Grossen Reise nach Jerusalem und Constantinopel* (Heilbronn 1879) pp 1–18 gives the Welsh version. The origin of the story is noticed by Williams p 224.

under that other Silvanus, the successor to Ailred.[72] The brother asked why the brethren were working in the fields because Mary had chosen the best part. So the abbot ordered him to be put in a cell with only a book for company. When the time for a meal arrived no one came to call him so the brother went to the abbot and asked whether the brethren were eating that day. Silvanus told him that they were and when he was asked 'Wherefore didst thou not call me?' he answered, 'Thou art a spiritual man, and thou dost not hold food to be necessary: but we being carnal have need to eat, and to that end we work: but thou hast chosen that good part.' At this the brother was ashamed and asked for forgiveness, at which the abbot explained 'So Martha is necessary for Mary, for because of Martha is Mary praised.'

It is clear that the early cistercians were very much inspired by the desert Fathers, their libraries contained the books which recalled them and their own works referred back to them. In the *Dialogue between the Cistercian and the Cluniac*, for example, the cistercian appeals to the examples to be found in the *Collations* of hermits who joined the contemplative life with using their own hands to support themselves.[73] The cistercians were not the only monks inspired by the desert, but they were the first considerable group to see there a justification for the place that hand work had in their own life. Among modern historians we may note at least one, Wilmart, who concluded that because 'heroic Cîteaux and all that it represents, intended a return to the sublime and dangerous life of the Fathers of the desert . . . it was foreign to the true thought of St Benedict'.[74] The desert tradition had, however, living exemplars on the fringe, so to speak, of the monasteries, from at least the time of St Romuald onwards: hermits. Their significance in the history of the eleventh and twelfth centuries has become clearer over recent years; to some extent they were an inspiration and an irritant to monastic circles, and at the same time they brought new ways of thinking about God and praying from the cloister out to the rural population.[75] The most famous English hermit, Godric of Finchale, exemplifies this process, and in the context of this investiga-

---

72 *Vitae Patrum*, bk III, 55. *PL* 73 (1878) col 768. The translation here is derived from Helen Wadell, *The Desert Fathers* (London 1936) pp 197–8. This story occurs in a sermon on the Assumption by Odo of Cheriton early 13th century: compare Leopold Hervieux, *Les Fabulistes Latins*, IV (Paris 1896) pp 144 ff. Hervieux seems to have thought it referred to a cistercian abbot. For Silvanus of Rievaulx see Wilmart, *Les Mélanges* p 55.

73 *Dialogus*, col 1622.   74 *Une riposte*, pp 308–9.

75 Compare *L'Eremitismo in Occidente nei Secoli XI e XII* (Univ del Sacro Cuore Milan 1965) being *Miscellanea del Centro di Studi Medioevali*, IV.

tion we may note how he cleared the ground around his cabin by the Wear so that he could raise his own corn and vegetables.[76] He, the friend of great cistercians like Robert of Newminster and Ailred, lived out the combination of work and contemplation of which they spoke, showing it forth to many from far and near who came to him for advice or healing.

The vision that the cistercians had of the positive spiritual value of manual work did not then appear in a world which had absolutely no currents flowing in the same general direction. These did exist and they certainly began to flow more strongly as the twelfth century progressed. The stream represented by Honorius, the 'secular' spring of the *Pélerinage*, the source welling up in the dry places of Egypt, from which from time to time earlier fountains had drawn their water, all joined with the new water from Cîteaux which, itself, was drawing on some of the same underground cisterns from which the other currents drew. The search for origins is in such matters an endless quest, but I would suggest that the cistercian contribution to the creation of a new appreciation of work was crucial, in the same way that it was vital to the creation of the human Jesus, *Dulcis Jesu memoria*.[77] It made its mark on the learned world of the twelfth century by writing as well as by example, and the influence of these written words, at least, continued to be felt throughout the middle ages.[78] The unlettered, on the other hand could only respond to example and for them throughout the twelfth century the order presented a life in which men from different stations found that part of their proper service to God and man was fulfilled by work. The example of the lay brothers particularly, whose dress was very similar to a peasant's, and who lived a life of consecrated labour, could have been peculiarly acceptable. Occasionally, as in the record of the life of the lay brother Simon at Villers in Brabant, or, nearer home, in the story of Sunnulph at Fountains guiding Ralf Murdac to his new life, we see how the message was passed to laymen, but generally the how and when is not revealed.[79] Certainly we may doubt whether, by the thirteenth century

---

[76] Reginald of Durham, *Libellus de vita et miraculis S. Godrici, heremitae de Finchale*, caps xxvi, xxxii, ed J. Stevenson, SS 20 (1845) pp 74–5, 83.

[77] Compare R. W. Southern, *The Making of the Middle Ages* (London 1953) p 233.

[78] Giles Constable, 'The Popularity of Twelfth Century Spiritual Writers in the Late Middle Ages', *Renaissance Studies in Honor of Hans Baron* (Florence 1971) pp 5–28.

[79] E. de Moreau, *L'abbaye de Villers-en-Brabant aux XIIe et XIIIe siècles* (Brussels 1909) pp 96–104; J. R. Walbran, *Memorials of the abbey of St Mary's of Fountains*, SS 42 (1863) pp 118–20, 123.

when the order was much more prosperous, it was so effective an example to the wider world. The picture must, of course, have varied across Europe depending on many different circumstances. Some English cistercian houses, for example, were wealthy in the thirteenth century, or at least comfortably off, whilst others were struggling to survive. But the very success of some, and the survival of others, must themselves have owed something to the way that the religious ideal of the white monks had part of its feet firmly planted in that understanding of the value of manual work which it has been my purpose to explain. Looked at in the broadest light that understanding seems to have a part to play in the emergence of attitudes and feelings which have been connected in the past, at least since Weber, with urban communities of a later period.[80]

[80] Robert Moore, 'History, economics and religion: a review of "The Max Weber Thesis" thesis', in *Max Weber and Modern Sociology*, ed Arun Sahay (London 1971) pp 82–96 for a review of the vast 'Weber' literature.

MULIERES SANCTAE

by BRENDA M. BOLTON

THE early thirteenth century was an extraordinary period in the history of piety. Throughout Europe, and especially in urban communities, lay men and women were seized by a new religious fervour which could be satisfied neither by the new orders nor by the secular clergy. Lay groups proliferated, proclaiming the absolute and literal value of the gospels and practising a new life-style, the *vita apostolica*.[1] This religious feeling led to the formation, on the eve of the fourth lateran council, of numerous orders of 'poor men' and shortly afterwards, to the foundation of the mendicant orders. From this novel interpretation of evangelical life women by no means wished to be excluded and many female groups sprang simultaneously into being in areas as far distant as Flanders and Italy. Yet how were such groups to be regarded because current attitudes to women were based on inconsistent and contradictory doctrines?[2] It was difficult to provide the conditions under which they could achieve their desire for sanctity as they were not allowed to enter the various orders available to men. How then were men to reply to the demands of these women for participation in religious life? That there should be a reply was evident from the widespread heresy in just those areas in which the ferment of urban life encouraged the association of pious women. And heretics were dangerously successful with them! For the church, the existence of religious and semi-religious communities of women raised, in turn, many problems, not least the practicalities involved in both pastoral care and economic maintenance. Only, after 1215, when it attempted to

---

[1] An account of the way in which these groups practised the *vita apostolica* is given by [M. D.] Chenu, *Nature, Man and Society* [*in the Twelfth Century*] (Chicago 1968). See also C. Violante, 'Hérésies urbaines et rurales en Italie du 11e au 13e siècle', in J. Le Goff, *Hérésies et sociétés dans l'Europe pré-industrielle 11-18 siècles*, Ecole pratique des hautes études. *Civilisation et Sociétés*, 10 (Paris 1968) who offers an analysis of the movement towards the *vita apostolica*.

[2] These doctrines placed woman either on a pedestal or in a bottomless pit; exalted her as the virgin mother of Christ or denigrated her as 'the supreme temptress, the most dangerous of all obstacles in the way of salvation'. See [E.] Power, 'The Position of Women', in *The Legacy of the Middle Ages*, edd C. G. Crump and E. F. Jacob (Oxford 1962) pp 401–3.

regulate and discipline them, did it realise the widespread enthusiasm on which their movement was based.

For men the problem was less difficult for an astonishing variety of new religious orders had begun to appear at the beginning of the twelfth century.[3] Premonstratensians, augustinians, grammontines and cistercians alike enjoyed an immediate and overwhelming success. In spite of this stimulus, there was no comparable, parallel attempt to enrich the religious life of women, with the possible local exception of the gilbertines in England.[4] Nunneries remained exclusive and few in number. Instead, many women attached themselves to itinerant religious leaders whose teaching had a wide appeal. The first such charismatic preacher was Robert of Arbrissel, who settled his large and heterogeneous female following in a new convent at Fontevrault in the Loire valley but, within a generation, it had become entirely aristocratic, looking no further than the northern French nobility for its recruits.[5] Another such preacher, Norbert of Xanten, received a most enthusiastic reception from women in the neighbourhood of Valenciennes in the early 1120s.[6] The premonstratensian order, which he founded, immediately assumed the protection of pious women and established a number of double monasteries. In 1137, the general chapter decreed the separation of monks and nuns for reasons of convenience, although successive popes repeated that adequate maintenance should be provided for women. Yet, by 1150, apparently undeterred by powerful influences at work against them, the women were said to number over ten thousand.[7] Finally, in 1198, Innocent III's bull *de non recipiendis sororibus* confirmed and commended the decision of the general chapter no longer to accept them into the order.[8]

The community at Fontevrault and the early premonstratensian nunneries had flourished initially because of the help which they had received from their male protectors. But other protectors of female communities appeared in different and unexpected guises. Large numbers of women began to form convents which followed the customs of Cîteaux and yet which held no formal place in the structure

---

[3] [R. W.] Southern, *Western Society [and the Church in the Middle Ages]* (Harmondsworth 1970) pp 240–72.

[4] R. Graham, *St Gilbert of Sempringham and the Gilbertines* (London 1901).

[5] PL 162 (1854) col 1053.

[6] PL 170 (1854) col 1273. See also [S.] Roisin, 'L'efflorescence cistercienne [et le courant féminin de piété au xiiie siècle'], *RHE* 39 (1943) pp 349–50.

[7] PL 156 (1853) col 997; Southern, *Western Society* p 313.

[8] PL 214 (1855) col 174; Potthast I no 168.

of the order.[9] In Spain, many great families, who were responsible for
the settlement of cistercian monks, also created large, aristocratic houses
of cistercian nuns. Possibly because of this noble patronage and because
of the grandeur of aristocratic Spanish women, individual cistercian
abbots appear to have supported and supervised these nunneries. The
abbesses enjoyed a remarkable degree of independence.[10] By the
1190s, the cistercian order, which had, at first, ignored the existence of
female intruders, became increasingly aware of the large number of
women who claimed its protection without being subject to its organisation or control. The contrast between the discipline of the male order
and the freedom of the large and rapidly growing female branch was
becoming very apparent.

In Flanders, too, there is evidence that the cistercians supported the
foundation of nunneries and that abbots, such as Walter of Villers, in
the diocese of Liège were responsible for their supervision and welfare.[11]
Of the popularity of these houses we are left in no doubt. The contemporary view of the situation in this diocese alone was that there
were three times as many pious women as there were cistercian houses
able to receive them.[12]

From 1213, the general chapter began an attempt to discipline them.
The number of nuns was limited; they were strictly enclosed; they were
forbidden to receive visitors and their opportunities for confession
were limited.[13] In 1228, the general chapter issued a peremptory
statute forbidding all further attachment of nunneries to the order and
refusing the benefit of visitation and pastoral care to existing communities.[14] But, the severity of this decree was more apparent than real for,
if they could support themselves economically, cistercian convents
could continue to exist and new foundations to be made.[15] Yet, despite
this, the cistercian general chapter had made the point most forcibly

9 Southern, *Western Society* pp 314–18.
10 They held their own chapters, undertook the benediction of their own nuns, preached
and had their own dependent houses. *PL* 216 (1855) col 356; Potthast I no 4143.
11 Roisin, 'L'efflorescence cistercienne' pp 354–5.
12 Jacques de Vitry, *Jacobi de Vitriaco libri due quorum prior orientalis sive Hierosolimitanae,
alter occidentalis historiae nomine inscribitur*, ed Franciscus Moschus (Duaci 1597) p 306.
13 E. Martène and U. Durand, *Thesaurus novus anecdotorum* (Paris 1717) c 2 p 1312; c 10
p 1324; c 4 p 1327; c 6 p 1340.
14 *Ibid* c 7 p 1348.
15 Between 1220 and 1240, almost fifty houses for women were incorporated into the
order in places as far apart as Castile and Hungary, Ghent and Marseilles. For a
comprehensive list of these foundations see Roisin, 'L'efflorescence cistercienne'
pp 351–61.

that there was no place for these women in its order and that they were accepted only with extreme reluctance.

There was, thus, a strong reaction in both the premonstratensian and cistercian orders against the large numbers of women who wished to join them. What is so difficult to explain is why this reaction should have occurred. The general ecclesiastical attitude to women was, at best, negative if not actively hostile. Nor, indeed, was a woman's vocation necessarily regarded in a serious light.[16] It was thought that women inevitably contributed to indiscipline.[17] As the church became increasingly institutionalised so it was less able to tolerate any disruptive force in its midst.[18]

Women were also considered to be receptive to all forms of religious prophecy and to be completely unrestrained in relationships with their leaders or patrons. Just as, in the first half of the twelfth century, orthodox and heretical preachers had become the founders of orders and sects, so later, the cathars confronted the cistercians and the mendicants. Sects were generally only too glad to accept women, and women accompanied preachers through the land, sometimes preaching themselves. Here was the dilemma. The church, in turn, had to provide some measure of approval for their aspirations or heresy would materialise amongst these women.

Women could not, however, under any circumstances, be allowed to regulate their own forms of religious life. In the view of the church, the only possible role for them was one of attachment to existing male orders. But these orders did not want them and were reluctant to provide pastoral care and administrative oversight. So the importance of a male protector to advance and secure their interests and, possibly, to ward off accusations of heresy, was increased for these communities of pious women.

Women who had, thus, been catered for erratically in the twelfth century, moved, by 1200, into a different situation. They began to demand recognition of their real and separate identity. The question

16 The cluniac nunnery of Marcigny, founded specifically for women whose husbands had already become monks, provided a refuge in which 'mature women, tired of matrimonial licence, might purge themselves of past errors', Southern, *Western Society* pp 310-11.

17 St Bernard, who was horrified at the dangers implicit in the association of men and women, was only expressing a common contemporary belief in feminine wantonness when he warned that 'to be always with a woman and not to have intercourse with her is more difficult than to raise the dead', *PL* 183 (1854) col 1091.

18 And women could be disruptive as we are reminded in the parody of the chapter of nuns at Remiremont by C. S. Lewis, *The Allegory of Love* (8 ed Oxford 1965) pp 18-19.

of their status in religion could no longer be answered solely by placing them in houses attached to the male orders, often as unwanted appendages. As enthusiastic women began to share the aspirations of the friars and like-minded religious groups, the logical outcome ought to have been the creation of a separate female order. Instead, in 1215, the fourth lateran council issued a decree which epitomised the contest between those who would have allowed new forms of religious life within the church and those who supported the forces of tradition and reaction. As a result of this, there were to be no more new orders and, henceforward, anyone who wished to establish a religious community had to do so within the framework and rule of an approved order.[19]

Although it may not have been possible to measure an increase in piety, yet contemporaries undoubtedly believed that female piety was increasing at the beginning of the thirteenth century. In 1216, Jacques de Vitry, protector of a group of pious women in the diocese of Liège, travelled to Perugia where the curia then was, and, in a letter to his Flemish friends, described those groups of religious women which he had seen in Lombardy and Umbria.[20] In Milan, among the *humiliati*, he found pious women, some who lived separate and ascetic lives in religious communities and others who lived at home and practised strict evangelical precepts by stressing the importance of family life, prayer, exhortation and manual work. Although they were called heretical by their enemies, he was convinced of their orthodoxy and reported that they alone were resisting and actively working against heretics in Milan.[21] In Umbria, he encountered the Poor Clares and early franciscan tertiaries who were following the example of the

19 Cap XIII, Lateran IV in *Conciliorum Oecumenicorum Decreta* ed J. Alberigo and others (2 ed Freiburg 1962) p 218. For a discussion of this decree see [M.] Maccarrone, 'Riforma e sviluppo [della vita religiosa con Innocenzo III]', *Rivista di storia della Chiesa in Italia*, 16 (Rome 1962) pp 60–9.

20 Jacques de Vitry, born c 1160–70, probably in Rheims, was a regular canon of St Nicholas of Oignies in the diocese of Liège from 1211–16, bishop of Acre from 1216–27, auxilliary bishop of Liège from 1227–9 and cardinal from 1229–40. See McDonnell, *The Beguines*, pp 17–21 (n 28 below). The text of his letters is from *Lettres [de Jacques de Vitry]*, ed R. B. C. Huygens (Leiden 1960) pp 71–8. But see also 'Les passages des lettres de Jacques de Vitry rélatifs à Saint François d'Assise et à ses premiers disciples', ed R. B. C. Huygens in *Homages à Léon Herrman, Collection Latonius*, 44 (Brussels 1960) pp 446–53.

21 On the *Humiliati* see L. Zanoni, *Gli Umiliati nei loro rapporto con l'eresia, l'industria della lana ed i communi nei secolo xii e xiii, Biblioteca historica italia*, Serie II, 2 (Milan 1911); Maccarrone, 'Riforma e sviluppo', pp 46–51; [H.] Grundmann, *Religiöse Bewegungen [im Mittelalter]* (2 ed Darmstadt 1970) pp 70–97, 487–538, and my article 'Innocent III's treatment of the *Humiliati*' in *SCH*, 8 (1971) pp 73–82.

primitive church in various hospices near the towns. They would accept nothing and lived entirely by the work of their hands. He reported that they were greatly distressed because, by clergy and laity alike, they were honoured more than they would have wished to be.[22]

Why was Jacques de Vitry so interested in female communities? Like many devout men of his day he eagerly gathered information about the variety and extent of such pious groups and individual female mystics. He wrote about them in his *Historia Occidentalis*, in his *Exempla* and in his *Sermon to the Beguines*.[23] Above all, he wrote about them in his life of the 'new' saint, Mary of Oignies, around whom centred female piety in the diocese of Liège.[24] Irresistibly attracted to voluntary personal poverty from an early age, she had eventually renounced her marriage, distributed her wealth to the poor and, together with her husband, served the leper colony at Williambroux, outside Nivelles. After several years, she had moved into a cell at the Augustinian priory of St Nicholas of Oignies, there living in complete poverty, save for what she earned at her spindle. In 1209, she prophesied the Albigensian crusade after a vision in which she saw a great number of crosses descending from heaven.[25] Jacques de Vitry, who himself preached this crusade in Flanders in 1211, was drawn to Oignies by Mary's renown and by his desire to identify himself with her work.

At her instigation, he was ordained in 1210 and remained in the community as her confessor. After her death in 1213 he continued to be the enthusiastic protector of her followers. To enhance her memory and expressly to counter heresy in the south of France, he wrote her *Life* and seems to have taken it with him on his journey to Perugia but there is no evidence that he showed it to Honorius III.[26] Mary exercised a considerable influence over him and he, personally, was very close to her, even carrying around with him her finger in a reliquary.[27]

22 [J] Moorman, [*A History of*] *the Franciscan Order* [*from its origins to the year 1517*] (Oxford 1968) pp 32–9, 205–25.
23 Jacques de Vitry, *Historia Occidentalis* pp 304–7, pp 334–37; *The Exempla of Jacques de Vitry*, ed T. F. Crane, *Folk Lore Society Publications*, 26 (1890); *Die Exempla aus den Sermones feriales et communes*, ed J. Greven (Heidelburg 1914); *Die Exempla des Jacob von Vitry*, ed G. Frenken, *Quellen und Untersuchungen zur lateinischen Philologie des Mittelalters*, 5 (Munich 1914) pp 1–153.
24 *Vita Maria Oigniacensis, ASB*, 5 (1867) pp 542–72.
25 *Ibid* p 556.   26 Grundmann, *Religiöse Bewegungen* p 173.
27 It was the possession of this to which he attributed his safe arrival in Milan in 1216, despite the hazards of crossing rivers in flood in Lombardy. *Lettres* p 72 lines 34–46.

The pious women whom Jacques de Vitry was protecting in Liège were known as beguines and were to be found also in France and Germany.[28] Their movement was essentially urban in character. They followed no definite rule of life; they had no real founder; at their inception, they sought no authority from the hierarchy and imposed no irreversible vows upon their adherents. Their objectives were two-fold: chastity or continence and the renunciation of worldly goods. They did not protest at the wealth of others but voluntarily renounced property and possessions to fulfil their evangelical ideal. They lived by the labour of their hands, for the injunction to work was essential to such semi-religious associations in their pursuit of a penitential life and it also enabled them to meet in some measure the religious needs of the new urban populations.

What other contemporary evidence may we use to match Jacques de Vitry's experience of the beguines? His manuscripts belong to the period of his cardinalate, 1229 to 1240.[29] At about the same time, between 1229 and 1235, Robert Grosseteste, bishop of Lincoln, declared privately to the franciscans at Oxford, that the beguines, who, unlike the mendicants, did not live on alms but only by manual work, had achieved through their way of life the highest degree of christian perfection through this poverty.[30] Shortly afterwards, Robert de Sorbon declared that, at the last judgement, the beguines would give a better account of themselves than many a learned *magister*, jurist or theologian.[31] And later still, in 1243, the English chronicler, Matthew Paris, wrote of those women 'who have adopted a religious profession, though it is a light one. They call themselves "religious" and they take a private vow of continence and simplicity of life, though they do not follow the rule of any saint, nor are they, as yet, confined within a cloister. They have so multiplied within a short time that two thousand have been reported in Cologne and neighbouring cities.'[32]

The beguine movement differed from heretical poverty in that

---

28 For a guide to the huge bibliography on the beguines see [E. W.] McDonnell, *The Beguines [and Beghards in Medieval Culture]* (Rutgers University 1954). Also a review by J. Van Mierlo in *RHE* 28 (1932) pp 377–83 of H. Grundmann, *Zur Geschichte der Beginen im XIII Jahrhundert, Archiv fur Kulturgeschichte*, 16 (1931) pp 292–320. Of special value have been Grundmann, *Religiöse Bewegungen* pp 170–98, 319–54 and [A.] Mens, 'Les béguines et béghards [dans le cadre de la culture mediévale']', *Le Moyen Age* 64 (1958) pp 305–15.

29 McDonnell, *The Beguines* p 21.

30 Southern, *Western Society* p 320.

31 Grundmann, *Religiöse Bewegungen* pp 322–3.

32 Translated by Southern, *Western Society* p 319.

it made no polemical demands on clerics and did not stress to the same extent, the merit of the priesthood.[33] Yet, beguines were often confused with heretics and it was probably from their supposed Albigensian affiliations that their name derived.[34] Jacques de Vitry discounted the accusations of heterodoxy against them and, in his role as protector, worked to save them from this charge. The beguines fascinated him by the fervour and spontaneity of their personal religion and he saw that, in common with the *humiliati* of Lombardy, they could provide an effective barrier against heresy if contained within the church. We know that he was not alone in this view from the whole-hearted admiration shown to the beguine communities by bishop Fulk of Toulouse, who arrived in the diocese of Liège in 1215 or early 1216.[35]

Jacques de Vitry was interested in pious women's communities because he saw them as being significant and potentially useful to the church. His enthusiasm for the beguines was, however, tempered by the possible dangers of their extra-regular status. He seems to have wished them to be completely incorporated into the ecclesiastical structure so that their obedience could be ensured. In spite of his representations to the curia on their behalf, no independent female order came into being. Perhaps he had hoped for assistance from Innocent III but his arrival in Perugia coincided with the death of the pope and he saw instead, Honorius III, whom he described as a kind and simple man, ready to aid the poor in any possible way.[36] But he only obtained from him oral permission for the beguines in Flanders, France and the Empire, to live together in religious communities and to assist one another by mutual exhortation.[37] Shortly before Jacques de Vitry's mission to the curia in 1216, John de Liro, a friend and preacher in the Liège area, had set out for Rome with much the same purpose, only to perish in the Alps.[38]

Jacques de Vitry obviously considered the Poor Clares of Umbria and the religious women's communities which he knew in Flanders as

---

[33] Grundmann, *Religiöse Bewegungen* p 197.

[34] For the origin of the word 'beguine', see R. P. Callaey, 'Lambert li Beges et les Béguines', *RHE* 23 (1927) pp 254-9, and Mens, 'Les béguines et beghards' p 309.

[35] Fulk of Toulouse, poet, *jongleur*, monk and then cistercian abbot of Florège, was created bishop of Toulouse in 1206. In 1212, he was driven from his diocese by heretics and went to preach the crusade in Flanders. His interest in religious women's communities as a bulwark against heresy led him to support Dominic's foundation at Prouille and it was at his request that Jacques de Vitry wrote the life of Mary of Oignies. [C.] Thouzellier, *Catharisme et Valdéisme* [*en Languedoc à la fin du xiie siècle*] (2 ed Louvain 1969) p 192.

[36] *Lettres* p 73 lines 61-70.   [37] *Ibid* p 74 lines 76-81.   [38] *ASB* 4 (1867) p 197.

a united, cohesive phenomenon for he said nothing about the generic and organisational differences between them. But were there, perhaps, differences which Jacques de Vitry did not see? Superficially, the two groups might have been similar, yet, from one emerged the order of Poor Clares, while the beguines were never officially organised. Why, if there was an order of Poor Clares, was there no order of beguines or, for that matter, of cistercian nuns? Perhaps we could approach the problem from two directions by first looking at the social composition of these groups and then at the institutional problems which the attempts to found one order raised.

Who were these women who, in the early thirteenth century, wished to live in poverty and humility in areas as widely separated as Flanders and Lombardy or Umbria? In the initial stages, they appear to be almost exclusively aristocratic. In 1218, cardinal Hugolino commented that the Italian women, whose cause he had adopted, were of noble birth, assured of a comfortable existence and yet, still wished to renounce the world to live instead in communities alongside their chapels.[39] Jacques de Vitry also describes the patrician status of beguines and cistercians alike.[40] Surely neither Hugolino nor Jacques de Vitry should have been surprised that these were aristocratic women. Such women were far more likely to question their way of life than those from lower classes and their natural self-assurance must have helped them to win acceptance.

Here, the religious factor seems to have been of prime importance. The religious poverty movement appeared to represent a reaction to landed wealth or newly acquired urban prosperity among those circles best placed to participate. Perhaps they felt that competition to achieve status was irreconcilable with their interpretation of the gospel. These women, whether beguines or Poor Clares, wished not only to be poor but to live with the poor. Against the natural order of society they deliberately chose to deny their noble or rich background and turned instead to a way of life scorned by those they had known. It seems likely that poverty and chastity represented for these women a personal and social *renovatio* – a spiritual renewal through the adoption of a new life-style – the *vita apostolica*.[41]

[39] Potthast I no 5896.
[40] Jacques de Vitry, *Historia Occidentalis* pp 305–6; J. Greven, 'Der Ursprung des Beginenwesens', *HJch* 35 (1914) pp 26–58, 291–318.
[41] For discussion of this question see [J. L.] Nelson, 'Society, theodicy and the origins of heresy: [towards a reassessment of the medieval evidence'], *SCH* 9 (1972) pp 65–77; Chenu, *Nature, Man and Society* pp 202–69.

Jacques de Vitry described two groups of women in these religious communities. There were those married noblewomen, who, with the consent of their husbands, had renounced their earthly marriage, together with lands and possessions, in favour of a spiritual marriage and a life of voluntary poverty. Mary of Oignies, the child of rich and respected parents, was married at the age of fourteen, but later separated voluntarily from her husband. Many other women like her, in the first half of the thirteenth century, parted from their husbands and became beguines or nuns, attached to a franciscan or dominican house.[42]

Jacques de Vitry also talked of young girls from the nobility, who, scorning not only their parents' wealth but advantageous marriage, preferred to live humbly, sparsely clothed and poorly fed, and to follow religious precepts outside their accustomed social circle.[43] Clare herself, at her conversion by Francis in 1212, gave away her property in order to serve God in voluntary poverty.[44] There were many examples of noble and unwilling brides-to-be who attempted to escape marriage in order to join a religious community. Christine of Stomeln, aged twelve, ran away to join a beguine group in Cologne. The beguines, however, received her coolly and sent her home. She endured several years of hardship and suffering, living as a beggar, before she eventually managed to convince them of her vocation.[45]

Was the number of pious women really increasing or was it that there were simply more women? Could the *Frauenfrage* be explained in demographic terms alone? Did these new religious groupings stem from women's social and economic needs at this time?[46] Such questions have received lengthy discussion elsewhere but it is perhaps worth making some points again. By 1200, the population of certain areas of western Europe was beginning to reflect an imbalance between men and women. Factors bringing this about were female longevity; a masculine proclivity to death in battle or permanent absence on crusade; and the large numbers of men entering the priesthood.[47] There may, thus, have been a high proportion of nubile women for whom there was no

---

[42] *ASB* 5 (1867) pp 547–50.   [43] Jacques de Vitry, *Historia Occidentalis* pp 305–6.

[44] Grundmann, *Religiöse Bewegungen* p 235.

[45] *ASB* 5 (1867) pp 236–7. Two of many other such examples are Ida of Nivelles, aged nine, who fled from home to avoid marriage, becoming a cistercian nun six years later, and Yolande of Vianden, whose noble family, which included the archbishop of Cologne, tried for years to persuade her to accept an advantageous marriage. They were unsuccessful and she eventually entered a dominican convent. See Grundmann, *Religiöse Bewegungen* pp 192–3.

[46] G. Koch, *Frauenfrage und Ketzertum im Mittelalter* (Berlin 1962).

[47] Power, 'The Position of Women' p 411.

prospect of marriage and who, therefore, sought release in a mystical, contemplative life. We may even wonder tentatively if the intense interest in virginity, expressed through devotional literature, did not create a strong aversion in the minds of many girls towards marriage.[48] Practical considerations may here have played some part for early marriage brought attendant risks in childbirth.

Possibly this women's movement towards religion was stimulated by the disadvantageous position which they appear to have held in feudal society. Primogeniture became more usual and depressed the independent status of some aristocratic women in land-owning families.[49] Nobles could no longer necessarily afford large dowries for their daughters. Such insecurity may often have provided an incentive to enter a religious house or join a beguine community. As a disadvantaged group in society women looked for anything which might improve their personal status. They turned to religion as nothing else was available for them. It is possible to argue that they might indeed achieve status through austerity in this world or if not that 'what they cannot claim to *be*, they replace by the worth of that which they will someday *become*'.[50]

The argument is thus circular, and returns constantly to religious factors. Poor Clares, beguines, cistercian nuns; all seemed to spring initially from the same social environment. Their motivation was basically religious but was, perhaps, complicated by other factors.

It is now worth examining the institutional differences between the Poor Clares and the beguines which led to the development of an order in one case but not in the other. One man alone grasped the significance of the feminine piety movement. In his treatment of Francis, Innocent III had taken a long step towards creating the possibility of an order for women. He had already enabled new religious movements such as the *humiliati* to develop within the church, and, by his far-sighted actions, had saved many groups from heresy. It was logical that Innocent III should have been in favour of adding a women's order to the church, to strengthen it in its struggle with heresy and its current political difficulties.

Francis had come to him in 1210, seeking approval for his way of life, yet, unwilling to accept a traditional rule.[51] In the face of

---

48 Southern, *Western Society* p 311.
49 Nelson, 'Society, theodicy and the origins of heresy' pp 71–2.
50 M. Weber, *The Sociology of Religion* (London 1965) p 106.
51 For a detailed account of Innocent's treatment of Francis see Grundmann, *Religiöse Bewegungen* pp 127–35.

considerable hostility from the hierarchy Innocent had to determine how this movement might be incorporated into the church and, thus, allowed Francis to continue on two conditions. He and his companions were to be tonsured and, as clerks, could then be given the *licentia praedicandi ubique*. The question of leadership was solved when Francis promised obedience to Innocent III and received oral approval from the pope.

The recognition of Francis by Innocent III had very wide implications for Clare. The oral permission given to him by the pope in 1210 contained no justification for the formation of a female order, nor was such permission subsequently issued. In 1212, after her conversion by Francis, Clare established her community in the church of St Damian in Assisi. The community did not follow any usual, recognised rule, but a simple *formula vitae* which Francis had given them and which was essentially similar to his in its profession of evangelical poverty.[52]

When, in 1215, the lateran council imposed on all new movements the obligation to accept an approved rule, the community at St Damian had to apply for a privilege to enable it to maintain its renunciation of property and its profession of strict poverty. At the same time, Clare was appointed as abbess of St Damian and strict claustration was introduced.[53] She received from Innocent III the *privilegium paupertatis*, a privilege which allowed the sisters of St Damian to live without an assured income.[54] All previously approved rules had been based on the presupposition that, although individuals were without property, houses would have to maintain themselves by a sufficient income from corporate possessions. So this privilege represented for Clare a guarantee that her community could not be obliged to adopt an existing rule. It seemed that Innocent had, therefore, helped her to create an entirely new form of convent community, which maintained itself on alms and the profits of manual labour in the same way as the franciscans.

Innocent may have issued this document in May 1216 at Perugia or possibly earlier, in 1215, when Clare was made abbess of St Damian.[55] Could he have been concerned, as, indeed, he was with Francis in 1210, that the question of leadership in the community should be regulated? What we do know is that Innocent actually wrote the privilege with his own hand *cum hilaritate magna* and that he, therefore, knew very

[52] *Ibid* pp 253–4.
[53] It seems that Clare may not have wanted strict claustration at all. See Moorman, *The Franciscan Order* p 36.
[54] Grundmann, *Religiöse Bewegungen* pp 149–51.
[55] For a discussion of dates *ibid* p 150 n 147.

well how unique it was.[56] At whatever time this privilege was issued, whether before, during or after the council, it was unquestionably opposed to the decree since it made possible a new form of religious community, not based on an existing order.

The beguines, however, did not have the same advantages. Jacques de Vitry might have received a similar reception from Innocent III if he had been able to tell this pope about the beguines. But there were other considerable difficulties. Mary of Oignies's death in 1213 had deprived the beguines of Flanders of a leader and they were soon to lose their protector as Jacques de Vitry, now bishop-elect of Acre, was about to depart for the Holy Land.[57]

Is it possible that Innocent III's intervention on behalf of the Poor Clares might have led to the creation of a separate male order? A separate order for women would have horrified most medieval ecclesiastics. For this reason, Clare represented a potential revolution within the church. Why, therefore, with Innocent's help, did not her community develop into an independent order? Perhaps Francis had hoped that this might happen for he certainly did not wish to be too greatly involved with the convent of St Damian. Nor indeed could he be. The Poor Clares lived in convents; the friars were mendicant preachers and as such were unable to live a stable, cloistered life.[58] Jacques de Vitry, in 1216, described how, after their annual gatherings, they would disperse throughout the year in Lombardy, Tuscany, Apulia and Sicily.[59] As they became more popular and spent more time in preaching over a wide area so Francis, beset by other problems, could devote less time to the community of St Damian.[60]

Yet, there was certainly no lack of interest in a community such as Clare's. All over Italy there was a tremendous demand from women to join similar religious groups, and in 1218 cardinal Hugolino applied to Honorius III on their behalf, asking that they should be placed under papal protection. He wished to institutionalise them but was not satisfied with simply congregating them under a nominal benedictine rule to fulfil the provision of the lateran decree.[61] They still lacked

---

56 *ASB* 2 (1867) p 757. Et ut insolitae petitioni favor insolitus arrideret, pontifex ipse cum hilaritate magna petiti privilegii primam notulam sua manu conscripsit.

57 *Lettres* pp 77–8,   58 Moorman, *The Franciscan Order* p 206.

59 *Lettres* p 76 lines 124–32.

60 The friars could not help the Poor Clares by collecting alms for them and the community of St Damian experienced great hardship, eking out a living from spinning and making altar linen. See Moorman, *The Franciscan Order* p 36.

61 [J. H.] Sbaralea, *Bullarum Franciscanum*, I (Rome 1759) p 264; Grundmann, *Religiöse Bewegungen* pp 258–9.

connection with a male order so Hugolino wanted all of them, including St Damian's, to adopt one uniform rule and also make the franciscans responsible for overall pastoral care of such communities. Francis appeared to agree that Clare's community should adopt Hugolino's rule as it made no statement about the possession of property and thus contained no essential contradiction to her original *formula vitae*.[62] On the issue of pastoral care, however, he was adamant.

St Damian was the only convent community which he would tolerate. He ordered that no others were to be founded or supported by his followers or attached to his order in any way at all. He rejected the use of the word 'sister' to describe the women saying 'God has taken away our wives, and now the devil gives us sisters.'[63] His violent reaction to Hugolino's attempt to involve the friars in the service of the women's convents during his absence has been reported by one of the brothers. Francis had said 'Up to now the disease was in our flesh and there was hope of healing but now it has penetrated our bones and is incurable.'[64] He managed to have this decision declared void and remained convinced that he had narrowly avoided the ruin of the order. Francis, like Innocent III, might have aimed originally at creating a separate female order under Clare. In the light of his hostility to women it would have given more coherence to his actions. Or did the possibility of a separate order for women come about almost by default – an attempt to prevent the friars from getting too involved with female communities? Whether this is so or not can only be a matter for conjecture.

What of Dominic's attitude to women? He had set out to create a new form of religious life for them long before he had created his own preaching order. The foundation of the nunnery at Prouille in 1206 was closely associated with the struggle against heresy in the south of France.[65] At first, Dominic attracted to Prouille the daughters of the impoverished lesser nobility whose education and upbringing were likely to be entrusted to the cathars.[66] Then older, aristocratic women, often former heretics, came to satisfy their demands for an austere life which, previously, catharism alone had offered in that area.[67] In 1215,

---

[62] *Ibid* p 260. Grundmann thinks that Francis agreed to the adoption of Hugolino's rule by the community of St Damian before he left for Egypt in 1218 or 1219.

[63] Moorman, *The Franciscan Order* p 35.   [64] Grundmann, *Religiöse Bewegungen* p 62.

[65] Thouzellier, *Catharisme et Valdéisme* p 253.   [66] *Ibid* p 200.

[67] These women confessed to Dominic that they had admired those who originally converted them to heresy for their ascetic form of life. See Grundmann, *Religiöse Bewegungen* p 209.

Prouille was taken into papal protection by Innocent III and, when the order of preachers was established, the convent became its property.[68] Other convents were also linked with Dominic. In 1218, he founded a house for nuns in Madrid which was supervised by his brother.[69] In 1219, he was given the task of reforming the convent of St Sisto in Rome.[70] While in Bologna in the same year, Dominic approved the suggestion of another house, on the lines of Prouille, which later became the convent of St Agnes.[71] All this activity in relation to foundations for women, and especially the community at Prouille, raises a particular question. Was it possible that Dominic was really trying to found a female order? This might have been so in the years immediately after 1206 but he certainly felt differently by the early 1220s. On his deathbed he warned his followers most urgently about communion with women, especially young women.[72] It seems likely that he was considering the future of his order and how far it should put itself at the disposal of women's communities, which might then draw it away from its greater task of preaching.[73]

Both Francis and Dominic had, thus, by the end of their lives, refused in highly emotive terms to allow the general attachment of women to their orders. Yet this represented a denial of their *raison d'être* as preachers. Everywhere they went they were met by a huge wave of female piety. Heinrich, first dominican prior of Cologne, specialised in preaching to women and enjoyed such success among 'virgins, widows and female penitents' that his early death was bewailed by women throughout the city.[74] There was considerable and constant pressure on the curia to recognise these women and incorporate them somehow within the church. But before such communities could exist they had to be institutionalised and firmly regulated. So, in 1227, the curia returned to the policy of creating female branches of male orders and turned its attention to the mendicants to examine how far it was possible to link the women to these orders. Thus ensued a struggle between the women supported by the curia and the orders. This struggle centred on two particular problems; the extent to which

68 *Ibid* p 211.
69 Jordanis de Saxonia, *De initiis ordinis*; [*opera ad res ordinis Praedicatorum spectantia*], ed J. J. Berthier (Freiburg 1891) p 19.
70 Grundmann, *Religiöse Bewegungen* p 213.
71 *Ibid* pp 213–19 for a full discussion of the foundation of this convent.
72 Jordanis de Saxonia, *De initiis ordinis* p 28.
73 Grundmann, *Religiöse Bewegungen* p 215.
74 Jordanis de Saxonia, *De initiis ordinis* p 25.

pastoral care could be provided without detracting from their original mendicant character, and the nature and extent of the economic support required by female communities.

In 1227, Gregory IX placed more than twenty central Italian convents of *pauperes moniales reclusae* in the care of the general of the franciscan order and henceforth grouped them under the title of the order of St Damian.[75] In the same year, the curia mediated with the dominicans to achieve the incorporation of the nunnery of St Agnes in Bologna and this process was repeated on many subsequent occasions.[76] Thus, within a short time of their deaths, the curia had succeeded in doing just what Francis and Dominic had striven so hard to prevent during their lives. But the orders resisted vigorously. In 1228, the year in which the cistercians, too, refused to accept nunneries, the general chapter of the dominican order forbade, not only the incorporation of women's convents, but also threatened with censure any brother who accepted their vows, tended to their pastoral needs or allowed them to wear religious habits.[77] This prohibition of pastoral care was completely ineffective against vigorous feminine demands. We know this from a bull of 1238, directed to the general of the order by Gregory IX, which reversed a previous chapter decision to release the brothers from the *cura mulierum* and thus to dissolve all connection between the order and its convents.[78]

At the request of the nuns of Prouille and Madrid, Gregory instructed that dominican friars should be reappointed to undertake care of souls but, in 1239, the order managed to secure an assurance that it would not, in future, be obliged to take on pastoral duties in convents or for other female groups, unless this was expressly permitted by an abrogation clause.[79] In 1242, an attempt was made to forbid any dominican activity within convents not legally in the care of the order which further diminished its responsibilities towards women.[80] Against this, Innocent IV and the dominican nuns launched a massive counter-offensive, and, from 1245 to 1250, thirty-two convents in Germany alone were incorporated into the order.[81]

The equally vain attempts of the franciscans to deny responsibility for women were likewise frustrated by Innocent IV, who, in 1246, authorised the incorporation of fourteen convents in France, Spain and

---

[75] Sbaralea, *Bullarum Franciscanum* I p 36.

[76] [T.] Ripoll, *Bullarum ordinis fratrum Praedicatorum*, ed A. Bremond (Rome 1729) VII p 7.

[77] Grundmann, *Religiöse Bewegungen* pp 218-19.

[78] *Ibid* p 241.   [79] Ripoll, *Bullarum ordinis fratrum Praedicatorum* I p 107.

[80] Grundmann, *Religiöse Bewegungen* p 245.   [81] *Ibid* pp 246-52.

Italy and also groups of *sorores minores* who were wandering, un-disciplined and unregulated, save for their desire to join the order of St Damian.[82]

The problem of economic provision of these convent communities faced both the curia and the mendicant orders. How far could religious women be allowed to live in absolute poverty without a guaranteed income? This was almost impossible to achieve. Dominican and fran-ciscan nuns and beguines alike attracted gifts and benefactions from patrons and admirers.[83] Clare, alone, managed to resist. In 1247, the question of convent property came to a head when Innocent IV attempted to impose uniform regulations in the convents of the order of St Damian by ordering them all, irrespective of any earlier and con-tradictory regulations, to accept property and income.[84] Clare reacted strongly to this threat to her privilege. Not only did she succeed in re-jecting this decree but used the opportunity to create a specific rule approximating as closely as possible to that of the friars. In 1252, she received confirmation of the *privilegium paupertatis* and also of the essential characteristic of her rule – the profession of the strict principle of poverty in accordance with the directions of Francis.[85] In a sense, therefore, she took her own community out of the order of St Damian to avoid the property regulations which the curia was attempting to impose.

The situation was complicated by the fact that by no means all female communities succeeded in gaining incorporation by the mendi-cant orders. Many women, therefore, remained in beguine communities with no uniform rule or defined leadership. Again there was the prob-lem of their supervision and pastoral care. The parish clergy, on the one hand, claimed them as part of their regular flock; the mendi-cants, on the other, resisted them by general legislation or by the appointment of special confessors from outside their orders.[86] But these beguine-type groups arose independently of the mendicant orders as a result of the movement towards the *vita apostolica*. In the Rhineland especially we find numbers of women who wished to lead a religious life, singly or in small groups, in inherited family houses or in those bought by pooling resources.[87] In Flanders, similar groups had close relations with the cistercians.

[82] Sbaralea, *Bullarum Franciscanum* I p 413; Grundmann, *Religiöse Bewegungen* pp 270–1.
[83] *Ibid* pp 224–6. [84] Sbaralea, *Bullarum Franciscanum* I p 476.
[85] *Ibid* I p 671. [86] Grundmann, *Religiöse Bewegungen* pp 274–5.
[87] Southern, *Western Society* pp 323–4.

Despite the statutes of the general chapter of the order many cistercian abbeys were spontaneously interested in the fate of religious women.[88] They defended them against the cathar adepts whose danger lay in their austere guise and pious way of life, and to whom women were easy prey. Two abbeys in particular, Villers and Aulne, both in the diocese of Liège, were noted for their patronage of pious women under a succession of abbots.[89] Why was there never an order of female cistercians? The answer, perhaps, is that there was no need for one, at least, not in Flanders. There, both the cistercians and the beguines seemed content with the situation as it was. The cistercians not only defended them against their detractors but supported them in difficulties as Jacques de Vitry had done previously. Abbot Walter of Villers wanted 'nothing more than to attract men to the religious life and to found convents for women'. But he saw the danger of an excessive multiplication of cistercian nunneries for 'he reflected that he was sufficiently occupied by the government of his own monastery'. Besides, 'he knew that if he sent the older, more enthusiastic monks to these convents to hear confessions, then the younger ones, missing their example, would become less humble and the discipline of the house would be weakened'.[90]

The cistercian general chapter remained firm in its attempt to keep women out of its order, yet, certainly in Flanders, it showed itself to be tolerant towards those abbots who themselves encouraged some degree of affiliation of convents and beguine groups. To the beguines of the diocese of Liège protection from the monks of Villers and Aulne was a valuable safeguard, not only against the penetration of heresy but as a defence against their detractors. Nor was this a one-way process. The beguines' lives embodied an idea of sanctity which was most attractive to contemporaries and especially to the cistercians in Flanders.[91]

The cistercians in Liège entered into spiritual relationships with nuns and beguines through which both sides benefited. St Bernard appeared to Mary of Oignies in a vision and she had a great admiration for his order.[92] But feminine emotion often went beyond the limit recommended by the abbot of Clairvaux. Diedala, a beguine, experienced a vision in which, one Christmas night, the Infant Jesus appeared and lay in her arms. She explained that she could not sufficiently wonder at this

[88] Roisin, 'L'efflorescence cistercienne' p 346.
[90] *Ibid* p 355.
[92] *ASB* 5 (1867) p 567.

[89] *Ibid* pp 358–60, 362–4.
[91] *Ibid* p 372.

marvel unless her friend, a monk at Villers, could enjoy it also. So, miraculously, she was transported to the abbey and there presented the child to the monk who was saying mass.[93]

The appearance of such large numbers of women in such diverse forms, demanding that they should be allowed to participate in the large-scale religious changes which were in progress in the early thirteenth century, perplexed the church and all those associated with it. A small number of like-minded men, whose activities covered a very wide area and who had influence with these women, attempted to deal with the problem. Jacques de Vitry in Flanders; bishop Fulk in Languedoc; some cistercian abbots in Spain and Flanders; Francis and Dominic in a wider European context; all had the interests of the church at heart. These interests were reflected, above all, by pope Innocent III, who led these men in their common aim to fight current heresies and to keep within the church any movements which might be of value. Alone, his far-sightedness, his breadth of vision and his skill in seeking out such movements, regulating and incorporating them into the church, might have made possible the creation of an independent female order, worthy of Clare or Mary of Oignies. But to recognise women in this way proved impossible in the face of antagonism from the traditional forces in the hierarchy. The lateran council of 1215, and Innocent's death in the following year, combined to hinder still more any progress towards meeting the demands of religious and semireligious women alike.

Subsequent popes indicated a willingness to support them but, by this time, the church was too rigid, the mendicants too widely dispersed and too preoccupied with their internal strife to care what became of them. Left to themselves, the women reverted, becoming branches of the male orders, some vigorous shoots such as the community of St Damian and the cistercian nuns and beguines in Flanders, others, such as the incorporated dominican and franciscan convents, proliferating like suckers and risking always severance from the main life-giving trunk of the church.

[93] Roisin, 'L'efflorescence cistercienne' p 373.

THE REPRESENTATION OF THE ENGLISH LOWER CLERGY IN PARLIAMENT DURING THE LATER FOURTEENTH CENTURY

by A. K. MCHARDY

'THE service of God in Church and State': in medieval England these two usually separate activities were combined in the parliamentary attendance of the clergy. Two methods were employed in summoning the clergy: parliamentary abbots and the bishops were called by individual writs of summons; the lower clergy were called indirectly.

The writ of summons to each bishop of England and Wales included a mandate, called, from its opening word, the *premunientes* clause, ordering the bishop to cause to appear in parliament the head of his cathedral chapter, one proctor for the cathedral clergy, all the archdeacons, and two proctors for the diocesan clergy.[1] After 1340, obedience to the *premunientes* clause was not enforced by the crown,[2] so technically the command to the lower clergy to be present in parliament was episcopal, not royal. It is not the intention to discuss here the theoretical and constitutional issues involved but to describe the execution of the *premunientes* clause between 1340 and 1400 as far as the limitations of the sources allow.

These sources are of three kinds: notes of execution found in episcopal registers and capitular act books; notices of the appointment of proctors preserved in the Public Record Office; and entries, among accounts, recording the payment of expenses to clergy attending parliament. Bishops' registers vary greatly in the amount of information they afford. In some episcopal chanceries it was not the practice, even before 1340, to enter the writs of summons in the bishop's register; in others, though the writs were registered, no notes of execution were appended. Thus in several dioceses the episcopal registers

---

[1] The *premunientes* clause was first used in 1295. R[eports from the Lords Committees touching the] D[ignity of a] P[eer of the Realm] (London 1820) III p 67.

[2] The provincial writs enjoining the attendance of the lower clergy were issued for the last time for the parliament of March 1340, the second of the three parliaments held in that year. *Ibid* IV p 518.

afford no evidence for the execution of the *premunientes* clause either before or after 1340. But even in the most informative registers the evidence is far from complete. Thirty-four parliaments met during the episcopate of John Buckingham of Lincoln (June 1363–July 1398); twenty-four writs are entered in his registers, sixteen being followed by notes of execution, and there is also, among the *Memoranda*, one note of execution of a writ which was not recorded. There is even less material in chapter act books. At York, for example, the apparent failure to enter information about parliamentary proctors is in marked contrast to the number of appointments actually made, as we know from PRO special collection 10. The same holds true of the Lincoln chapter act books. Such seeming carelessness may be explained by the fact that the episcopal mandates to execute the *premunientes* clause soon came to be couched in common form. Once the form of the mandates was established it was often the practice to add only a brief note indicating that they had been dispatched. From the writing of no more than a brief and stereotyped note it was but a short step to writing nothing at all.[3] The general reluctance of chapter members to record the appointments of parliamentary proctors in their act books may be accounted for by the limited time these proctors held office.

The second source of information, the notices of the appointment of proctors, is contained in PRO special collection 10. A valuable source of information about the parliamentary attendance of both bishops and abbots,[4] this class also affords evidence relating to the execution of the *premunientes* clause. Deans and priors of cathedral churches, their chapters, archdeacons and the diocesan clergy – notice of the appointments of proctors representing all these categories are to be found among the files of special collection 10. But the collection, which is arranged in roughly chronological order in files each containing fifty documents, is by no means complete. For some parliaments there is no information at all; others are imperfectly represented. This is true of the material on abbots' and bishops' proctors;[5] but even more serious are the losses of material relating to the lower clergy, as a comparison with other extant sources indicates, and conclusions based on the evidence of this class can be only tentative.

Even more scanty is the evidence to be gleaned from financial

---

[3] See, for example, Guildhall Library, London, MS 9531 no 3 (*Register* Braybrooke) fols 441ᵛ, 443, 443ᵛ, 444ᵛ.

[4] J. S. Roskell, 'The Problem of the Attendance of the Lords in Medieval Parliaments', *BIHR* 29 (1956) pp 153–204.   [5] *Ibid* p 173.

records, but accounts, both capitular and manorial, do occasionally identify payments to meet the expenses of clergy going to parliament, and it is not too much to hope that further investigation of accounts will yield fresh evidence.

The scarcity and incompleteness of the evidence here reviewed has led some writers to doubt whether any clerical proctors attended parliament during most of this century since they made no mark on the political scene.[6] This view was modified, at least as far as the diocesan clergy were concerned, by four historians working on economic aspects of the fourteenth century. In 1927 A. E. Levett showed that the accounts of the manors of Gamlingay (Cambs) and Wootton (Hants) provided evidence about the attendance of clerical proctors in parliament in the early fourteenth century.[7] In 1933 E. C. Lowry published material from the Gamlingay accounts of the later fourteenth century,[8] and the following year F. M. Page produced evidence of attendance during the same period from another Cambridgeshire manor, Oakington.[9] Finally, Marjorie Morgan, in *The English Lands of the Abbey of Bec* stated that the records of the manor of Combe in the bailiwick of Ogbourne showed payments being made towards the expenses of clerical proctors for parliament in the years 1306–7 and 1308–9.[10] In the light of these studies it could no longer be held that the clergy refused to attend parliament, and that, in particular, 1340 marked the end of any such attendance. Some later writers conceded that the clergy did attend, but did so only rarely, and thus let slip the opportunity of making their voice heard at the centre of political life.[11]

There is, however, enough evidence to be derived from the class of parliamentary proxies to show that the clergy were attending parliament in the 1330s more than occasionally. Of the last eleven parliaments to which the lower clergy were called before their attendance ceased to be enforced there is evidence of the appointment of proctors for ten by the clergy in ten dioceses. The largest known number of

---

[6] A. F. Pollard, *The Evolution of Parliament* (2 ed London 1924) pp 74, 122.

[7] 'The Financial Organisation of the Manor', *Ec.HR* 1 (1927) p 70.

[8] [E. C.] Lowry, ['Clerical Proctors in Parliament and Knights of the Shire, 1280–1374'.] *EHR* 48 (1933) pp 443–55.

[9] *The Estates of Crowland Abbey* (Cambridge 1934) p 63.

[10] (Oxford 1946) p 58 n 5.

[11] [M. V.] Clarke, [*Medieval Representation and Consent*] (London 1936) pp 140, 150; A. M. Reich, *The Parliamentary Abbots to 1470* (Berkeley, California, 1941) p 361; but see also Edward Miller, *Historical Studies of the English Parliament* (Cambridge 1970) I, p 17 for the view that the proctors of the lower clergy had withdrawn from parliament.

appointments is twelve and relates to the parliaments both of February 1334 and of 1335. But the figures show no tailing off towards 1340.[12]

Could it be held, then, that 1340 marked a turning point and that from this date clergy attended parliament only occasionally? Fifty-one parliaments were held from July 1340 to 1400, and special collection 10 provides evidence for the attendance of proctors of the lower clergy at thirty-six of them. It is true that the number of appointments for any one parliament never reaches double figures, but the blank years are interspersed through the whole period, and again, there is no evidence of a tailing off of attendance at the end of the century.[13] Closer examination of this and other evidence allows a more positive conclusion than that of 'occasional attendance' to be reached.

The first command of the *premunientes* clause was that the bishop should order the head of his cathedral chapter, whether dean or prior, to attend parliament in person, and the members of the chapter to send one suitable proctor to represent them. This order was sent directly to the chapter in all dioceses except, apparently, Carlisle and Durham, where the bishops wrote to their officials who then informed the chapter.[14] It was laid down also in the episcopal mandates, that the chapter was to submit, in the form of a letter patent to its bishop, a report of what action it had taken. In the dioceses of York and Worcester a deadline was imposed for the return of this information.[15] At Lincoln bishop Buckingham sometimes went further, specifying not only the date but also to which episcopal manor the certificate was to be forwarded.[16] He allowed between twenty and thirty days for the operation. A letter announcing the appointment was then addressed to

---

[12] The numbers of appointments are: March 1332 4; Feb 1334 12; Sept 1334 0; 1335 12; 1336 8; 1337 4; 1338 1; Feb 1339 2; Oct 1339 6; Jan 1340 2; March 1340 6. The lower clergy were not summoned to the parliaments of Sept and Dec 1332. The list of parliaments used is that given in *Handbook of British Chronology*, edd F. M. Powicke and E. B. Fryde (2 ed London 1961) pp 519–28.

[13] For the fifty-one parliaments from July 1340 to 1399 the numbers of appointments extant are: 0; 1; 0; 7; 0; 5; 1; 1; 9; 5; 4; 7; 5; 1; 0; 9; 6; 0; 0; 0; 0; 8; 5; 6; 2; 6; 1; 1; 6; 1; 4; 3; 0; 1; 1; 0; 0; 4; 3; 5; 5; 0; 0; 0; 5; 7; 7; 2; 4; 1; 1.

[14] Carlisle: Carlisle Castle *Register* Appleby pp 147, 293–4, 305–6; Durham: The Prior's Kitchen *Register* Hatfield fols 168, 171ᵛ.

[15] Borthwick Institute York *Register* 10 (Zouche) fol 246, *Register* 11 (Thoresby) fol 45; Worcester Record Office *Register* Barnet (Worc) p 23, *Register* Brian p 230.

[16] Writing from Stow Park (Lincs) on 30 Aug 1382 Buckingham ordered the return to be made to Sleaford (Lincs) before 22 Sept. L[incolnshire] A[rchives] O[ffice] Lincoln *Register* 12B (Buckingham, Royal Writs) fol 35; on 7 Sept 1383 a mandate issued from Nettleham (Lincs) asked for the certificate to be sent to Sleaford by 29 Sept. *Ibid* fol 38ᵛ.

the king by the chapter, while the proctors were provided with letters patent as proof of their status. Occasionally both types of letters are extant.[17]

Evidence survives that Worcester cathedral priory was represented at twenty-one parliaments, the earliest being in January 1348, the latest in 1399.[18] On each occasion the prior and chapter issued separate letters of appointment, and for eleven parliaments the letters of both prior and chapter have survived. Durham, too, was represented at twenty-one parliaments as may be seen by examining both the PRO material and the register of the priory.[19] Again the evidence is spread over a wide period; the first dates from 1357, the last from 1399. Sometimes – there are eleven instances – the prior and chapter acted together in choosing their proctors; sometimes they acted separately – there is evidence of eight instances of separate action by the prior and of six instances by the chapter. The variations in practice do not coincide with changes in priors and have no obvious explanation. At Carlisle, John Horncastle, prior of the augustinian cathedral, appointed proctors to represent him in five parliaments from 1344 to 1362;[20] and on two of these occasions his cathedral chapter is known to have appointed proctors also.[21] At Ely, the prior and chapter are known to have appointed proctors for the parliaments of 1362 and 1373.[22]

A similar pattern is revealed by examination of the material relating to secular cathedrals. York chapter appointed proctors for twenty-one parliaments during this period from 1344 to 1394. Next comes Lincoln whose sixteen appointments, all but one made by the chapter alone, range in time from 1354 to 1399.[23] Evidence on a lesser scale comes from Bangor, though the five[24] surviving records of appointment

---

[17] Both the York chapter's letters of appointment of proctors for the parliament of 1344, PRO MS SC 10/23 nos 1146 (letter patent), 1147 (letter close addressed to the Crown); the prior of Durham's appointments for 1393, PRO MS SC 10/38 nos 1859 (letter patent), 1896 (letter close addressed to the Crown).

[18] PRO MS SC 10/25–40 *passim*.

[19] The Prior's Kitchen Durham Prior and Chapter *Register* II fols 114, 195, 332ᵛ.

[20] 'Bro. John de Horncastle O.Can.S.A.', occurs as prior on 10 Jan 1353, and resigned on 10 Nov 1376. [J.] Le Neve, [Fasti Ecclesiae Anglicanae,] (3 ed London, 1962–7) VI, p 100.

[21] These were 1354, PRO MS SC 10/26 nos 1269 (prior), 1272 (chapter); 1357, SC 10/27 nos 1321 (chapter), 1339 (prior).

[22] PRO MS SC 10/28 no 1400; SC 10/30 no 1485.

[23] In nine instances the evidence is drawn from the chapter accounts. LAO Bj/2/7 fols 29, 48ᵛ, 71, 118–118ᵛ, 138, 159ᵛ; Bj/2/8 fols 10ᵛ, 97; Bj/2/10 fol 11.

[24] In addition, in 1379 an appointment was made on behalf of the dean, to which reference will be made below.

made by the dean and chapter all date from early in our period;[25] from London whose four examples, three emanating from the dean and chapter, one from the chapter alone, range in time between 1371 and 1393; and from Chichester whose dean and chapter were represented in the parliaments of January 1377 and 1379.[26] The dean of Lichfield is known to have appointed a proctor for the parliament of 1363, and the dean of Wells for the parliament of February 1388.[27]

It is worthy of note how scanty is the evidence for the appointment of proctors by the deans of secular cathedrals compared with that for appointments by priors of monastic cathedrals. The explanation must lie in the fact that most of the secular deans were king's clerks. As such they might well attend parliament in person, perhaps as part of their administrative duties; but it is equally feasible to conjecture that they might be beyond the reach of episcopal mandates, for few were resident in their cathedral closes. Thus, on several occasions, the canons of Lincoln, when appointing parliamentary proctors, reported that their dean was absent.[28] Here one might mention that to one of the absent deans, master John Stretele, belongs the distinction of receiving two summonses to the same parliament, that of 1365. He received an individual writ of summons, probably in connection with his work in Gascony,[29] and an indirect summons as dean, through the *premunientes* clause.[30] But the dean's absence need not necessarily have meant that he was unrepresented in parliament: John Martin, dean of Bangor, was at the Roman curia in 1379, but his *locum tenens* as dean, John Pagge appointed three proctors for parliament.[31]

In respect of parliamentary duties archdeacons bore certain resemblances to deans of secular cathedrals. Among archdeacons, too, there were king's clerks, and there were those who were absent when the time came for them to be apprised of their parliamentary obligations.[32]

---

25 The earliest in 1344, the latest in 1357. PRO MS SC 10/24 nos 1169, 1191, SC 10/25 no 1237, SC 10/26 no 1296, SC 10/27 no 1323.

26 London, chapter, PRO MS SC 10/29 no 1438; dean and chapter, SC 10/34 no 1651, SC 10/38 nos 1854, 1874. Chichester, SC 10/31 no 1538, SC 10/32 no 1556, SC 10/33 no 1602.

27 Lichfield, PRO MS SC 10/29 no 1409; Wells, SC 10/36 nos 1797, 1800.

28 For example, 1363, PRO MS SC 10/29 no 1403; 1373, SC 10/30 no 1494; Jan 1397, SC 10/40 no 1962.

29 RDP IV, p 641; he was chancellor of Guyenne, 1362–c Sept 1364, [A. B.] Emden, [*A Biographical Register of the University of*] *Oxford* (Oxford 1957–9) III, p 1804.

30 He was dean 1361–9, Le Neve I, p 4 (from the corrected copy in the LAO).

31 PRO MS SC 10/33 no 1614.

32 The official of the archdeacon of Worcester, in answer to a mandate of bishop Barnet

In the southern province the information came to the archdeacon in a mandate directly from the bishop, and in the northern through a mandate transmitted *via* the episcopal official.[33] The archdeacon had two duties: the first was to attend in person or, if this were not possible, then to appoint a proctor. The probability is that many archdeacons did attend parliament, often both in their own right and as proctors for others.

Few commissions from archdeacons to their parliamentary proctors are known to me, and most emanate from the northern province. On 7 January 1352 William Rothbury, archdeacon of Carlisle, commissioned proctors to represent him in the parliament beginning six days later. He also commissioned proctors for parliament in 1358.[34] His successor, master John Appleby, appointed one proctor in 1368, 1369 and January 1377. On the first occasion, in 1368, the letter patent of appointment was sealed with the bishop's seal; this bishop was Thomas Appleby, the archdeacon's brother.[35] In 1362 and 1363 the archdeacons of both Durham and Northumberland were represented in parliament by proctors,[36] while William Ferriby, archdeacon of Cleveland, appointed representatives for four parliaments.[37] The three examples from the southern province concern the archdeacons of Cornwall, Buckingham and Colchester.[38]

The second duty of an archdeacon was to warn the clergy in his jurisdiction to cooperate in electing two suitable proctors to represent the diocesan clergy in parliament. How this mandate was obeyed varied both from place to place and from time to time. In Durham diocese proctors were chosen by the clergy of the two archdeaconries acting independently in 1344 and 1394; but in 1362 one appointment was made by the clergy of the whole diocese.[39] Similarly, the York

---

dated 14 Sept 1362, replied that his archdeacon was overseas so could not be warned to attend the forthcoming parliament, *Register* Barnet (Worc) p 23.

[33] Carlisle: *Register* Appleby pp 147, 293–4, 305–6; Durham: *Register* Hatfield fols 168, 171v; York: *Register* 10 (Zouche) fol 246, *Register* 11 (Thoresby) fol 44v, *Register* 12 (Alexander Nevville) fol 102v.

[34] PRO MS SC 10/25 no 1249, SC 10/28 no 1359 (see Le Neve, VI, p 102 where the earliest occurrence of Rothbury as archdeacon of Carlisle is given as 11 June 1355).

[35] *Register* Appleby pp 170, 194; PRO MS SC 10/32 no 1552; Emden, *Oxford* I, p 41.

[36] PRO MS SC 10/28 no 1387, SC 10/29 nos 1402, 1412, SC 10/30 no 1456.

[37] 1371, PRO MS SC 10/29 no 1425; 1372, SC 10/30 no 1467; 1373 SC 10/31 no 1508; Jan. 1377, *ibid* no 1550.

[38] Nicholas Newton, 1371, PRO MS SC 10/29 no 1429; William Gynewell, 1376(?), SC 10/31 no 1513; John Carlton, 1393, SC 10/38 no 1873.

[39] PRO MS SC 10/24 nos 1160, 1176, SC 10/39 nos 1911, 1912, SC 10/28 no 1380

diocesan clergy acted as one body in choosing proctors in 1341 and 1352, whereas for the parliament of February 1388 two of the archdeaconries, Cleveland and York, sent separate notice of the appointment of proctors to represent them. In 1394, however, the proctors were again chosen by the clergy of the whole diocese.[40] The only clergy in the diocese of London, which contained four archdeaconries, who are known to have appointed any representatives were those of the archdeaconry of Colchester.[41]

Some details of the organisation of proctorial elections may be gathered from the registers of bishop Buckingham of Lincoln. Buckingham's mandates, addressed to the archdeacons or their officials, ordered them to summon their clergy to a meeting to elect proctors for parliament. The size of Lincoln diocese, however, meant that, as in the diocese of Coventry and Lichfield, preliminary elections had to be held. The archdeacons or their officials ordered the rural deans to cause a proctor from each deanery to come to an archidiaconal meeting to elect one representative. The eight proctors, one from each archdeaconry, then assembled at a place named by the bishop to elect two men to represent the diocesan clergy.[42] By the time of Buckingham's episcopate two centres had become traditional for diocesan meeting of all kinds, St Mary's Church, Stamford (Lincs)[43] and All Saints' Church, Northampton. In ten cases out of eleven Buckingham chose Northampton for the meetings to elect parliamentary proxies.[44]

The meeting, held on a day chosen by the bishop, was presided over by his commissaries, two or three in number. The names of the commissaries are known in seven instances and in all but one the abbot of St James's, Northampton, was of their number.[45] Their duties were fourfold:[46] to receive certificates about the preliminary elections; to

[40] PRO MS SC 10/23 no 1113, SC 10/25 no 1235; SC 10/37 nos 1808, 1815, SC 10/39 no 1930.
[41] In Nov 1384, PRO MS SC 10/35 no 1735; 1385, SC 10/36 no 1767; 1393, SC 10/38 no 1894. [42] Clarke pp 327–8.
[43] Ibid p 328; see LAO Lincoln Register 12 (Buckingham, Memoranda) fol 136 for a diocesan meeting, held in St Mary's, Stamford, to discuss the tax grant of £50,000 in 1371.
[44] Compare the elections of proctors for convocation during Buckingham's episcopate, of which ten out of thirteen were held at Northampton.
[45] He was usually joined by a secular clerk who was also a magister and engaged in diocesan administration. Examples are master John Banbury, official of the archdeacon of Northampton, Lincoln Register 12B fol 42, Register 12 fol 292; or master James Brigg, sequestrator in the same archdeaconry, Register 12B fol 52ᵛ.
[46] Commission were not entered in the registers. The execution note after the writ of 18 July 1397 is particularly full, ibid fol 72.

ensure parliamentary proctors were elected; to arrange for the proctors' expenses; and to send the bishop a written report of the proceedings before a given date, usually within seven days of the meeting. The proctors elected received payment for their expenses. The payments were probably levied, as were those for proctors in convocation, on all assessed benefices, at the rate of a halfpenny in the pound.[47]

There is evidence that the clergy of Carlisle diocese sent proctors to eight parliaments from 1344 to January 1377.[48] It is known that the clergy of York diocese, sometimes the whole of it, sometimes parts only, were represented in four parliaments, the earliest in 1341, the latest in 1394,[49] while the clergy of both Durham and Ely dioceses were represented three times.[50] In November 1384, in 1385, and in 1393 the clergy of Colchester archdeaconry appointed proctors,[51] as did their counterparts of Bangor diocese on two occasions.[52] In 1363 the clergy of Coventry and Lichfield commissioned proctors to represent them,[53] and those of Winchester and Exeter dioceses chose proctors in 1371.[54]

On the other hand there is evidence that some of the diocesan clergy refused to cooperate. In response to a writ of summons to the parliament of 13 October 1363 John Barnet, bishop of Worcester, ordered both his archdeacons to warn the clergy in their jurisdictions to elect proctors. The archdeacon of Gloucester replied that in accordance with the bishop's mandate he had caused his clergy to be warned of their obligations, but the official of the archdeacon of Worcester – the archdeacon was abroad – made a very different report; he had called the clergy of the archdeaconry together at a certain day and place to elect a proctor, but with one voice they replied that they were neither bound nor accustomed, from time immemorial, to send a proctor to parliament or any other council unless summoned thereto by the archbishop of Canterbury.[55]

---

[47] Lincoln *Register* 12 fols 186ᵛ, 422ᵛ.

[48] 1344, 1348, 1352, 1355, 1357, 1358, 1362, 1377, PRO MS SC 10/24 nos 1154, 1200; SC 10/26 nos 1261, 1295; SC 10/27 no 1319; SC 10/28 nos 1356, 1390; SC 10/32 no 1557.

[49] The other occasions were 1352 and Feb 1388. PRO MS SC 10/23 no 1113, SC 10/25 no 1235, SC 10/37 nos 1808, 1815, SC 10/39 no 1930.

[50] Durham: 1344, 1362, 1394, PRO MS SC 10/24 nos 1160, 1176, SC 10/28 no 1380, SC 10/39 nos 1911, 1912. Ely: 1366, 1371, 1373, Lowry p 453.

[51] PRO MS SC 10/35 no 1735, SC 10/36 no 1767, SC 10/38 no 1894.

[52] 1352, PRO MS SC 10/25 no 1240; 1379, SC 10/32 no 1594.

[53] PRO MS SC 10/29 no 1408.

[54] *Ibid* nos 1427, 1430.   [55] *Register* Barnet (Worc) p 23.

Such a response, however, was exceptional: the evidence shows that the clergy of a majority of the English dioceses were prepared to execute the *premunientes* clause, and it may well be asked why the proctors of the lower clergy made no impression on the parliamentary scene.[56] One can but speculate, but three possible or at least contributing causes may be advanced. First, a large number of appointments did not necessarily mean there was a large number of attenders, for one person might be chosen as the representative of several groups or individuals. In 1363, for instance, the dean of Lichfield commissioned master Thomas Rippeley as sole proctor while the clergy of the diocese made him co-proctor.[57] In 1371 the clergy of both Winchester and Exeter dioceses chose master Robert Wikeford as one of their two proctors.[58] Master John Blanchard, bound to attend parliament as archdeacon of Worcester, was commissioned to represent, in the parliament of 1373, the chapter of Worcester, the bishop of Salisbury, the abbot of Evesham and the abbot of Glastonbury;[59] and his situation was not unique.

Second, it is probable that some parliamentary proctors were not recognised as such, because they were already bound to attend parliament in another capacity. Thus the widespread use made of royal chancery clerks as proctors is to be explained by the central part they played in parliamentary business: as far as is known, all the receivers of petitions to parliament were chancery clerks,[60] and their attendance at parliament was guaranteed by their obligations to the crown. The advantage of choosing such men as proctors is obvious, but they would be recognised as chancery clerks first and only secondly as proctors.

Third, the proctors did not form a cohesive and homogeneous group; it was a mixture of monks[61] and of seculars such as king's

---

56 During the period under review only one clerical proctor, Thomas Haxey, seems to have played any significant role: in 1397 when proctor for the abbot of Selby, as indeed he had been on four previous occasions, he achieved notoriety by presenting a petition condemning extravagance in the royal household, PRO MS SC 10/37 no 1847 (1391); SC 10/38 no 1872 (1392); SC 10/39 no 1916 (1394); SC 10/40 nos 1952 (1395), 1964 (1397).

57 PRO MS SC 10/29 nos 1408, 1409.

58 *Ibid* nos 1427, 1430.

59 PRO MS CS 10/30 nos 1483, 1486, 1491, 1497.

60 H. G. Richardson and George Sayles, 'The King's Ministers in Parliament, 1272–1377, III, The Parliaments of Edward III', *EHR* 47 (1932) p 379.

61 The chapters of both Durham and Worcester often commissioned fellow-monks to represent them.

clerks,[62] canon lawyers,[63] and diocesan officers.[64] The clergy of both Carlisle and Durham dioceses appointed laymen;[65] but on one occasion the clergy of the archdeaconry of Colchester committed the archbishop of Canterbury to represent them.[66]

To sum up: it has been shown that for some dioceses, notably Carlisle, Durham, Lincoln and York there is evidence that the *premunientes* clause was being executed on a considerable scale.[67] Less activity seems evident in dioceses such as London, Worcester, and Bangor. In a third group, of which Ely, Exeter and Chichester are examples, the evidence enables us to say only that response to the summons to parliament was made sporadically. Some other dioceses may not have responded at all. Differences of method and extent of execution have been noted even within dioceses, especially where the diocesan clergy were concerned. No claim is made that representatives of all the lower clergy attended every parliament, but, by describing sixty years of the story of the attendance of the lower clergy in parliament, a story that does not end in 1400[68] nor even in 1500,[69] I hope to have shown that the lower clergy were more assiduous in undertaking their parliamentary duties than has been assumed hitherto.

[62] For example, master Robert Wikeford, already mentioned, Emden, *Oxford* III pp 2045-6; or Richard Piriton, exchequer clerk and archdeacon of Colchester, proctor for the clergy of his archdeaconry, PRO MS SC 10/36 no 1767.

[63] Such as master Thomas Rippeley, compiler of the canon law formulary, Gonville and Caius MS 588/737; and master Richard Coningston official of the court of Canterbury, proctor for the clergy of the archdeaconries of Cleveland and York, PRO MS SC 10/37 nos 1808, 1815.

[64] The official of the archdeacon of Merioneth was a proctor for the clergy of Bangor diocese, appointed 3 April 1379, PRO MS SC 10/32 no 1594.

[65] PRO MS SC 10/32 no 1557, SC 10/39 nos 1911, 1912.

[66] William Courtenay, PRO MS SC 10/35 no 1735.

[67] Some of the material for these dioceses has almost certainly been lost. Thus though there is considerable evidence in bishop Buckingham's registers that proctors for the diocesan clergy of Lincoln were appointed, none of these commissions survive in SC 10. The five notices of execution in the register of bishop Appleby of Carlisle correspond to only one notice of the appointment of proctors by his diocesan clergy, and to none by the prior and chapter of Carlisle cathedral.

[68] The numbers of appointments of proctors for the first five parliaments after 1400 are: 5; 7; 7; 12; 3. PRO MS SC 10/40-42. Evidence of the execution of the *premunientes* clause is also to be found at Lincoln, in the registers of Philip Repingdon, *The Register of Bishop Repingdon 1405-1419*, ed Margaret Archer, Lincoln Record Society 58, II (Lincoln 1963) pp 378-9, LAO Lincoln *Register* 15B (Repingdon, Royal Writs) fols 11ᵛ-12; and at Durham in Durham Priory *Register* III fols 15, 32, 68.

[69] There is evidence for the sending of proctors in the sixteenth century by the chapter of Wells, Eric Kemp, 'The Origins of the Canterbury Convocation', *JEH* 3 (1952) p 142; and for the parliamentary attendance of the dean of Lincoln in 1536, LAO Lincoln Dean and Chapter Wills II, fol 44.

PAPAL WITCHCRAFT: THE CHARGES
AGAINST BENEDICT XIII

by MARGARET HARVEY

THE charges with which I shall deal in this paper were almost
certainly a tissue of nonsense. Indeed a recent – hostile –
account dismisses them as containing *motifs presque folkloriques
rappellant la legende de Sylvestre II*.[1] The folklore is itself interesting
however, and so are the circumstances in which it could be delivered
solemnly as fact to auditors at a general council by a powerful group
including doctors of law and even a cardinal.

The circumstances in which the charges were brought were as
follows:[2] In 1409 popes Gregory XII and Benedict XIII were tried by
the council of Pisa, with the intention of deposing them to end the
schism. First, 37 charges were brought against them, giving a fairly
detailed and damning account of the recent behaviour of both in
failing to keep their oaths to end the schism.[3] Some members of the
council must have felt that these charges were not adequate, however,
because on 17 May 1409 the council gave permission for new charges
to be added if necessary.[4] Ten new charges were indeed prepared and
heard from May 27–30, so we have the full account of the evidence of
the witnesses.[5] Among these charges are accusations of witchcraft
against each pope.[6]

Gregory was said to have consulted a jewish doctor, to foretell his
future as pope. The evidence here was meagre and I will not trouble
you with the details.[7] The charge against Benedict XIII read:

> Item, ut ipse posset per phas et nephas papatum retinere, et que
> sibi et circa papatum ipso vivente ventura erant prescire valeret,

---

[1] FM, XIV (1962) p 152.

[2] [N.] Valois, [*La France et le Grand Schisme d'Occident*] (Paris 1902 repr 1967) IV, pp 94–7
gives the charges with some comment. [S] Puig y Puig, [*Pedro de Luna, ultimo Papa
de Aviñon 1387–1430*] (Barcelona 1920) pp 208–14 repeats Valois with a few additions.

[3] [J.] Vincke, ['Acta Concilii Pisani'], *Römische Quartalschrift* 46 (Rome 1938) pp
213–94.   [4] *Ibid* p 163.

[5] *Ibid* pp 185–208. Valois is worth consulting because in some cases his transcriptions are
better than Vincke's.   [6] *Ibid* pp 183–5.   [7] *Ibid* pp 192, 205

multos nigromanticos, divinatores, magicos et libros nigromancie et alios perquiri mandavit et perquisivit ac habuit, et multociens malignos demoniorum spiritus tam per se quam per alios invocavit et consuluit ac invocari et consului fecit, ac eciam quendam librum nigromancie in terris Sarracenorum perquiri fecit, quoniam alibi ipsum reperire non poterat, et ipsum librum ab ipsis Sarracenis habuit, et pro ipso perquirendo et habendo exposuit circa mille francos.

The evidence offered in the case of Benedict was much more interesting than in the case of Gregory. First of all there was the attempt to prove that he employed necromancers and *divinatores*. Here the aim seems to have been to exploit the ill-repute of some of Benedict's associates – ill-repute not firmly founded – and to try to suggest that these were merely the centre of a larger circle. The most maligned member of the inner circle was Francisco Aranda, a most important counsellor of the pope. Aranda was an interesting person in his own right.[8] He had been a knight and had become a councillor to the royal house of Aragon. Then he became a carthusian lay-brother, without however losing his former influence with the king. In 1403 Benedict summoned him from his monastery in Catalonia to be his adviser. It is clear that the pope relied on him greatly, which explains the hostility to him at Pisa. Several witnesses actually admit that he was thought to be a necromancer because he was too close to Benedict. Aranda was thought to be able to see distant events (which may be a tribute to his sources of information). The bishop-elect of Fréjus, Gilles le Jeune,[9] had been active in the curia and in a position to know those concerned. He said that Aranda had told the pope of the death of the duke of Burgundy on the very day it happened (in 1404) though the curia was in Provence and the death occurred in Brabant. When official news came 15 days later all suddenly realised that he had got the day correct.[10] Le Jeune continues:

> et ex hoc et quia ipse dominus Franciscus totaliter videtur regere ipsum dominum Benedictum, insurrexit fama publica in curia

8 *DHGE* III col 1420.

9 Vincke p 186. His evidence was suspect. He was litigating to obtain Fréjus and was probably relying on Pisa to ratify his title, C. Eubel, *Hierarchia Catholica Medii Aevi* (Münster 1913) I, p. 263. He was not disappointed. He was consecrated by Alexander V. Vincke pp 214, 216, 233 shows him active in Benedict's service and speaking with pope and cardinals.

10 Valois III p 367. The death was on 27 April 1404. Philip was Benedict's chief opponent.

ipsius domini Benedicti, quod dictus Franciscus utatur arte nigromancie . . .

I have been able to find no evidence of Aranda's activities which might
have been a firm foundation for this charge of witchcraft. Indeed he
seems to have been in some ways a rather saintly man. On the other
hand he seems to have had an interest in alchemy, and this could have
started the stories going.[11] Furthermore Aranda had in his service a
very sinister Spanish knight of St John, tall, thin, with (naturally) a
long beard. Several witnesses had had him pointed out as the chief
invoker of demons in Aranda's service. Evidence for this was given by
the dean of Tours, a lawyer called Jean de Seilhons;[12] Pierre Fabre,
provost of Riez, and a writer of papal letters and abbreviator;[13]
François de Chissé, a layman from Geneva[14] and Charles de Auzac
from Maguelonne, a servant of the cardinal of Viviers.[15]

Another suspect from the pope's immediate circle was the Catalan
franciscan Francesco Eximenis, whom Benedict made patriarch of
Jerusalem in 1408.[16] Jean Guiard, archpriest of Poitiers, accused him of
teaching the pope to invoke demons and of writing to him about such
things when they were apart. This witness had acted as a messenger
between the cardinals and Benedict in 1408 and early 1409 and had
eventually been ejected from Perpignan by the papal side when
negotiations finally broke down.[17] Eximenis is well known as a pro-
lific writer in Catalan and Latin. The basis for this story is no doubt
his interest in and writing on the prophecies of the abbot Joachim.[18] He
certainly was interested in Joachim's ages of the world even though he
did not try to give them a date. Such an interest was of course a far
cry from invocation of demons, but it would in some eyes have placed
him in the ranks of those holding dubious beliefs.

As well as naming certain individuals, the witnesses tried to show
that there was a wider group in the service of the papal witch. So one
finds mention of a beguin in Portovenere and Perpignan, a hermit in

[11] Puig y Puig app no LXXXVI, p 534, a letter from Diego Navarro.
[12] Vincke p 191.   [13] *Ibid* p 196.
[14] *Ibid* p 194.   [15] *Ibid* p 204.
[16] A convenient summary of information in *DHGE* XVI cols 252–5.
[17] Vincke p 202. See also *ibid* p 154, Valois IV pp 45–6 and [Martin de] Alpartil, [*Chronica actitatorum temporibus d. Benedicti pape XIII*] ed F. Ehrle, Görres Gesellschaft (Paderborn 1906) pp 375 ff for his activity as a letter carrier. Valois IV p 309 shows him as notary for the French nation at Constance.
[18] [M.] Reeves, [*The influence of prophecy in the later Middle Ages. A study in Joachimism*] (Oxford 1969) pp 222–3.

Avignon and a Spanish fraticello of the third order called Alvarez who was in the house of cardinal Amadeo of Savoy.[19] This last man was said by Jean Poncet,[20] clerk of the sacred college, a lawyer and a canon of Besançon, to be in touch with a whole group of minorite magicians in Provence. The reason for mentioning these sinister personages becomes clearer from some further evidence. Jean Guiard, the archpriest,[21] said he had often spoken with a minorite brother John Benedict de Bergerac, whom he described as a *divinator* who was always with the pope. This man showed Guiard two books in which were many figures of popes, kings, angels, demons, ships, turrets and waters. He said that Benedict would fly to a corner of land but that afterwards there would arise a king of Sicily of the house of Aragon, who would be emperor. As emperor he would bring Benedict to Rome by sea and there Benedict would crown him emperor and both would rule the world and hold it in subjection. This sounds like not witchcraft, but joachimist prophecy. The two books were almost certainly the 'pope prophecies', one group of which Miss Reeves described elsewhere.[22] Miss Reeves has pointed out also the frequency of such prophecy among the beguins, especially in Provence, and among the friars minor both orthodox and fraticelli in Aragon and Catalonia at this time.[23] This may lend colour to the stories about beguins and sinister fraticelli and groups in Provence.

As well as using *divinatores* Benedict was accused of using books of necromancy and of searching out one special book in the land of the saracens. Under this head the witnesses produced much circumstantial evidence, though some of it is contradictory. The bishop of Nîmes[24] claimed to have met the minorite master of theology (called Gilles Vanalatte) who had procured the book from the saracens for the pope. But no less a man than the prior general of the order of St John of Jerusalem Walter Crassus[25] had a much more intriguing tale, which must have happened about 1405. Crassus had travelled from Savona[26] to Avignon with a young theologian of Bologna, a native of Cordova. The student said that in Bologna he had heard that Benedict was looking for a book compiled by a Jew. He had found it in the Bologna

[19] Jean Guiard refers to Eximenis, a beguin, a hermit and friar John Benedict de Bergerac (Vincke p 202).
[20] *Ibid* p 197.   [21] *Ibid* p 203.
[22] [M.] Reeves. 'Some Popular Prophecies [from the fourteenth to the seventeenth centuries'], *SCH* 8, edd G. J. Cuming and D. Baker (Cambridge 1971) pp 107–34.
[23] Reeves pp 203–7, 221–4.   [24] Vincke p 204.   [25] *Ibid* pp 187–9.
[26] Benedict XIII was in Savona from 8 October 1405, Valois III p 415.

area, borrowed it, had two copies made, and had then taken it to the pope. Benedict was truly delighted and had rewarded him with a vacant parochial church in Cordova, with money to travel home. When Crassus met him he was actually on his way to take possession of his church, taking with him in his saddlebag his own copy of the book in two volumes. Crassus asked him what the book was about, and he said it was full of magic and showed that Christ's miracles were done by necromancy. He offered to show it to Crassus but the latter *omnino et penitus abhorrens materiam libri supradicti . . . plus optabat dictum librum igne cremari . . .* a lack of scientific curiosity which the historian cannot but lament. On the other hand one can discover from other witnesses what sort of books were thought dangerous and unsuitable for the pope to own. Jean Guiard[27] mentioned two or three books. Benedict had from the saracens *unum librum consecratum* which may be the same as what Guiard calls *claviculam Salamonis*. This he used to raise demons. The *clavicula Salomonis* is a genuine book which was also called *Sacratus*.[28] It has information on how to obtain one's wishes, how to control spirits and shut them up, and how to control the weather. Guiard also thought that the pope used a book beginning *Incipit mors anime*. This is a work which Albertus Magnus ascribed to Aristotle.[29] He said it was the worst of all books of magic images and later writers refer to it as a depraved, obscene and detestable work, though no copies survive for one to verify this reputation. Pierre Margant,[30] a young benedictine monk from Chaise Dieu, Clermont, said that the servants of the chamber in the house of Benedict's steward had showed him a book which they said contained necromancy. In Benedict's bed when he left Nice in 1407 was said to have been found a book of necromancy.[31] This was probably the work called *librum consecratum* or *Yeezael*, by one witness,[32] who said he had his information from a Catalan with whom he had travelled from Avignon to Montpellier. Benedict was said to have slept with *Yeezael* under his pillow to show the future. This was probably one of the works of Zahel Benbriz or

---

27 Vincke pp 202–3.
28 *A Catalogue [of Incipits of Medieval Scientific writings in Latin]*, edd L. Thorndike and P. Kibre, The Medieval Society of America, 29 (London 1963) pp 227, 458; [L]. Thorndike, [*History of Magic and Experimental Science*] (New York 1923) II pp 280–9.
29 *A Catalogue* p 449; L. Thorndike 'Traditional Medieval Tracts Concerning Engraved Images', *Mélanges Auguste Pelzer* (Louvain 1947) p 255; Thorndike II p 258.
30 Vincke p 200.
31 Valois III p 548, for the date of leaving Nice. Vincke p 191.
32 Pons Gaude, a minorite from Aubenas in the diocese of Viviers, *ibid* p 306.

Zael,[33] a jewish astrologer of the ninth century. His works were very popular in the west and included information on how to choose a favourable time for a journey and the like.

The truth of any of these accusations is hard to ascertain. None of the books named appears in the list of books in the papal library in Peñiscola. On the other hand that library did contain several astrological works as well as works by the abbot Joachim of Fiore.[34] This merely shows that the pope shared with most of his contemporaries a belief in astrology and an interest in prophecy. He clearly also believed in the power of black magic, as can be seen from the seriousness with which he treated the plot to kill him by magic in 1406.[35] All the witnesses no doubt shared these beliefs. Pierre D'Ailly pointed out the contemporary need to distinguish between 'true astronomy and superstitious magic',[36] which would have included astrology used in an acceptable way and used to do harm or to know what was forbidden. The dividing line was none too clear and this was useful no doubt when one wished to accuse the pope of overstepping it.

The rest of the evidence at Pisa is of interest to show what sort of powers fairly or very well-educated men attributed to evil magicians in the early fifteenth century. Witnesses solemnly affirm that Benedict knew events in advance or knew of distant events as they happened.[37] He could influence the weather. Master Albert Andree, MA and licenciate in medicine,[38] and cardinal Pileo de Marini, archbishop of Genoa,[39] were both prepared to believe that he stirred up storms. Guiard thought that among the spirits working for him was the god of winds,[40] and Jean de Seilhons was shown in Nice a tower which the devils had destroyed, apparently during a thunderstorm.[41] Benedict also consulted 'the finder of hidden treasure' according to Guiard, who also thought that he kept two little demons shut up in a box to consult

33 F. J. Carmody, *Arabic Astronomical and Astrological Sciences in Latin Translation* (Berkeley and Los Angeles 1956) pp 40 ff; C. H. Haskins, *Studies in the History of Medieval Science* (repr New York 1960) p 44.

34 Valois IV p 95 n 3; M. Faucon, *La Librairie des Papes d'Avignon*, 2, *Bibliothèque des Ecoles Françaises d'Athènes et de Rome*, L (Paris 1887) pp 49, 51, 141. The work by Ali Abenragel called *De judiciis stellarum*, is by a muslim astrologer Ibn-L-Rijal. It was a most popular book on horoscopes. Compare G. Sarton, *Introduction to the History of Science*, I (Washington 1948) pp 715–18.

35 P. Luc, 'Un complot [contre Benoit XIII'], *Mélanges d'archaeologie et d'histoire* 55 (1938) pp 374–402.

36 J. Gerson, *Œuvres Complètes* II, *l'œuvre Epistolaire*, ed mgr Glorieux (Paris 1960) p 222, *inter veram astronomiam et superstitiosam magicam*.

37 Vincke pp 186, 207.

38 *Ibid* p 207.   39 *Ibid* p 199.   40 *Ibid* p 202.   41 *Ibid* p 191.

when he needed them.[42] The readiness to believe in witchcraft is seen again and again. Jean de Seilhons[43] had a circumstantial story about going one evening to visit master Stephen Taberti de Arbrella in Portovenere, no doubt in 1408. While in the entrance hall the witness heard voices, and hesitated to enter, thinking Taberti was engaged. Then he heard a sound as of mill wheels, and he bethought himself that Stephen was indulging in witchcraft. Stephen already had a reputation in this because he was supposed to have predicted the result of a duel. After a while the witness called out and Taberti came to the door, looking stupified, saying he had been studying. He was all alone. It is interesting that de Seilhons, hearing a noise 'as of wheels', waited to hear more, 'since I have heard that divinations are made with wheels'. One wonders if this was a partial understanding of the use of wheels in illustrations in books of divination.[44]

All the evidence produced at Pisa, however, tells one more about the beliefs of the witnesses than about the magical practices of the pope or his followers. By modern standards the evidence was extremely weak especially since there were no witnesses for the defence, and it may even have seemed weak to contemporaries. The charges found no place in the definitive sentence, and were only noticed by one contemporary chronicler.[45] In the background of course there was a great deal of talk. Again and again witnesses say *publica vox fuit*, and there was a good deal of gossiping in inns.[46] One influence in the background was probably the plot to kill Benedict by witchcraft in 1406.[47] Some of the evidence in 1409 suggests that witnesses had heard of the previous case. A character in the 1406 plot had been a student of Avignon, who had kept some of the nasty materials for the plotters and was used by the pope to track them down. This had involved the pope in being privy to some very mirky dealings, including trying to persuade the plotters to make their lethal magic circle in the Provençal area and not elsewhere. A name that crops up inexplicably in 1406 is that of Jean Poncet, who is found in 1409 giving evidence that a friar in the house of cardinal Amadeo de Saluzzo was in touch with a whole group of Provençal magicians.[48]

---

[42] *Ibid* p 202.   [43] *Ibid* pp 191-2.   [44] Reeves, 'Some Popular Prophecies' p 117.

[45] Valois IV, p 97, n 3, referring to Konigshofen, *Chroniken der deutschen städte*, IX, p 613.

[46] Evidence of Jean de Brogny cardinal of Viviers, Dominic Petit, Pileo de Marini archbishop of Genoa, Regucius Symonis de Ancona (a writer of apostolic letters), Pierre Fabre, Jacobus Cabassolis chamberlain to cardinal Amadeo de Saluzzo, François de Chissé, Gilles le Jeune; Vincke pp 186, 194, 196, 197, 199, 206.

[47] See note 35 above.

[48] One of the items in the box left by the plotters was a letter from the cardinal of St

Clearly none of this proves a charge of witchcraft. What then was the point of it all? Evidently, as Noel Valois saw, some members of the council of Pisa feared that the evidence against the popes was not enough to prove a charge of heresy,[49] which alone would be sound traditional ground for deposing a pope. Nor was it enough in some eyes to prove 'other notorious crimes'.[50] It may be then that a charge of witchcraft was brought in because Gratian had assembled material on the use of magic which might even satisfy traditionalists.[51] His authorities equated the consultation of augurs or the stars in order to foretell things, with idolatry. There is also a general condemnation in Gratian of the use by the clergy of such things, either personally or by use of others. Bishops transgressing this were to be deprived of their office. Hence no doubt the emphasis in the evidence on the people around Benedict. It is worth remembering that Nogaret's charges against Boniface VIII included one of witchcraft[52] and his case was one of the precedents for Pisa.

The justification for dealing with this topic in a volume concerned with sanctity and secularity is that it illuminates a little the shadowy area where religion shades into politics, and prophecy is a political matter as well as a religious one. The later middle ages abound in charges of witchcraft which have an ulterior motive . . . one thinks of the cases of Eleanor Cobham or Joan of Arc. On the other hand one must remember that Eleanor had done at least one of the things of which she was accused, though under other circumstances she might have got away with it.[53] The Pisa case gives one an excellent picture of the conditions in which such charges could be brewed up . . . secret conversations years before with sinister Catalan friars in inns, and visits late at night to dubious scholars easily produced charges of witchcraft if necessary in an atmosphere where prophecy abounded and where no one doubted the possibility of astrological prediction.

Angelo, Pierre Blau, to cardinal Amadeo de Saluzzo about ending the schism. Poncet is mentioned in it as their go-between. Luc, 'Un complot' p 391.

[49] Valois IV p 92.

[50] B. Tierney, *Foundations of the Conciliar Theory* (Cambridge 1955) pp 8, 60-7, 214-15.

[51] Causa XXVI q 2 c 9; q 5 *passim* and esp c 5. Pedro de Saluzzo (Vincke p 194) represented himself as saying to friar Alvarez 'Since that art is forbidden to all and is especially shameful in a pope why is it used?'

[52] P. Dupuy, *Histoire du differend d'entre le pape Boniface VIII et Philippe le Bel, Roy de France* (Paris 1655) pp 324, 331 ff.

[53] A. R. Myers, 'Captivity of a Royal Witch' *BJRL* 24 (1940) pp 263-84, esp 273-5.

THE FIFTEENTH-CENTURY EPISCOPATE: CAREERS AND BEQUESTS

by JOEL T. ROSENTHAL

IN this paper I wish to show a possible line of relationship between the careers of some fifteenth-century English bishops and their deathbed bequests. This attempt to correlate episcopal secularity, as revealed by the 'careerism' of the bishops, and episcopal sanctity, as revealed by their philanthropy, touches three major themes of historical inquiry. One of these is gift-giving. Anthropologists have taught us to see how the giving of gifts in pre-industrial societies can illuminate the role of symbolic relationships, of ties between lineages, of the bonds of social solidarity, status and hierarchy.[1] Medieval historians know from their own work the importance of gift-giving in the economic sphere.[2] I am also attempting to carry out a 'group study', one particular form of sociological history. The purpose of such endeavours is not, as Elton asserts, to reopen the quarrel as to whether history is or is not scientific.[3] It is rather to ask questions about the past which the people of that day did not think to ask about themselves. As such I believe it to be a legitimate and proper form of historical inquiry. Lastly, I seek to shed some light on a particular aspect of medieval espiscopal activity. Anything we can learn about the ecclesiastical élite is that much more known about medieval people and medieval society.

Eighty men reached episcopal office in the seventeen English sees between 1399 and 1485.[4] Of the eighty, only thirty-eight were kind enough to leave extant wills.[5] I propose to examine the wills of these

---

[1] M. Mauss, *The Gift*, trans I. Cunnison (New York 1967) written 1925.

[2] P. Grierson, 'Commerce in the Dark Ages: A Critique of the Evidence', *TRHS*, 5 series, 9 (1959) pp 123–40.

[3] G. Elton, *The Practice of History* (London 1967) pp 27–8.

[4] I include those men who reached the episcopacy, in English sees, between the accession of Henry IV and the death of Richard III. Excluded are Welsh bishops, men who held English sees after 1485 though they held Welsh ones before, and men who became bishops for a second time after 1399, for example, Thomas Arundel and Roger Walden.

[5] The wills are to be found in: [E. F. Jacob, *The Register of Henry*] *Chichele* (Oxford 1938) II—William Barrowe pp 433–4; John Catterick pp 178–82; John Chaundler

thirty-eight men – thirty-two seculars and six regulars[6] – to look for testamentary bequests left to institutional recipients on the basis of relationships which stemmed from the bishop's pre-episcopal career experience. Such a focus is admittedly a narrow one, but in an exploratory study such as this anything as diverse as an episcopal will must be placed under strict controls in terms of the questions addressed to the data. Otherwise we can wander into a maze of bequests to various people, institutions, and causes, and relating them becomes not only a complex but a lengthy process. Accordingly I am not concerned here with bequests or gift-giving from the man's lifetime, nor with gifts made to recipients other than the three dealt with below.[7] If this rigid definition of my subject gives us an over-all picture that is too

---

pp 346–53; Richard Clifford pp 224–6; Robert FitzHugh pp 540–1; William Grey pp 544–6; Robert Hallum pp 126–30, 162–3; John Langdon pp 556–8; Philip Morgan pp 530–2; Stephen Patryngton pp 133–5, 137; Thomas Polton pp 485–95; Philip Repyngdon pp 285–7; John Rikynghale pp 415, 419; Simon Sydenham, pp 559–60; Henry Ware pp 195–7; Roger Whelpdale pp 237–40.

    T[estamenta] E[boracensia], edd J. Raine and J. Raine, *SS* 4 (1836) pp 398–403 Henry Bowet; 45 (1865) pp 60–1 William Strickland; pp 65–8 Roger Whelpdale (the will in *Chichele* is better); pp 248–50 Lawrence Booth; 53 (1869) pp 138–48 Thomas Rotherham.

    Sede Vacante Wills: ed C. E. Woodruff, Kent Archaeological Society, Records Branch, 3 (1914) pp 112–15 E. Story; pp 105–12 Thomas Langton; pp 85–93 John Morton. *Somerset Medieval Wills*, ed F. W. Weaver, Somerset Record Society, 16 (1901) pp 326–9 Nicholas Bubwith; pp 202–7 Thomas Bekynton. *Archaeologia Cantiana*, 24, pp 244–62 Thomas Bourchier. *Registrum Johannis Stanbury*, ed A. T. Bannister, *CY* 25 (1919) pp vii–ix John Stanbury. R. Chandler, *Life of William Waynflete* (London 1811) pp 379–88. F. Blomefield, *An Essay towards a Topographical History of the County of Norfolk* (London 1805–1811) III, pp 537–8 for Walter Lyhart, and for James Goldwell, *ibid* pp 539–43.

    Stafford's *Register*, at Lambeth Palace: fols 131–4 Thomas Brouns; fol 165 R. Gilbert; fols 128–9 Richard Praty; fols 122–3 William Wells; fols 178–9 William Alnwich. PRO, Prerogative Court of Canterbury Wills: 16 Stokton Reginal Boulers; 4 Logge Richard Beauchamp; 32 Godyn John Lowe; 7 Wattys Walter Lyhart; 28 Milles Thomas Kemp; 21 Vox John Russell.

    Three wills are extant but so jejune as to be of no value: Richard Scrope, *TE*, III, p 169; Philip Repyngdon, John Catterick, in *Chichele*. All the others are rather extensive. I wish to acknowledge the help of the Henry E. Huntingdon Library and to Miss J. A. Rosenthal for their aid in obtaining and transcribing the wills.

6 The regulars were Boulers, Langdon, Lowe, Patryngton, Stanbury and Wells.

7 As well as the basic biographical information there is a guide to the bishops' main lines of benefaction in A. B. Emden, *A Biographical Register of the University of Oxford to A.D. 1500* (Oxford 1957) 3 vols and *A Biographical Register of the University of Cambridge to A.D. 1500* (Cambridge 1963). Many major building projects are ignored here, for example, Scrope's bequests to York cathedral, Strickland's aid to his native area, Rotherham's school at Hull, Waynflete's creation of Magdalen college, and many others.

jaundiced against the bishops, I apologise. In the absence of the systematic analysis of any sizable group of related medieval wills, a small start is a not improper beginning.

The fifteenth-century episcopate was composed of men who devoted long careers to their church, whatever the level of piety and sanctity which marked them. The thirty-two secular bishops had had pre-episcopal careers which averaged 21·2 years, as measured from the date of the first recorded benefice or academic status to the moment of first (confirmed) episcopal nomination.[8] They went on to episcopal careers which averaged 19·7 years, roughly equal to their earlier period of service.[9] The six regulars, whose earlier career duration cannot be calculated with any accuracy, averaged but 14·7 years in the episcopate, the shorter career probably being a reflection of greater age at the moment of first nomination. The thirty-eight bishops together averaged 18·8 years in the episcopate. In their earlier careers, amidst all the variety of experience and opportunity, the bishops had had three forms of common experience: they had all been to university, they (if they were seculars) had almost all held churches connected with prebends, and (if they were seculars) had all been rectors. The advantages and revenues which accrued as a result of these positions were instrumental in no small way in their subsequent success. Did they remember these early bonds when they made their wills?

Not only had all the bishops been either to Oxford or Cambridge, but the majority had doctor's degrees, mostly in law but not infrequently in theology. Such 'graduate work' meant not only serious intellectual purpose but a long duration of academic residence and contact. Furthermore, many of the bishops had been active as administrators, either in the university as a corporation or within their college or hall. Their ranks included former chancellors, vice-chancellors, proctors, arbitrators, provosts, wardens, masters, etc. So in short, between the dying bishop and his former university there had often been lengthy and responsible contacts and a whole network of reciprocal services.

In the case of fifteen of the thirty-eight bishops the 'old school tie' touched a responsive and tangible chord. The fifteen loyal alumni

---

[8] The early careers of the fifteenth-century bishops are dealt with in J. T. Rosenthal, *The Training of an Elite Group: English Bishops in the 15th Century* (Philadelphia 1970) American Philosophical Society, new series, 60, part 5.

[9] The pre-episcopal career was longer in seventeen instances, and in eight of the seventeen it was longer by ten years or more. The episcopal career was longer in thirteen cases, and in six cases of the thirteen it was longer by ten years or more.

included eight men with doctorates, eight former college fellows or college officials. The bequests of the fifteen men took two directions, either to the university as an entity or to a single college or hall. Bequests of the former sort took varied forms. Thomas Bourchier left £100 to both Oxford and Cambridge for the creation of a loan chest. He had been a resident of Neville's Inn and chancellor of Oxford. Robert FitzHugh, also of noble family and a former chancellor (though of Cambridge), gave books to the Cambridge library: *lego librarie communi universitatis Cantebrigie textum moralis philosophie, item Codeton super 4^or libros Sentenciarum.* Morton simply left £126 6s. 8d. in cash for prayers, Bubwith 250 marks.[10] These were generous gifts, even for such wealthy men as bishops, especially as no stipulation beyond the obligation to say prayers was affixed to the bequests.

Another type of academic gift was that which coupled the legacy to a local bias of the donor. William Alnwick, a Cambridge man, left £30 for the support of honest secular clerks, half at each university, provided they came from his diocese of Lincoln. Thomas Bekynton left money for prayers and for the support of scholars, and both categories of funds were to be dispensed with a special concern for boys from Bath and Wells. Bekynton was both a native of that diocese and its bishop.[11] Thomas Brouns left money for six poor boys of his diocese who were to become exhibitioners at Oxford: 100 marks, for boys in great need (*magnis indigentis*). He also left 20 marks for the university (from which he held doctorates in both civil and canon law), as Alnwick had given £50 in cash outright to each university beyond his more particularised bequests.

A sizeable group of men left gifts to a specific subdivision of the university. Richard Clifford, a cadet of the aristocratic northern family, had once rented Burnell's Inn at Oxford. On his death in 1421 he left a handsome gift: *lego mille marcas pauperibus scolaribus meis presentibus et futuris Oxonie in hospicio meo vocato Burnell' In . . . magistro et sociis . . . pro eorum sustentacione quadraginta libre annuatim ministrentur quousque summa dictarum mille marcarum sic ut predicitur sit soluta et plenarie consummata.* Thomas Langton had had an extensive education, with

---

[10] Bubwith's bequest ran: '250 marks for the celebration of masses in the University of Oxford by priests unbeneficed or poorly beneficed who are studying there.'

[11] Bekynton's money was 'to ten honest priests of good conversation, apt and disposed to study, and either staying or about to stay in the University of Oxford, not having a sufficient exhibition, and especially those who belong to my diocese . . . To the exhibition of ten poor scholars not having a sufficient exhibition . . . to be selected from my diocese.'

two doctorates from Oxford, the office of senior provost at Cambridge, and time at Padua. He left 1s. to each friar in the two universities, 3s. 4d. to each priest at Pembroke Hall, 6s. 8d. for each fellow of Queen's, Oxford, and 2s. apiece to other scholars and residents there. The elemosinary chest at Queen's received £40 in cash, plus vestments, and there were further bequests to St Clement's Inn and Oxford. Walter Lyhart left an antiphonary and other books to Exeter college, vestments to All Souls, £5 each to Gonville and Trinity Hall, and the residue of his goods to Oriel and Exeter.[12] Rotherham left capes, robes and £100 for repairs to King's college. John Russell, former sub-warden of New college, left money to Magdalen, Oxford. Waynflete left small bequests to Magdalen:[13] his great gifts of foundation had been made during his lifetime. Roger Whelpdale, a northerner, left the bulk of his books, £10 for vestments, and £36 16s. 4d. for a loan chest to Queen's: Balliol, with customary northern ties, received a few of the most valuable books from his library.[14] Bekynton left some valuable gifts to New college in addition to his general university bequests.

As a group bishops were generous donors to their universities. Of the thirty-eight, fifteen left something in their wills, and this ratio of 39% donation is more than modern educational institutions are likely to realise from a selection of their most successful sons. The bequests were often large, being of substantial help to the recipient instead of just a token of remembrance. When we remember that we have totally ignored the often princely gifts made earlier in life, we can hardly fault the bishops for their generosity in this direction.

Of the thirty-two secular bishops, thirty had been canons and had held prebends: only Waynflete, in a career of thirty-two years, and Whelpdale in one of seven had not held prebends. The other thirty men had held a total of 163 prebends: an average of 5·4 apiece. The actual spectrum of acquisition was from the one prebend each that three men had acquired to the twelve of Bubwith, the thirteen of

---

[12] Of the residue, 'all his clothes were to be divided between Oriel and Exeter Colleges, and the overplus of his personals he ordered his executors to expend in maintaining poor scholars at Cambridge and Oxford'.

[13] Waynflete left 6s. 8d. to the president of the college, 2s. to each scholar and chaplain, 1s. 4d. to each clerk, and 1s. to each chorister, plus the manor of Sparshold and the residue of his goods.

[14] Balliol was to receive a *Speculum Historiale* of Vincent of Beauvais, Gregory's *Moralia* and a work on Ezekiel, some works of Egidius Romanus, a set of the decretals and a fancy goblet and some lesser trinkets.

Bekynton, or the fourteen of Clifford. Of the thirty former prebend-aries, only seven left testamentary bequests to these early affiliations or to such related aspects as the people of the parish, the mother church of the prebend, or another institution within the parish. They were Bekynton, Brouns, Chaundler, Morgan, Polton, Russell and Ware. Chaundler left bequests to six of his former churches, the others to but one each. The fortunate recipients were selected from among Bekynton's thirteen prebends, Broun's seven, Morgan's three, Polton's eight, Russell's six, and Ware's four. The latter six men had held forty-one positions, and they gave to but six of them. If Chaundler is included, twelve among fifty-one potential beneficiaries were re-membered. This is a much lower scale of donation than we saw from the universities.

In most cases the bequests to prebendal churches were respectable but markedly smaller than the academic gifts. Bekynton gave £5 to the poor of Bedwyn parish. Brouns left 13s. 4d. to each clerk within Flixton parish. Morgan gave vestments to Abergwelli parish church and others to the college there. Polton remembered Milverton parish church: *lego c s. ad faciendum ymaginem Sancti Michaelis*. Ware left some theology books to Llandaff Cathedral, where he had once occupied a stall.[15] John Chaundler gave to six of his former prebends, but separ-ately each bequest was rather small. He left 6s. 8d for work on the fabric at Calne, 13s. 4d, for the poor there, 13s. 4d. for the poor at Milton Manor, but 6s. 8d. for paupers at Leckford, and 20s. to be divided among the poor of Netherbury, Beminster and Slape. The benedictine nunnery within Wherwell parish was to get £2, but this was a narrow form of philanthropy as far as his former parishioners were concerned. The gift of 6s. 8d to the hospital of St John the Baptist, Wilton, was a bit more in the direction of christian social work. But all of Chaundler's bequests together barely amounted to £10. None of these seven men showed the sort of personal interest in this form of benefaction that the academic donors had, either in quantitative terms or as revealed by the detailed direction of the bequest.

All thirty-two of the secular bishops had held rectories. Their aggregate of 138 rectories comes to an average of 4·3 per man, with the range of acquisition running from one rectory (for four men) to twelve (for James Goldwell), and five men held seven or more. Of the thirty-two bishops concerned, only five left testamentary gifts to their

---

15 'Item volo quod liber decretalium necnon liber decretorum et Gorham super epistolas Pauli et super psalterio qui sunt libri ecclesie Landavensis restituantur eidem ecclesie.'

old churches or to related institutions or people. They did give a bit more generously than to prebendal churches. Two of the five donors gave to one rectory each: Bekynton to Sutton Courtenay (alone of his four rectories) and Chaundler to Warblington. Bekynton left £5 to the poor, plus the usual assortment of vestments and copes to the parish church, 'of which I was once rector'. Chaundler left 6s. 8d. for the fabric of the church, and another 6s. 8d. for the poor. Goldwell endowed three of his twelve rectories, including an antiphonary to Harrietsham parish church.[16] Lyhart gave to three of his five: £10 to each, to repair the fabric at Nettleton, West Tilbury, and Bradwell on Sea. Rikynghale endowed two places, the church at Fressingfeld (with vestments and £2 to the poor) and that at Thorpe Abbots (with five marks to the fabric, £1 to the poor, and some service books).

This was limited generosity at best. Of the fifteen men endowing the universities, seven their former prebends, and five their former rectories, a total of twenty different individuals emerge. Only five of the university benefactors gave to one of the other types of recipient, while five of the seven giving to prebends and three of the five to rectories gave in more than one category. Seen differently, only six from among the twenty donors gave to more than one category. Twenty of thirty-eight men is not a bad record, but if we take into account the number of potential recipients, the picture takes on a different hue. Most of the former churches were ignored.

Each bishop thought of himself as a free agent, dispensing his largesse as he pleased. But this does not prevent us from seeking some key to the patterns which prevailed. Freedom of action does not necessarily mean amorphous or hopelessly eccentric behaviour. Why did these bishops tend to follow certain similar pattern of action, even in the realm of their voluntary behaviour? It can be seen that there was a descending order of generosity, going from those giving to universities to former prebends to former rectories. This is not hard to understand. The ties with universities were not ephemeral ones, to be snapped forever once a new benefice came along and an old one was discarded. Connections between the great alumni and the universities continued through the episcopal careers.[17] The early ties merely marked the

[16] He had once been rector of Great Chart, Kent, and during his lifetime he helped rebuild the church, found a chapel and endow a chantry for his parents' souls: J. Weever, *Funeral Monuments* (London 1767) pp 91–2. The only testamentary bequest towards Great Chart was a gift of 6s. 8d. to James Le Vyndales, Goldwell's godson, who lived there.

[17] For the continuing ties and obligations, see E. F. Jacob, 'English University Clerks in

beginning of a long bond. Since some at least of the academic bequests went to branches of the university other than those at which a man had studied, we can see that there was always room for new attachments.

The ties with the other types of beneficiaries went back almost exclusively to the early career. There is no way of determining why the fortunate recipients were chosen from amongst the many potential ones, any more than there is of telling, on an individual basis, why one bishop gave and another chose not to. The donors were not bound to their beneficiaries in any obvious way. They systematically gave neither to their first benefices nor to their last ones. Bekynton gave to Bedwyn, the seventh of his thirteen prebends. Brouns gave to Flixton, the fifth of the seven churches he acquired. Morgan, a Welshman, gave to his first prebend, of five: it was his only Welsh benefice, and this tie was probably the operative one. Polton gave to his first church and ignored the remaining seven in his will. Russell gave to St Paul's cathedral, a tie which probably sprang from his possession of a stall there. Ware, like Morgan, gave to his only Welsh prebend and ignored those outside his native land. Chaundler gave to six of his ten prebends, but in order of acquisition they were his first, second, fourth, fifth, seventh and tenth. It is generally impossible to make a case for order of acquisition as a critical determinant in plotting the gift giving.

Was social origin linked to the propensity to donate to the institutions of the early career? It seems that to a small degree there is an inverse relationship, that is, the men of higher social origin did not give to former prebends or rectories while those of humble birth were more likely to. Fourteen of the bishops, all seculars, were of aristocratic or 'upper middle class' background.[18] Of these, six gave to the universities, none to their prebends, only one to a rectory. As these fourteen men averaged twenty-two years in the church before coming to the episcopate, and they averaged five prebends and 4·3 rectories, they hardly lacked opportunity to make contacts that they might some-day repay. But men like Thomas Bourchier or Richard Beauchamp

---

the Later Middle Ages', *Essays in the Conciliar Epoch* (Manchester 1963) pp 207–39, and J. T. Rosenthal, 'The Universities and the Medieval English Nobility', *History of Education Quarterly* (1969) pp 415–37.

[18] Beauchamp, Bourchier, Clifford, FitzHugh and Grey seem to have been related to aristocratic families, while Strickland, Alnwick, Lawrence Booth, Bowet, Goldwell, Thomas Kemp, Morton, Sydenham and Waynflete were probably from well established land-owning families.

were merely marking time, rather than fighting to climb a steep and competitive ladder. Their thoughts were directed, from an early date, towards the top, and their memories seem to have been focussed in this direction as well.

There was no significant change in episcopal gift-giving through the course of the century. Eighteen of the secular bishops died before 1461 and thirteen afterwards. Of those who died before, eleven were donors (61%). Of those who died later, nine were donors (69%). The difference is insignificant, and it at least shows that, within the narrow time span we are dealing with, no new customs, no revolution in social aspirations, is to be found, at least not at the top levels of society. Other factors, for example, the total number of benefices held or the length of episcopal careers, also seem to have had no effect on episcopal action.

The length of the pre-episcopal career does seem to offer some clue to the propensity to donate. Bishops who gave to the universities had short pre-episcopal careers (an average of 19 years) but those who gave prebendal or rectory benefactions had longer than average early careers (23·4 and 28·2 years respectively) and shorter than average episcopal careers (13 and 17·2 years respectively compared with 21·9 years for university donors). More years of dependence and fewer years of grandeur represent a believable combination of circumstances. A moderate but not insignificant differential can be shown between the length of early careers and the propensity to donate. About half the men with short pre-episcopal careers were donors, while over three-quarters of those with longer than average careers had donated: seven of fifteen as against thirteen of seventeen, respectively. Of the twenty donors, thirteen had long pre-episcopal careers, while of the twelve non-donors only four had had long early careers. A comparison of this sort does not prove a case, but it suggests a strong likelihood of association between the separate sets of data. That it also seems to offer a reasonable explanation is that much more grist for the mill. Given the small number of men being treated in this study is it impossible to do more than make some suggestions.

By way of contrast we should note that the bishops handsomely re-membered the last stages in their careers. Of the thirty-eight, thirty-seven chose burial within their cathedrals,[19] and these burials meant that bequests of cash, ornaments, vestments, books, lands and other

---

[19] After mentioning that Morgan kept his attachment for Wales, it should be noted that he requested burial within the London charterhouse. This is of note because he was bishop of Worcester and then of Ely, never of London.

possessions all came to the cathedral, as did gifts to members of the chapter, the priests in attendance at the funeral, etc. Furthermore, in seventeen of the thirty-eight wills other institutions within the diocesan city were remembered: lesser churches, regular and mendicant houses, colleges, hospitals, anchorites, the poor, the sick, prisoners, members of the bishop's familia, personal friends and others. Twenty-one of the thirty-eight bishops had held more than one see in their lives, and ten of them left bequests to their previous cathedral. So if the early steps towards the bishopric were apt to be treated in a cavalier fashion, the top and final rungs made an impression which was manifested through the distribution of a tangible thanks-offering.[20]

What emerges from this case study is another example of the way that careerism ran as a theme through the course of these long and ultimately distinguished lives. An ecclesiastical system which gave men benefices in which they were not expected to reside and which offered them considerable administrative help in the collection of revenues from those benefices was hardly likely to inculcate a deep feeling for the churches and parishioners so used. Though a few of the bishops had real ties with their prebendal churches and their rectories, most knew them as little more than names.[21] So, accordingly, few were likely to have done much by way of service while holding the benefice, and it is hard to expect them to be too compassionate when they made their last bequests. Pluralism and absenteeism were easy to practice. The type of men who rose to the episcopacy in the fifteenth century were mostly capable and tough, and they were always thinking of the next step forward. The story of bishops is the study of success stories, and it is possible that I am looking for gifts where they could not reasonably have been expected to give them in their wills.

But some asperity of judgement must be registered. Any social system works on a web of reciprocal relationships. This study shows that the successful careerists among the clergy were getting far more

[20] Many other channels of benefaction could be explored. Though none of the six regulars gave to any of the three categories we are concerned with, three (Boulers, Langdon and Wells) gave bequests to their former monasteries. Eight bishops had been wardens or masters of hospitals, and three (Bekynton, Praty and Bouchier) left bequests to them.
[21] In the fourteenth century many bishops were local men: Kathleen Edwards, 'The Social Origins and Provenance of the English Bishops During the Reign of Edward II, *TRHS*, 5 series, 9 (1959). This was not the case for the fifteenth century men. Furthermore, with the exception of a few northerners, few bishops had many of their pre-episcopal beneficies concentrated in either their native region or within the diocese which they eventually held. It was very much a church of 'foreigners'.

from their early benefices than there is reason to believe they re-invested, either when they held them or in later life. This is in striking contrast to their own behaviour towards the institutions of their later days, and with that of local clerks and canons as illustrated in any collection of fifteenth-century clerical wills, with their abundance of chantries and local charities. If it is unfair to say that the bishops 'should' have endowed their former benefices, it is at least fair to point out the existence of an ecclesiastical structure which turned their thoughts towards their future rather than towards their flocks. These bishops were not ungenerous or callous men: their wills contain innumerable provisions for the re-distribution of wealth. What gifts they did give to their old benefices were welcome and often substantial.[22] But the bishops (and their wills reflect this) were part of an institutional order, a 'system' that did not emphasise a circular passage of material goods from the humble to the mighty and back again to the humble.

[22] Gifts in kind to a parish church were a boon to the parishioners because it relieved them of the obligation to provide the vestments, service books, and plate. I wish to thank Miss K. Wood-Legh for drawing this point to my attention.

BLOOD AND BAPTISM:
KINSHIP, COMMUNITY AND
CHRISTIANITY IN WESTERN EUROPE
FROM THE FOURTEENTH TO THE
SEVENTEENTH CENTURIES

by JOHN BOSSY

ISTORIANS of west-European christianity in its late medieval and early modern phases have recently been much concerned with the relations of the church and the devil. Our subject here, the church and the world, may seem by comparison, and notably for the period immediately preceding the reformation, a well-worn topic; inspired by the achievements of historical demography, we may be tempted to abandon it for more promising researches into the relations of the church and the flesh. This is indeed what I shall be doing here, at least to the degree that 'flesh and blood' can be considered as falling under the last heading. Yet, since it may be argued that 'flesh and blood' formed, for the average western christian of this time, a major constituent of his 'world' or social environment, I do not feel that I am stretching a point in offering, within the present context, some comments on the subject indicated in my title. I am concerned with the connections of the Church and the 'world', meaning by that the complex of human relations it lives in. I am particularly concerned with the structure of one such society, that of western Europe in the immediately pre- and post-reformation age. And I am finally interested in pursuing or criticising some socio-historical arguments about what happened to European christianity in and after the sixteenth century.

A word about these. In the first place I wish to pursue in this paper a suggestion made in an earlier piece on the social consequences of the counter-reformation: that a particular social characteristic of the pre-reformation church, as distinguished from what succeeded it on either side of the confessional divide, was that it admitted a variety of forms of the extended kin-group, natural and artificial, as constituent elements in its life.[1] In investigating the application of tridentine catholicism in rural communities, I was struck by some recurring difficulties which arose in the enforcement of this more rigorous code of religious observance, for example that people refused to come to church at the same time as others with whom they were in a state of social hostility. These difficulties suggested to me that there were two social problems in pre-reformation popular christianity which required investigation: its relation to the bonds of kinship, and its relation to the practice of feud. I have taken the opportunity offered here to examine these topics at greater length. On the negative side, I am anxious to offer some constructive criticism of a conception of the relations between the church and the 'world' which underlies a good deal of recent writing about English religion in the sixteenth and seventeenth centuries, and is prominent in the work of Christopher Hill: that the pre-reformation rural parish was a unified community broken up by the progress of economic individualism during the sixteenth century, and that, just as the social function of the traditional church (or traditionalist churches) was to embody traditional community, so the role of innovating forms of christianity, like puritanism, was to dissolve it.[2] I should also like to make a collaborative contribution to the work of recent historians like Keith Thomas, who have been trying to understand popular religious and allied attitudes in this period with the help of ideas derived from anthropology. While I am sympathetic to their point of view, and have learnt a very great deal from them, I am worried by what strike me as weaknesses and over-simplifications in the social dimension of their work which derive, I think, from an attempt to read in the light of the model described above evidence which cannot really be assimilated to it.[3] A different pattern would, I suspect, provide a more appropriate background for what they have to say. These critical considerations explain why, though the general scope of my argument is European, an undue proportion of the evidence adduced is English.

If we are going to argue for the primacy of kin-relationships in the popular religious practice of the late middle ages, to envisage the groups formed by such relationships as amounting to constituent cells of

---

[1] [J.] Bossy, ['The Counter-Reformation and the People of Catholic Europe], *PP* 47 (London 1970) pp 56 ff, 68.

[2] [Christopher] Hill, [*Society and Puritanism in Pre-Revolutionary England*] (London 1964) esp cap xiv, 'Individuals and Communities'.

[3] [Keith] Thomas, [*Religion and the Decline of Magic: Studies in Popular Beliefs in Sixteenth and Seventeenth Century England*] (London 1971) caps vi, xvii; [Alan] Macfarlane, *Witchcraft [in Tudor and Stuart England*] (London 1970) for example p 197.

the christian community as a whole, we must first investigate the process by which such groups were constructed, and the part played by christian rituals in constructing them. I propose to look at two of the christian *rites de passage*, those of marriage and baptism, and the social environment in which they were celebrated.

On marriage, we may be fairly brief, because the position is fairly well understood.[4] There is nothing very original in saying that in medieval popular practice the sacrament of matrimony was understood by reference to a system of collective social relations, as the concluding point of a process of alliance between two groups of kin. A contractual collectivist view of marriage with extremely deep roots had been juxtaposed to the sacramental theory of the church, whose individualistic implications had been stressed by canon lawyers since about 1300, and a rather unstable mixture had been produced; so far as catholics were concerned, this was not resolved in law until the council of Trent, and in practice until long after. For a picture of how things worked in practice during the earlier period we may resort to a well-known study of English rural life.[5] Here we find a pithy description of the marriage-process from *Piers Plowman*: –

> And thus was wedlock y-wrought with a mean person [mediator]:
> First by the father's will and the friends' counsel,
> And then by assent of themselves [the parties], as the two might accord;
> And thus was wedlock y-wrought, and God himself it made.[6]

We find evidence that betrothal or trothplight, which I take to be the ritual embodying popular collectivist theory in its traditional form, was understood as entailing legal and effective marriage, acceptable in the customary law of manorial courts. We also find a good deal of relevant liturgical evidence. The church ritual itself indicates that what is occurring is an alliance of two kindreds. The bride, who is passing from one to the other, is accompanied by bridesmen and bridesmaids, and given by her father or a near kinsman. In the course of the wedding proper at the church door, or during mass, or both, the bridegroom and bride exchange the kiss of peace; peace being made between the two

---

4 There is a valuable recent discussion in [F. R. H.] Du Boulay, [*An Age of Ambition*] (London 1970) pp 80–108.

5 [G. C.] Homans, [*English Villagers of the Thirteenth Century*] (Cambridge, Mass, 1942) pp 160–76, 'Trothplight and Wedding'.

6 B Text, Passus ix, 11. 113–6, following Du Boulay's modernised version.

kindreds, they may hope to come safely together through the festivities of the bride-ale.[7]

In emphasising certain aspects of the medieval marriage-rite I have been influenced by the remarkable study by J. K. Campbell of contemporary social relations in a pastoral village of northern Greece, and in particular by his explanation that in this environment one is assumed to be at enmity with those to whom one is not related, and that marriage is therefore, almost by definition, 'a contract between two hostile groups'.[8] That this description is of some relevance here is suggested by the need felt for a 'mean person' or mediator in launching marriage-negotiations, as well as by the peace-ritual. It is easy, too, to recognise in western experience his account of the wedding-feast as a celebration of the new relations formed and of a consequent release, not always successful, from the tensions of social hostility. One might cite the famous case of the Buondelmonte murder in Florence in 1216, allegedly the origin of guelf and ghibelline factions: a marriage arranged by kinsmen as a means of settling a dispute which might otherwise escalate into feud; Buondelmonte, stung by the taunt that he is only marrying because he fears the vengeance of the Uberti, his intended bride's family, repudiating the marriage without consulting his own kinsmen, leaving the bride waiting at the church, and marrying elsewhere; the Uberti murdering him on the way home.[9] Admittedly, this occurred among the nobility; I suspect that Campbell's Greeks have a more rigid and formalised system of relations than would have obtained among the west-European peasantry in the late middle ages, save in pastoral and mountain communities; but I also suspect that the difference is only a difference of degree.

Like the sacrament of matrimony, the sacrament of baptism brings into play the bonds of existing kinship, and creates new ones. It seems easier to approach it from the second point of view, and to look at the new community into which a child is baptised, that of his *godsib*, godparents or spiritual kindred. Godparenthood seems to me an important subject which has been too little studied. I venture four exploratory remarks about the character of the relation in the late medieval west.

[7] Homans pp 170-2; [E.] Delaruelle, [E. -R. Labande, P. Ourliac, *L'Eglise au temps du Grand Schisme et de la crise conciliaire*], FM XIV.2 (1964) p 740; unlike the provençal rite there described, the Sarum rite has the spouses simply joining their right hands at the church door, and not kissing until the *pax* during the mass: *The Sarum Missal*, ed J. Wickham Legg (Oxford 1916) p 413.
[8] [J. K.] Campbell, [*Honour, Family and Patronage*] (Oxford 1964) pp 39 ff.
[9] F. Schevill, *History of Florence* (New York/London 1961) pp 106 ff.

First, in this context *parentes* seems to have meant, to ordinary people, not 'parents' in the modern sense, but kindred: in popular pre-reformation practice the spiritual kindred seems to have been a comparatively large group, as one may gather from the widespread evidence in ecclesiastical legislation of efforts to restrict it. The thirteenth- and fourteenth-century diocesan statutes of Tournai, Cambrai and Lisieux imposed a limit of three godparents (two of one sex and one of the other, depending on the sex of the child); those of Cambrai in 1550 went to four (two of each sex). The council of Basel legislated to the same effect; the council of Trent finally came down to one, or at most one of each sex, though there is plenty of seventeenth-century evidence that these limits were not observed.[10] Second, one may ask what was the relation between a child's spiritual kin and his or her natural kin. Evidently the relation is not one of conflict: the question is whether, to use the language of anthropologists, spiritual relationship was understood as intensifying or as extending natural kinship relations: whether, that is, a child's spiritual relations were likely to be chosen from among his natural relations or not. One finds evidence of both. The council of Soissons of 1403 permitted the admission of children as godparents provided they were close kindred of the child baptised, implying or at least encouraging a practice of intensifying existing relations. On the other hand, the universally experienced difficulties about people marrying within forbidden degrees of spiritual relationship show that parents were choosing as godparents for their children people whom they would have been otherwise free to marry: a practice, in other words, of extension. It would appear that extension was the predominant mode, in the sense either of making firm connections between kin whose relationship might otherwise have been too distant to be effective, or of establishing them where they had not existed hitherto.[11] Thirdly, we need to inquire exactly what the functions of spiritual kinship were. The least significant of these seems to have been the religious education of the child, a notion which was itself in any case but dimly envisaged at this time. My impression is that the chief object in view was the creation of a formal state of friendship between the spiritual kin and the natural kin; the effect would somewhat resemble that of blood-

---

10 [P.] Adam, [*La vie paroissiale en France au XIVᵉ siècle*] (Paris 1964) pp 104 ff; [J. Toussaert, [*Le sentiment religieux en Flandre à la fin du Moyen Age*] (Paris 1963) pp 94 ff; Delaruelle p 739; Bossy p 58.

11 [S. W.] Mintz and [E. R.] Wolf, in [*Kinship*, ed J. Goody] (London 1971) p 350; Adam pp 104 ff; an introduction to the literature of the subject in [Alan] Macfarlane, [*The Family Life of*] *Ralph Josselin* (Cambridge 1970) pp 144 ff.

brotherhood, or of fraternity in general. Thus in early seventeenth-century Ireland people were forbidden to recruit more than two god-parents 'for the sake of forming a friendship or for any other cause'; and members of religious orders were prohibited from acting as godparents, on the grounds that this would mean contracting an *amicitia* or *mundana, sodalitas* with secular persons which would pull against the obligations of their rule.[12] The assumptions here seem similar to those involved in the modern practice of *compadrazgo* in Spanish America, where the relation to the child is relatively unimportant, but parents and god-parents enter into an intimate relationship of mutual assistance.[13] Possibly this was already the case in fifteenth-century Iberia, but as a general explanation it is difficult to square with the widespread evidence for the choice of children as godparents; this indicates rather a concern on the part of parents to lay the foundations of a new group which would sustain the child in his or her adult life and perhaps make up for the anticipated ravages of death among brothers and sisters. That this ambition was not always fulfilled, is suggested by fifteenth-century complaints that a child-godparent might well have forgotten his spiri-tual relationship by the time he and the baptised had grown up, and that if they were of opposite sexes they might seek to marry; though one might of course interpret this as a too-successful rather than an unsatisfactory relationship. At this point we have reached the problem of the negative consequences of godparenthood in the bar to marriage which it instituted; all I can say is that this subject seems to me to raise extensive difficulties on which I can shed no light.

To conclude: the social effect of baptism in late-medieval Europe was, so far as I can see, to create what an anthropologist has called a 'polyadic horizontal coalition', a kinship-group partly natural and partly artifi-cial;[14] its horizontality might be primarily relevant to the parents or to the child. One might deduce that, in this society, the kin-relation was taken as the model of all effective social relations, but that natural kin-ship itself was not considered as providing an individual with adequate social support. One might further deduce that, like the fraternity,

12 John Bossy, 'The Counter-Reformation and the People of Catholic Ireland', in *Historical Studies, VIII: Papers read before the Irish Conference of Historians*, ed T. D. Williams (Dublin 1971) p 163 – in the passage quoted in n 22, *ad* should read *ab*; *Definities van der Generale Kappitels von de Orde van het H. Kruis*, ed A. Van de Pasch, Koninklijke Commissie voor Geschiedenis (Brussels 1969) pp 196, 408: note that the relationship envisaged here is primarily with the parents.
13 Mintz and Wolf pp 346 ff, esp 351-2.
14 E. R. Wolf, *Peasants* (Englewood Cliffs, N.J., 1966) pp 84 ff.

godparenthood was a more important institution at the popular level than among the nobility, who might expect adequate support from their natural kinsmen. It seems appropriate to return to *Piers Plowman* for a passage which may both bring some support to the description given, and also indicate that a system of social instincts which does not seem to have much connection with christianity was at least patient of a higher interpretation. At the close of Piers's vision, Christ invokes his kinship with Adam and his descendants as entitling him to bring retribution on Lucifer by rescuing man from hell at the last judgement:

Fendes and fendekynes   bifor me shulle stande
And be at my bidding   where so evre me lyketh
And to be merciable to man   thanne my kynde it asketh;
For we beth brethren of blode   but noughte in baptesme alle.
And alle that beth myne hole bretheren   in blode and in baptesme
Shal noughte be dampned to the deth   that is withouten ende.

Here the fiend or enemy was interpreted as the devil and his minions; the implication remained that, on earth – and barring those exceptional men for whom universal kinship entailed universal community – a formal system of friendship implied a formal system of enmity.[15] I propose to take up this point again later.

In spite of Langland, the *rites de passage* may be felt to lie somewhat on the fringes of religion properly considered: they tell us more of the social units which practised religion than of the religion they practised, and could be considered irrelevant to the practice of more central religious acts. I do not believe that they are so irrelevant, but to be sure of this we need to investigate the principal act of medieval worship, the mass. Two lines of thought have occurred to me in this connection; or rather one line of thought has found some encouragement in two sorts of evidence. The subject is that most flourishing feature of late medieval devotion, the practice of masses satisfactory, and the general instinct of mutuality in salvation which lay behind it. I should like to say something about the boundaries within which the obligation of mutual assistance in salvation was felt to be operative, first by looking at the details of some chantry foundations, and second by looking at some developments in the liturgy of the mass.

It is obvious that only the wealthy were in a position to found

15 B Text, Passus xviii, 11. 371–6: commentary in *The Pelican Guide to English Literature: I, The Age of Chaucer*, ed B. Ford (London 1954) pp 344 ff; Norman Cohn, *The Pursuit of the Millennium* (London 1970) p 200.

chantries; it is possible that their instincts in these matters differed somewhat from those of other people, but I see no reason to suppose that they differed very much.[16] The first purpose of a chantry foundation was the saving of an individual's soul, or of that of a man and his wife, through a perpetual offering of masses; but this object was rarely distinguished from that of distributing the efficacy of the principal aid to salvation through a group usually identified with some form of kinship community. This could be envisaged as vertical, a lineage community existing through time – a man makes a foundation 'for the souls of his ancestors' or his descendants – or as horizontal, a contemporary community of relations centred on the founder. Thus a London founder in 1521 specified that the priests were 'to sing for him and his friends by name', for their good estate during life and for their souls after death. William Whaplode of Chalfont St Peter stipulated for a prayer at the end of each foundation mass: *Animae regum Angliae, Willelmi Whaplode, patris, matris, fratrum, sororum, uxorum [sic], consanguineorum, amicorum et benefactorum requiescant in pace. Amen.* The implications suggested are underlined in the foundation of John Anstey of Cambridgeshire, intended, after his family, 'for the souls of all those persons being in purgatory who have few and weak friends to deliver them from thence': that is to say, that since the bond of kinship is the most effectual means of securing mutual support in salvation, one's chance of eternal life, as well as one's welfare in the present, will depend on the size, cohesiveness and wealth of one's kindred.

These foundations strike me as shedding a good deal of light on the kind of kinship-community within which effective obligations were mainly felt. On the whole, and even at this level of society, the lineage community as such seems of comparatively minor importance. What seems to matter is a mainly horizontal body of relations without much depth in time and, like the godparent group, composed of two main elements, the *consanguinei* and the *amici*. What precisely is meant by 'friends' in this context seems open to discussion: the term may possibly, as Marc Bloch indicated for an earlier period, have some particular reference to affines or relations by marriage, but apart from wives these do not seem to figure very prominently; on the other hand, some formal relation, rather than a purely emotional or sentimental one, seems to be indicated.[17] The nuclear family, as such, does not seem to

[16] All my evidence here comes from K. L. Wood-Legh, *Perpetual Chantries in Britain* (Cambridge 1965): cases cited at pp 30, 34, 42, 289 ff, 309 ff.
[17] Marc Bloch, *Feudal Society* (London 1965) pp 123–4; Macfarlane, *Ralph Josselin* p 143.

carry much weight, or at least it does not seem to function in the way we should nowadays expect. There seems little specific mention of children, and where they do appear it is more usually as benefactors to their parents than *vice versa*. I would deduce that the group is essentially considered as a group capable of giving mutual assistance, and that a foundation is partly a return for services rendered; hence the reference to benefactors and the neglect of children. This account would confirm the general picture of the development of the family and of attitudes to children given by, among others, Philippe Ariès; the nuclear family as a primary religious community seems a later invention.[18]

The recognition of the groups outlined above as constituent bodies of the church is indicated by the place made for them in the liturgy of the mass itself. The later middle ages seem to represent the high-water mark of the tendency to convert the mass from a public ritual offered by those present for themselves and the whole community of christians, into a private ritual offered by the priest for the benefit of a specific group of individuals, living or dead. Hence the commemoration of the living, and the commemoration of the dead, inserted at strategic positions in the canon of the mass, before and after the consecration. Originally inserted only in 'private', weekday masses, not in the public Sunday mass, these seem by the fourteenth century to have become universal in all masses, and so remained. Consider in the present context the commemoration of the living, inserted before the consecration. So far as I can see the original Roman ritual contained at this point a brief prayer for those present, who were conceived as offering the sacrifice; in something like the form: 'Remember, O Lord, thy servants here present, whose faith and devotion are known to thee, and who offer thee this sacrifice of praise, etc.' As expanded through the encroaching influence of the private mass, this had become by the close of the middle ages a complicated, awkward, and rather incoherent prayer, which attempted to combine at least two notions:

Remember, O Lord, thy servants N. and N., and all those present, whose faith and devotion are known to thee: for whom we offer, or who offer to thee this sacrifice of praise, for themselves and all theirs (*pro se suisque omnibus*), for the redemption of their souls, for the hope of their safety and salvation (*pro spe salutis et incolumitatis suae*), etc.

18 Philippe Ariès, *Centuries of Childhood* (London 1962); compare Du Boulay pp 87 ff.

Three points about this prayer seem worth making. In the first place it incorporates the general principle of the private mass into the public liturgy through the mention of specific persons and the form *pro quibus tibi offerimus*; this is uncomfortably juxtaposed to the original notion of the public mass offered by those present. Secondly, an indication is given of the nature of the group intended to be beneficiaries of the mass offered: the phrase *pro se suisque omnibus* was interpreted by commentators at the time as referring to the kind of group whose outlines we have seen in the chantry foundations; as rendered in the *Lay Folks' Mass Book* it meant 'sib and well-willing', *consanguinei* and *amici*. It is understood by the chief modern commentator on the Roman ritual as primarily a reference to kin. Finally, as in one of the chantry foundations already mentioned, the benefit conferred is conceived as temporal as well as spiritual: *incolumitas* means preservation from earthly harm, and even *salus* in this context seems only dubiously spiritual in its reference.[19] Altogether the commemoration of the living seems an unmistakable sign of the introduction of the kinship principle, at a very profound level, into the social constitution of the church; it is hard to think of anything which could more dramatically reveal it–if I may borrow a phrase I have already used elsewhere – as a 'conglomerate of autonomous communities'.

Throughout the discussion so far I have been implying that the system of formal friendship implied a system of formal hostility, of what one may loosely describe as feud. The direct evidence for the presence of feud in late medieval Europe seems overwhelming and more or less universal: though it found its most dramatic expressions among the nobility and princes, and in mountain regions, it seems in some form or other to have transcended all social, geographical and racial barriers. In the fifteenth-century Italy described by Burckhardt it appears as a major, if not the major principle of social relations. The Netherlands of Huizinga and Toussaert convey the same impression: the right of private vengeance was not abolished at law until the late fourteenth century, and was freely exercised in practice until the sixteenth. In much of northern Germany and Scandinavia elaborate systems of kin-responsibility and *wergild*-payment remained in force until the late

---

[19] [J. A.] Jungmann, [*The Mass of the Roman Rite*], 2 vols (New York 1951) II pp 159–69 (living), 237–48 (dead); *The Lay Folks Mass Book*, ed T. F. Simmons, EETS (London 1879) pp 34 ff, 44 ff; [H.] Maynard Smith, [*Pre-Reformation England*] (London 1965) p 99.

seventeenth century. Elsewhere, instincts survived though institutions might decay.[20] Resort to the law, as is well understood, was commonly the pursuit of private warfare by other means; witchcraft, as it has been revealed by Keith Thomas and Alan Macfarlane, was a form of social hostilities understood to be practised by a particular type of person employing a particular kind of weapon – notably by poor old women who had nothing more effective at their disposal.[21]

In this social environment the parish priest, the parish church, and the institution of the church in general had a very clear role to play, but it was scarcely the role which has been assigned to them by a number of historians of sixteenth- and seventeenth-century England. I do not think that they were there to represent the solidarity of a society of geographically defined rural collectives. They were there, socially speaking, to assist in the creation of peace in the feud.

Throughout the rural parishes of Europe, from the fourteenth to the seventeenth century, in countries that remained catholic and in countries that turned protestant, the primary social task entrusted to the parish priest or his equivalent was that of a settler of conflicts. At one end we have, for example, the statutes of the diocese of Tournai of 1306, according to which the priests *diligenter investigent omnes controversias et discordias quae sunt in parochiis suis, ut amicabili compositione amicorum utriusque partis irae, rixae, odia, seditiones, et injuriae manifestae cooperatione Sancti Spiritus gratiae de cordibus fidelium expellentur.*[22] At the other end, we have George Herbert's country parson in *A Priest to the Temple*, going around his parish on Sunday afternoons 'reconciling neighbours that are at variance', trying to stop his parishioners taking each other to law by arbitrating between them, and if nothing can be done doing his best to persuade them to go 'even as brethren, and not as enemies, neither avoiding therefore one another's company, much less defaming one another'; seeing 'much preaching' in 'friendliness'.[23] Between the

---

[20] J. Burckhardt, *The Civilisation of the Renaissance in Italy* (London 1951) pp 265–8; [J.] Huizinga, [*The Waning of the Middle Ages*] (London 1952) pp 12 ff, 20; Toussaert, see index under *faide*, and p 789; B. Phillpotts, *Kindred and Clan* (Cambridge 1913) caps iv, v; R. Mandrou, *Introduction á la France moderne* (Paris 1961) pp 112 ff.

[21] For example Macfarlane, *Witchcraft* pp 161 ff.

[22] Gabriel le Bras, *Institutions ecclésiastiques de la Chrétienté médiévale* FM XII (1964) p 407, n 11 – reading *ut* for *et*.

[23] [*The English Works of George*] *Herbert*, ed G. H. Palmer, I (Boston/New York 1915) pp 229, 274, 316: compare Patrick Collinson, 'The Godly: Aspects of Popular Protestantism in Elizabethan England', papers of *Past and Present* conference on popular religion (1966) typescript, p 6; Macfarlane, *Ralph Josselin* pp 30 ff; Thomas pp 154 ff; Peter Heath, *The English Parish Clergy on the Eve of the Reformation* (London/Toronto 1969) pp 97 ff.

two, no doubt before and certainly after, the theme recurs with a monotonous insistence which indicates the limits of what could be achieved.

Just as the medieval church had accommodated the liturgy of the mass to the existence and requirements of the bodies of 'sib and well-willing' which formed the units of the society in which it functioned, so it had modified it to take account of the endemic hostility which reigned between them: with the difference that here it modified with the object not of reinforcing but of counteracting the *mores* of the population; or, more exactly perhaps, of providing the countervailing weight without which the stability of the total system could not be ensured. The modifications seems to be somewhat earlier than the one already discussed, to have been substantially completed before the private mass got under way, and to reflect a situation in which the church had been obliged to recognise the presence of a new social environment, but was not yet prepared to give it a positive sanction. It occurred between the fifth century and the eleventh, though the fuller elaborations seem to date from the close of this period, and involved the interpolation into the liturgy, between the close of the canon and the communion, of a formal peace-ritual in which the congregation was to participate. The alterations were quite extensive. In its final form the ritual was carefully prepared for by a series of events beginning with the *Pater noster*, where the emphasis would seem to have lain on the petition to 'forgive us our trespasses as we forgive them that trespass against us'. The point was then taken up by an explanatory prayer, the *Libera nos*, containing in particular a petition for 'peace in our days', and concluded with a modification of the ancient response *Dominus vobiscum* in the form *Pax Domini sit semper vobiscum*. This led into the communion ritual, which began with the invocation of Christ in the eucharist – *Agnus Dei, qui tollis peccata mundi . . .* ; the last of the three invocations was altered to *Dona nobis pacem*. This came at a fairly late date to be followed by a prayer, introduced in German liturgies from the eleventh century:

Lord Jesus Christ, who didst say to thine Apostles, Peace I leave with you, my peace I give unto you [It is possibly of some significance that at this point the prayer does not continue with the quotation: 'Not as the world giveth . . .], consider not my sins but the faith of thy church, and deign to keep her in peace and unity according to thy will.

This prayer was immediately succeeded by the giving by the congregation to one another of the kiss of peace, to which later the words *pax tecum* were added. This was then meant to be followed by the communion of the congregation in the eucharist: the English rites say 'Receive the bond of peace and charity that you may be apt for the most holy mysteries of God.' However, as the reception of the eucharist became increasingly confined in normal circumstances to the priest, the *pax* tended to become a substitute for it, a kind of natural communion which, for the congregation, marked in practice the culmination of the mass.[24]

This may seem an uncalled-for excursion into the dark ages; and it seems very likely that the final elaboration of the peace-ritual in the mass had a close connection with the 'peace of God' and 'truce of God' movements discussed by Marc Bloch, which date from about 1000 and were concerned with the restriction or suppression of feud and violence.[25] Yet the ritual remained a vigorous reality at least until the reformation, as one may gather from the modifications which it underwent during the later medieval centuries. Beginning with the Roman liturgy about 1000, a hierarchical order was introduced into the kiss: instead of being exchanged at random between neighbours, it passed from the priest through the clerks to the higher ranks of the laity, and thence down the scale of status. From a somewhat later date, actual kissing began to go out, and more conventional gestures were substituted, less suspect in the eyes of post-gregorian ecclesiastical puritanism. In England, by the early thirteenth century, the position was that a wooden or other object, known as the *pax* or *pax-board*, was passed around, and people kissed it in turn. There are numerous literary references to the ceremony in late medieval literature which indicates its continuing vitality and necessity; many of them refer to quarrels among the congregation about the order in which the *pax* was to be kissed.[26] English protestants attacked the ceremony as a substitute for the eucharist and an occasion of discord. There is one reformed version from the north of England, dating apparently from the close of the reign of Henry VIII, according to which the parish clerk, taking the *pax* around, was to say: 'This is a token of joyful peace which is betwixt God and men's conscience: Christ alone is the Peacemaker, which straitly commands peace between brother and brother.' But with the adoption of a reformed

[24] Jungmann II pp 275-350 *passim*, esp pp 321 ff (*Pax*); *Lay Folks Mass Book*, pp 114 ff (York use).   [25] Bloch, *Feudal Society* pp 408 ff.
[26] Jungmann II pp 325 ff; Maynard Smith pp 96 ff; Huizinga p 37.

liturgy it was abolished in England. However, if Cranmer abandoned
the ritual, it was not because he felt that the object it had been intended
to secure was no longer relevant. His preface to the communion service
of 1549 contains two instructions about the conditions in which people
are to be excluded from communion. The first is immoral living

> The same order shall the Curate use with those betwixt whom he
> shall perceive malice and hatred to reign, not suffering them to be
> partakers of the Lord's Table until he know them to be reconciled.
> And if one of the parties so at variance be content to forgive from
> the bottom of his heart all that the other hath trespassed against
> him, and to make amends for that he himself hath offended, and
> the other party will not be persuaded to a godly unity, but re-
> main still in his frowardness and malice; the Minister in that case
> ought to admit the penitent person to the Holy Communion, and
> not him that is obstinate.

Similar sentiments were expressed in the liturgy itself, in the 'Exhortation for those Negligent to Come to Communion'.[27] Hence in
England the medieval tradition was in substance continued. In the
Roman liturgy the *pax* ceremony of course persisted, though it did so in
an increasingly etiolated form; as a popular ritual it seems to have been
disused by about 1700.

My argument, then, on both direct and liturgical evidence, is that,
over a span of centuries which includes those with which we are
concerned, the parish was not conceived by the church as a homogeneous unit, but as an assemblage of actually or potentially hostile
entities among whom its function was to maintain a precarious peace.
In so far as one can detect a trend in the situation, it would seem to be
towards unity rather than away from it; in contrast to the historians
I have mentioned I would see the reformers, and the sixteenth century
in general, as seeking to impose, and to some extent successful in imposing, a more rigorous and effective unity than had prevailed before.
I conclude with a comment on two institutions which have been used
to illustrate the notion of the parish as a community, and of the church
as a representative of communal values. The first is Rogationtide, the
days before Ascension Day, when the parish went in procession to beat

[27] Maynard Smith p 96; *The Prayers and Other Pieces of Thomas Becon*, ed J. Ayre, Parker
Society (Cambridge 1844) pp 279-81, 256; *Liturgies of Edward VI*, ed J. Ketley,
Parker Society (1844) pp 76, 87; repeated in 1552, pp 265, 274.

the bounds and to invoke the blessing of God on the harvest. The ritual is commonly accepted as a survival of pre-christian fertility religion, and I am certainly not qualified to question this assumption. But what one may ask is whether, even in a matter so crucial to everybody's survival, the community spirit was necessarily strong enough to override contrary social instinct. On this point I refer once again to George Herbert who, in contrast to contemporary puritans, was a strong supporter of the ritual, as a token of friendship. His country parson was to extol 'charity in loving walking and neighbourly accompanying one another, with reconciling of differences at that time, if there be any'; he was to require all to be present at the perambulation, and to reprove those who would not come as uncharitable and unneighbourly.[28] Considering how closely Herbert's testimony agrees with pre-reformation evidence in other respects, I see no reason for supposing that it would not correspond in this one. The second is the church-ale, which was evidently in aspiration a parish-feast in the same sense that a bride-ale was a kindred-feast. The argument for church-ales as it was conducted by anglicans in the early seventeenth century was the same as Herbert's argument for beating the bounds: they were not understood as expressing an existing sense of community, but justified as a help towards creating this sense among people to whom it did not come naturally. They were, it was argued, 'feasts of charity'; they helped to encourage a 'civil conversation' among the parishioners, to compound controversies, to appease quarrels, to persuade the rich and the poor to love one another.[29] How far these aspirations corresponded with reality I have no idea, and I suspect that it would be too cynical to suppose that bastards were the only fruits of mutual love to issue from church-ales. It would certainly be going beyond what I know to claim that the European parish of the fourteenth, fifteenth, sixteenth or seventeenth centuries was never felt as a collective entity like those described earlier, or like the fraternities which were modelled upon them. But I do have the impression that a sense of parochial community was an exceptional, temporary and precarious feeling, and that it belonged, if anywhere, to a few specific moments of ritual petition or festivity inserted in brackets in the prose of everyday life, and possibly helpful in ridding that life of tensions which might otherwise have proved intolerable.[30]

[28] *Herbert* I pp 316 ff.   [29] Hill p 192.   [30] Compare Campbell p 123.

OVERCOMING THE WORLD:
THE EARLY QUAKER PROGRAMME

by GEOFFREY F. NUTTALL (*presidential address*)

FEW religious leaders have provided us with so clear a record of what may be called their 'marching orders' as the seventeenth-century quaker, George Fox. It is true that the passage in question was composed some thirty-six years later than the time to which it refers, that (like most of his *Journal* as published) it was probably not written by him but dictated to an amanuensis, and that for the first pages of the *Journal* in which it comes the manuscript is not extant; so that critical questions arise.[1] In itself, however, the passage has a simplicity, directness, trenchancy and integration which go far to assure us that it is genuine. What Fox says is this:—

> I was to bring People off from all their own ways, to Christ the new and living Way; and from their Churches (which Men had made and gathered) to the Church in God . . . ; off from the world's Teachers, made by Men, to learn of Christ . . . ; and off from all the World's Worships, to know the Spirit of Truth in the inward Parts. . . . And I was to bring People off from all the

---

[1] Fox's *Journal* has appeared in three forms: in 1694, edited by Thomas Ellwood; in 1911, edited by Norman Penney; and in 1952, by J. L. Nickalls. Penney's edition, reproduced from Friends House Library, Spence MS, *verbatim* and *literatim*, reveals considerable interference with the text by Ellwood; Penney indicates, and classifies, Ellwood's omissions from the text but not his alterations nor, systematically, his additions to it. Nickall's edition normally follows Penney, modernising spelling and punctuation, but sometimes follows Ellwood, and also supplements from other sources.

The first sixteen of the MS's numbered pages are missing. Penney observes that, if written in the same hand as the greater part of the narrative portion of pp 17–20 (an unidentified hand, not the hand of Fox's stepson, Thomas Lower, in which the narrative portion is written from the middle of p 20 onwards), the missing pages would contain about 7,500 words less than are in the corresponding pages in Ellwood, but what sources Ellwood may have used by way of supplement, as is his practice elsewhere, has not been investigated. Further, Ellwood's constant alteration of the text elsewhere makes it likely that his reproduction of the missing pages also contains alterations; but a critical examination of his alterations elsewhere, which might suggest the nature and extent of alterations to the missing pages, has not been undertaken.

World's Religions, which are vain; that they might know the pure Religion, and might visit the Fatherless, the Widows and the Strangers, and keep themselves from the Spots of the World: And then there would not be so many Beggars; the sight of whom often grieved my Heart, to see so much Hard-heartedness amongst them, that professed the Name of Christ. And I was to bring them off from all the World's Fellowships, and Prayings and Singings, which stood in Forms without Power; that their Fellowships might be in the Holy Ghost, and in the Eternal Spirit of God; that they might Pray in the Holy Ghost, and Sing in the Spirit, and with the Grace, that comes by Jesus; . . .[2]

Off from the world: this is the refrain and the burden. The rhythms and the resonance are those of a particular man; but in general the theme is familiar. As professor Frend has reminded us, a longing for holiness shows itself in perfectionist sects throughout history.[3] In the phrase chosen by William Penn as the catchword of the title of his book expounding *the Faith and Practice of the People called Quakers*, published in 1696, what they aimed at was *Primitive Christianity Revived*.[4] In this endeavour they were neither the first nor the last; and like others they found in christianity's original documents a good deal of condemnation of, and of warning against, 'the world': this present world, its god, its prince and its darkness; its spirit, its friendship and, above all, its wisdom (whence, presumably, Mr Worldly-Wiseman in *The Pilgrim's Progress*).

This negative attitude to 'the world' is one of the themes of the briefer account of the beginnings of quakerism, and of the place in it of George Fox, which Penn contributed by way of preface to the first (posthumous) edition of Fox's *Journal* (1694), and which remains the most illuminating near-contemporary analysis of the movement. Penn's education permitted him to adopt the strategy of setting the movement in the perspective of the history of the church. First, he relates how, from the time of Constantine, 'having got at last the Worldly Power into their Hands', the Christians 'changed what they could, the Kingdom of Christ, which is not of this World, into a Worldly Kingdom; or at least stiled the Worldly Kingdom that was in their

2 [G.] Fox, *Journal*, ed [T.] Ellwood (London 1694) p 23.
3 W. H. C. Frend, 'Heresy and schism as social and notional movements', *SCH* 9 (1972) pp 37–56.
4 For the ambivalence of *Primitive Christianity Revived*, note its use (1711) by William Whiston.

Hands the Kingdom of Christ, and so they became Worldly, and not true Christians.... Thus the False Church sprang up, and mounted the Chair.' Coming to the age of the reformation, Penn acknowledges some steps towards' recovery. 'But yet', he observes, 'there was too much ... of worldly Authority and worldly Greatness in their Ministers, especially in this Kingdom, Sweden, Denmark and some Parts of Germany.' Turning to the independents of his own time, though initially it was not so with them, he remarks that through 'tasting of Worldly Empire' and falling 'under the Weight of Worldly Honour and Advantage', 'they degenerated'. Way was thus opened for the quakers, whose minds, he writes, using the present tense, 'are turned off from the Vanity of the World and its Lifeless ways and Teachers, and ad-hear to this blessed Light in themselves, which discovers and condemns Sin in all its appearances, and shows how to overcome it if minded and obeyed'.[5]

Here we have a fresh note: not only *off from the vanity of the world* but *how to overcome it*. It is correct elucidation; and it points to an important differentia between the quaker movement and others at first sight similar. The idea of *overcoming the world*, it is true, was specially precious to Penn. His own conversion (in quaker language, convincement) had come about when, in 1667, he had heard an Oxford tradesman turned quaker missionary, Thomas Loe, deliver a powerful address in Cork. 'There is a Faith that overcomes the World,' Loe said, 'and there is a Faith that is overcome by the World.'[6] Something in Loe's message or manner pierced the worldliness in the young courtier, reducing him to tears; and though Loe died the next year Penn never forgot him. Faith worketh by love; and Penn's reference in *Primitive Christianity Revived* to 'that Love and Patience [that] must in the end have the Victory'[7] may be seen as one remembrance, and interpretation, of Loe's words.

Apart from his own experience, Penn was correct in his explication of Fox and of infant quakerism. Psychologically and theologically, its message – and, while an excessive emphasis on it may fairly be termed perfectionism, it does appear to be part of the message of the New Testament – was of liberation and triumph: triumph, in the

5 [W.] Penn, in Fox, *Journal*, ed Ellwood, preface fol A2ᵛ–C1ᵛ. Penn's historical analysis antedates G. Arnold, *Unparteiische Kirchen- und Ketzergeschichte* (Frankfurt am Main 1699) by three years.
6 W. Penn, *Collection of the Works* (London 1726) I, p 2.
7 *Ibid* p 117.

first place, over evil within the heart, within one's self, over sin. If theology were our interest, I would point here to one of James Nayler's most popular tracts – published in 1657, by 1665 it was in its fourth or fifth reprint – which is entitled, plainly enough for him who runs to read, *How sin is strengthened, and how it is overcome*. Our present interests, however, are different; leaving sin on one side, we will return to 'the world', and, for the moment, to George Fox.

And what must be said first, and at once, is that the early quakers were not, as they later became, 'the quiet of the land'; were not, as is often erroneously supposed, a people detached, other-worldly or world-fleeing (to use von Hügel's terms in delineation of monasticism and the sect-type). On the contrary, they were world-seeking, world-overcoming, concerned (in von Hügel's rather grandiose phrase) with 'the Spiritualising of Civilisation'.[8] In Fox's own case – and it is difficult to exaggerate his influence in moulding the movement – personality and temperament played their part: he was a man of great courage and assuredness. Neave Brayshaw, who in this century brings us nearest to an understanding of the man, rightly says that not other-worldliness but over-worldliness was Fox's native air and that the dominant note of his life was 'the note of victory'.[9]

> Look over that which maketh to suffer . . .
> Look over all Prisons . . .
> Have power over your own Spirits . . .
> Keep your Feet upon the Top of the Mountains . . .
> Live in the Authority of the Son of God, and his Power,
>   whereby ye may be kept on Top of the World.[10]

These are among the quotations from Fox with which Neave Brayshaw makes his point. Any reader of Fox's letters could multiply them indefinitely. Equally, when his life ended, Penn tells how Fox was 'so full of assurance . . . that he Triumpht over Death . . . as if Death were hardly worth Notice or a Mention'.[11]

Now in the record of his 'marching orders' there is one phrase which stands out, as unlike anything else in the paragraph and as not strictly

8 F. von Hügel, *Essays & Addresses on the Philosophy of Religion: first series* (London/ Toronto 1928) p 270.
9 [A. N.] Brayshaw, *The Quakers [their Story and Message]* (3 ed London/New York 1938) pp 41, 40.
10 [G.] Fox, [*Collection of Many Select Christian*] *Epistles* (London 1698) pp 401, 198; *Journal*, ed Ellwood p 597; *Epistles* pp 152, 63-4.
11 Penn, in Fox, *Journal*, ed Ellwood, preface fol I1r.

relevant to its argument. The phrase is this: 'And then there would not be so many Beggars; the sight of whom often grieved my Heart.' Fox's marked social conscience and passion for justice, and in particular his concern for beggars and the poor, have their place here at the heart of his mission and in the moment of his commission. Even before this summary of it we find, a few pages earlier, that he 'exhorted the Justices, Not to oppress the Servants in their Wages' but 'to leave off Oppression', while at the same time he exhorted 'the Servants, To do their Duties, and serve honestly, &c.'.[12] Turn on instead of back, and we see him almost at once 'going to their Courts to cry for Justice', 'warning such, as kept publick Houses for Entertainment, that they should not let People have more Drink, than would do them good', and in fairs and markets declaring against their 'Cheating and Cozening; warning all to deal Justly, and to speak the Truth'.[13] The historian William Charles Braithwaite, with his unrivalled knowledge of quaker ephemera, draws attention to a number of these 'warnings' which, like a latter-day Luther, Fox set up as placards on church doors or in the market-place, thereby 'clearing his conscience', as he says himself, to drunkards, liars, swearers, brawlers and all who fight and cheat.[14] Or turn on a few pages more, and Fox is writing 'to ye Judges concerneinge there puttinge men to death for Catle & for Money'.[15] 'I alsoe writt to ye Judges what a sore thinge it was yt prisoners shoulde lye soe longe in goale.'[16]

Other quakers besides Fox were soon doing the same thing. As early as July 1652, in a letter of which the original is preserved, Thomas Aldan wrote to Fox from York, where he was in prison for refusing to pay tithes and on other charges, telling how he had followed Sir Thomas Harrison (later a high sheriff for the county), warning him 'of being partiel in Iudgement and of takeinge gifts and rewards', and adding 'that all their gifts and rewards takeing was from a law held up by the divil in them & all oppression acted by them was of the devell'.[17] In 1656 another quaker leader in the north, Gervase Benson, himself a justice of the peace, published *The Cry of the Oppressed From under their Oppressions*, with a postscript by Fox. Three years later a Somerset quaker, Thomas Morford, put out a tract with

---

[12] Fox, *Journal*, ed Ellwood p 17.

[13] *Ibid* p 25.

[14] [W. C.] Braithwaite, [*The*] *Beginnings* [*of Quakerism*] (2 ed Cambridge 1955) pp 49–50, where the reference to Boswell Middleton Collection should be p 49 and the reference to Samuel Watson Collection should be p 23.

[15] G. Fox, *Journal*, ed N. Penney (Cambridge 1911) I p 13.

[16] *Ibid* p 14.   [17] [Friends House Library], Swarthmore MS I fol 373.

the similar title, *The Cry of Oppression . . . with a true discovery of the unjust proceedings of those called Magistrates of Bathe.*

Indeed, if one goes no further than Fox's own writings other than his *Journal*, especially some of the many tracts by him not reprinted, one soon perceives how much (not all, of course) of what he intends to denote by his often repeated term 'the world' lies in this sphere of oppression and injustice. 'O ye earthly minded men!', he writes in *The Vials of The Wrath of God, Poured forth . . . Upon all professors of the World* (1654), 'give over oppressing the poor, exalt not your selves above your fellow-creatures; for ye are all of one mold and blood; you that set your nests on high, joyne house to house, field to field till there be no place for the poor, woe is your portion. The earth is the Lords, and the fulness thereof.'[18] Again, 'O England, and the Islands,' he writes in *A Warning to the World* (1655), 'and such as be about thee, whose Judges judgeth for rewards, and Priests preach for hire, and Prophets prophesie for money, and whose Divines divine for money . . . for this cause is England on heaps, as Jerusalem became.' This is followed by a series of tremendous *Away withs*, which, if placed alongside the *off from* series, strengthen their claim to be a genuine reflection of early conviction; to take a single example – 'Away with all such that take Tythes from poor people, and get treble damages if they will not pay them.'[19] One further example may be taken from an earlier piece, the *Severall Papers* published in 1653 by Fox and Nayler jointly; in this case the words are Nayler's. 'Woe unto you that live upon deceit in your weights and measures, by your sleighty words arising from the Serpents wisedome, which makes a prey on the simple; and when you have got great estates . . . you are set up above them, who are made poore by you; now is the Lord come to search you out, and you shall restore for your Theft foure-fold.'[20]

The early quakers were certainly no strangers to the art of invective. 'Admitting no weapon but the tongue,' it has been said, 'they used it unsparingly.'[21] Richard Baxter spoke for many others when he complained, 'They have called me Dog and Devil, and abundance of such names.'[22] This habit of rebuke they learned, to be fair, from the exhortation to it which is reiterated in the New Testament; they saw it as a

18 G. Fox, *The Vials of the Wrath of God* (London 1654) p 3.
19 G. Fox, *A Warning to the World* (London 1655) pp 5–8.
20 [G.] Fox and [J.] Nayler, *Severall Papers* (n.p. 1653) p 22.
21 *DNB* under G. Fox.
22 R. Baxter, *One Sheet against the Quakers* (London 1657) p 5.

natural, and a necessary, part of the reviving of primitive christianity; and it could, as we shall see, act as a healing knife in overcoming the worldly, if not the world. For their habit of challenging society with a series of 'woe's the quakers found equal precedent in the prophets of the Old Testament; and 'a more sure word of prophecy'[23] was precisely what they believed themselves called to exercise. The passages so far cited may be seen as intended to minister to society something of what in the experience of the individual is administered by conscience; and to conscience the quakers did often appeal. In another early piece (1653) issued jointly by Fox and Nayler, Nayler's part is entitled *A Lamentacion (By one of Englands Prophets,) Over the Ruines of this oppressed Nacion, To be deeply layd to heart by Parliament and Army*, Fox's *A Warning to the Rulers of England Not to usurp Dominion over the Conscience*. This is why the tone of very many of these pieces is so negative. They are enlargements, or specifications, of the over-all burden *off from, away with*. What later became known as 'the nonconformist conscience' has come in for its share of abuse; but there is sometimes virtue in pinpointing what is wrong, even though what should be done, positively, is not yet clear. A broadside by Isaac Penington has the frank title *A Brief Account of Some Reasons . . . why . . . Quakers cannot do some things*. Conscience, public as well as private, especially in a time of revolution and reform, will often act like Black Beauty in the dark pulling up sharp at a broken bridge.

In any case, while unhesitant in their condemnation of what was wrong with 'the world', the early quakers were very ready with advice, or demand, for its reformation. They not only continued to 'warn' judges and magistrates when they met them face to face – and their increasingly frequent appearances in court, charged with a variety of offences, made it the less necessary for them to 'go' to judges – they had personal interviews with Cromwell himself.[24] They also addressed tracts to Cromwell, to Parliament and to magistrates in general. Before Nayler's withdrawal in 1656 some of these pieces, like two already noticed, were issued jointly by Fox and Nayler, who in 1655 put out one entitled *To thee, Oliver Cromwell, into whose hands God hath committed the Sword of Justice*. Other tracts claimed the authorship of a group of quakers writing under common concern. Others again, such as *Some Papers Given forth to the World* (1655), addressed to the 'Rulers of this

---

[23] Fox, *Journal*, ed Ellwood p 26; for comment, see G. F. Nuttall, 'Juan de Valdés: fresh light on a Quaker forerunner', *Friends' Quarterly* 17, 3 (1971) p 120.
[24] For a list of such interviews see Braithwaite, *Beginnings* pp 435–6.

nation', were issued without any name or names at all. This puts difficulties in the way of compiling anything like a *catalogue raisonnée*; but the stream was constant. Fox alone issued, in 1654, *A Message from the Lord, to the Parliament of England*; in 1656, *This for each Parliament-man* and *Omnibus Magistratibus Gubernatoribusque*; in 1657 or 1658, *An Instruction to Judges and Lawyers* and *To all the Magistrates in London*; in 1658, *To the Protector and Parliament of England* and *The Law of God, the Rule for Law-makers*; and in 1659, *To the Parliament of the Common-wealth of England, Fiftynine Particulars laid down for the Regulating things* and also a postscript to *An Epistle To all the Christian Magistrates*, to which a group of five quakers, two of them women, had set their hands.

This year 1659, with the recall of the Rump, saw the flood-tide of quaker tracts of this nature, when at least sixteen quakers put out well over twenty pieces. Among their titles are these: *To the Supream Authoritie (under God) of the Common-wealth*; *Oh ye Heads of the Nation Who are set in the supream Authority Thereof, and are at this time Assembled in Parliament*; *To all present Rulers, whether Parliament, or whomsoever* (this was written by one woman Friend and printed for another); *Love, Kindness, and due Respect, By way of Warning to the Parliament*; *A Few words in true love written to the old long sitting Parliament*; and *The Real Cause of the Nations Bondage . . . presented unto the Parliament of the Common-wealth of England*. In some ways the most remarkable of all these pieces was *The Copie of a Paper Presented to the Parliament; And read the 27th of the 4th Moneth, 1659. Subscribed by more than fifteen thousand hands*, together with the document which followed closely on its heels, *These Several Papers Was sent to the Parliament The twentieth day of the fifth Moneth, 1659. Being above seven thousand of the Names of the Hand-maids and Daughters of the Lord, And such as feels the oppression of Tithes, in the names of many more*, the first eight signatures being those of Margaret Fell, who later married Fox, and of her seven daughters by her first husband, the youngest of them no more than six years old.

The general stance adopted by the writers of these manifold addresses to parliament is revealed in the titles of three of them, all published in 1659, by Richard Hubberthorne, Isaac Penington and Francis How-gill respectively, each of whom was a recognised quaker leader: *The Good Old Cause Briefly demonstrated*; *To the Parliament, the Army, and all the Wel-affected in the Nation, who have been faithful to the Good Old Cause*; and *An Information and also Advice . . . to the late Parliament; and also to all People who seeks peace and righteousness, and are for the Good old*

Cause – for 'the advancement of Christ's Kingdom', that is, together with 'the liberty of the subjects, and an equal distinction of justice'.[24a] So far as this aspect of the movement is concerned – to use the words of Alan Cole, who has given it close attention – 'in the first phase of its history, Quakerism was essentially a movement of protest against the suppression of the "good old cause"'.[25] This judgement is substantiated by three pieces containing summaries of the main positive reforms which the quakers confidently demanded, if 'the world', and the evil in it, was to be overcome: namely, the one by Fox already mentioned as laying down 'Fiftynine Particulars ... for the Regulating things'; a second by E[dward] B[yllinge], a future governor of West New Jersey, entitled *A Mite of Affection, Manifested in 31. Proposals, Offered to all the Sober and Free-born People within this Common-wealth*;[26] and a third by T[homas] L[awson], a noted botanist, whose name is preserved in that of the plant *Hieracium Lawsonii*, entitled *An appeal to the Parliament, concerning the Poor, That there may not be a Beggar in England.*[27]

'The main legal reforms suggested' in these three tracts 'were to publish all statutes in English, to decentralize and shorten law procedures for the sake of poor plaintiffs, and to end capital punishment for theft'.[28] Lawson 'planned that each parish should employ competent undertakers to relieve those who could not work, and to arrange with manufacturers and tradesmen for the employment of others', and 'also suggested a labour bureau'.[29] Byllinge's programme 'includes demands for annual parliaments, equal constituencies, annual rotation of officers'.[30] Among Fox's 'Fiftynine Particulars' numbers thirty-two and thirty-three read: 'Let all those Fines that belong to Lords of Mannors, be given to the poor people, for Lords have enough'; and 'Let all the poor people, blinde and lame, and creeples be provided for in the

---

24a *A Word for God* (London 1655) as reprinted in [*Collection of the State Papers of John*] *Thurloe*, [ed T. Birch] (London 1742) p 382.

25 [Alan] Cole, ['The Quakers and the English Revolution'], *PP* 10 (1956) p 44, and in *Crisis in Europe* [*1560–1660*, ed T. Aston] (London 1965) p 348.

26 This tract has also been attributed to another quaker, Edward Burrough. For attribution to Byllinge and a summary of its thirty-one proposals, see J. L. Nickalls, 'The Problem of Edward Byllinge: II. His writings and their evidence of his influence on the first constitution of West New Jersey', *Children of Light: in honor of Rufus M. Jones* ed H. H. Brinton (New York 1938) pp 20–3.

27 This tract has also been attributed to a baptist, Thomas Lambe.

28 [H.] Barbour, [*The Quakers in Puritan England*] (New Haven/London 1964) p 200.

29 [W. C.] Braithwaite, [*The*] *Second Period* [*of Quakerism*] (2 ed Cambridge 1961) p 559.

30 [W.] Schenk, [*The Concern for Social Justice in the Puritan Revolution*] (London/New York/Toronto 1948) p 125.

Nation, that there might not be a begger in England'[31] – he has not forgotten his 'marching orders'.

The first thing that strikes one about these pieces is the distance at which they set the early Quakers from the conventional picture of them as inward-looking and pietistic. 'The Kingdom they heralded' might be 'not *of* this world, but it was to be set up *in* this world'.[32] At least equally remarkable is the absence of any marked distinctiveness or originality in the positions they adopt or the policies they recommend. 'Concerning all these reforms the early Quakers were at one with a large body of radical opinion in the Puritan Revolution',[33] namely that represented by the levellers, 'the chief exponents of Puritan democracy', as they have been styled, and to a lesser extent by the diggers, 'who carry over from politics to economics the Levellers' feeling for justice and equality'.[34] In particular, the campaign against tithes, which in the unfolding of history became indelibly associated with the quakers, was a leveller interest before it was inherited by the quakers; it was a concern, the weight of which, not only originally, was economic as much as religious. What we have in these quaker tracts is, to quote Cole again, largely 'echoes from the past', 'the authentic tones of the Leveller pamphleteers of the previous decade'.[35] The very titles we ran over just now carry us back to the levellers' leader, John Lilburne: they repeat and continue his pieces *For every member of the House of Commons* (1647), his *Earnest petition of many free-born people of this kingdome* (1648), his *Discourse of the present power of magistracy and justice* (1649), his *Addresses* (1653) to Cromwell, and the *Petitions* on Lilburne's behalf *of divers afflicted women* (1653). Nor must it be supposed that quaker 'tracts echoing the Leveller platform'[36] are in any way limited to those already mentioned; a number were written, in particular, by George Fox the younger (a quaker not related to the other Fox but younger in convincement).

It is consequently not surprising that the quakers were sometimes taken to be levellers *redivivi* under another name.[37] Links of a personal nature are few but can be traced. In a tract published jointly by Fox and Nayler in 1654, entitled *A Word from the Lord, unto all the faithlesse Generation of the World*, Fox addresses 'You who are called Levellers'

---

[31] G. Fox, *To the Parliament* (London 1659) pp 8–9.
[32] Schenk p 129.　　　　　　　　　　[33] *Ibid* p 124.
[34] [*Puritanism and Liberty*] [ed A. S. P.] Woodhouse (London 1938), introduction, pp 98–9.
[35] Cole pp 42–3, and in *Crisis in Europe* p 346.
[36] Barbour p 193.　　　　　　　　　[37] Swarthmore MS I, fol 36.

more in sorrow than in anger, as if he had parted from them with
regret. 'You had a flash in your minde,' he writes, 'a simplicitie, and
your minds run into the earth and smothered it, and so got up into
presumption.'[38] In the following year one, or possibly two quakers, each
a man of influence, are thought to have taken part with Wildman and
Henry Marten in the meetings in London prior to Wildman's leveller
plot.[39] In 1659, among five names commended by Northamptonshire
quakers as those of 'men in this county that have estates & that are
free from persecution and louing towards friendes', and thus as suitable
to be put in commission as justices of the peace, is one described as
'William Raynsborrow, his Brother yt were murthered'.[40] This mur-
dered brother is Thomas Rainborow, the republican and advocate of
manhood suffrage, whose statement in the Putney debates, 'Really I
think that the poorest he that is in England hath a life to live, as the
greatest he'[41] A. D. Lindsay used to quote with such relish. William
Rainborow himself, a major in the parliamentarian army and a justice
till dismissed in 1650, also took part in the Putney debates.[42] Another
name commended in the same Northamptonshire list is Thomas
Nottingam, his 'seuen Children and his wife' being described as 'reall
freindes';[43] and Nottingam, it has been pointed out, was one of the
'rich men' whom the Wellingborough diggers praised for having 'freely
given us their share in the local common'.[44] But of course the main link
between the quakers and the levellers is to be found in John Lilburne
himself; for Lilburne, originally a member of a baptist congregation
and a devout man, not averse to language about himself which in
Nayler's mouth would be regarded as messianic,[45] ended his stormy
career as a quaker. (The evidence that Gerrard Winstanley, the diggers'
leader, also became a quaker is attractive but is not wholly convincing.[46])

[38] G. Fox and J. Nayler, *A Word from the Lord* (London 1654) p 13.

[39] Braithwaite, *Beginnings* p 175 n 2, following S. R. Gardiner, *History of the Common-
wealth and Protectorate 1649-1656* (2 ed London 1903) III p 228 n 3; but the captain
Bishop mentioned may have been not the quaker George Bishop but a Henry Bishop:
see M. Ashley, *John Wildman* (London 1947) p 86.

[40] [N.] Penney (ed), *Extracts [from State Papers relating to Friends 1654-1672]* (London/
Philadelphia/New York 1913) p 7.

[41] Woodhouse p 53.   [42] *Ibid* pp 52, 67.   [43] Penney, *Extracts* p 7.

[44] R. T. Vann, 'Diggers and Quakers – a Further Note', *JFHS* 50, 2 (1962) pp 67–8;
Vann suggests further identifications.

[45] Schenk pp 25–6.

[46] R. T. Vann, 'From Radicalism to Quakerism: Gerrard Winstanley and Friends'
JFHS 49, 1 (1959) pp 41–6.

In view of the overlap at this point between the levellers and the quakers, Lilburne's convincement offers an inviting avenue for considering the nature of the quaker differentia. Let us look at this more closely. We happen to possess the quakers' account of it as well as his own. In October 1655 Lilburne was in prison in Dover castle. An interview initiated by himself led to an invitation to attend the quaker meeting for worship in Dover from 'the father'[47] of the meeting, as he has been called, Luke Howard. Visiting the meeting that day was George Harrison, a travelling preacher from Westmorland, aged about twenty-five, who had the gift of rebuke and believed in using it. After his 'Declaration & Prayer', observing that Lilburne liked 'the Words & sound of the Truth . . . But his Wisedome was aboue it', as Lilburne was 'passeing away out of ye Meeting, George Harrison runs after him, in ye Entry, with these Words, "Friend, thou art too high for Truth". Which Words . . . Gaue him (as he said) "such a Box on ye Eare", that stund him againe, Insomuch that he could neuer get from vnder them; but liued & dyed in ye profession of ye Truth.'[48]

This is the quaker account. Lilburne's we have in the form of two letters which he wrote from Dover castle in December 1655, one to his wife, the other to a friend who had been with him during his recent imprisonment in Jersey. Both letters are printed in his tract *The Resurrection of John Lilburne*, which came out twice during 1656.

Lilburne confirms the quaker account by references which he makes to Luke Howard, whom, after reference to his 'Priscilla', he describes as his 'Aquilla (being a contemptible, yet understanding, spiritually knowing, & single hearted Shoomaker)'. Harrison he does not mention; but what he writes is consonant with the effect Harrison's rebuke – 'Friend, thou art too high for Truth' – was believed to have had on him. For he acknowledges that he has 'lost all manner of ability to consult with one grain of Machivel'[49] – a confession the more telling because in an earlier tract he had praised Machiavelli as 'one of the most wisest judicious and true lovers of his country of Italies liberties and freedomes, and generally of the good of all mankind that ever I read of'.[50] Now, he writes, he is called to live 'with a real weanedness from

---

[47] Braithwaite, *Beginnings* p 396.

[48] [N.] Penney (ed), [*The*] *First Publishers* [*of Truth*] (London/Philadelphia/New York 1907) pp 144–5.

[49] [J.] Lilburne, [*The*] *Resurrection* [*of John Lilburne*] (n.p. 1656) pp 4, 9.

[50] J. Lilburne, *The Upright Man* (London 1653) p 7; quoted by Schenk, p 34; see also P. Gregg, *Free-born John: a biography of John Lilburne* (London/Toronto/Wellington/Sydney 1961) p 313.

worldly or fleshly honour, applause, glory, riches, or creature-fulness'.[51]

Lilburne also tells his correspondents of three quaker tracts which he had found 'most convincingly, instructive' to his soul, and by which, as he puts it, he had 'been knock'd down'. These were: 'in the first place Iames Naylor . . . his *Something in answer unto . . . John Jackson . . . his book called, Strength in Weakness*'; and secondly, two works 'cald, *The Discovery of the great enmity of the Serpent against the Seed of the woman*, and . . . [*The*] *Discovery of mans return*', by William Dewsbury '(to whose precious and heavenly spirit,' he writes, 'although I never see his face, mine in indearedness of love is glued unto)'.[52]

Read today, these three pieces are not instinct with convincing power; but they were then newly out. To Lilburne the writings of Dewsbury would be made *actuel* by the fact that Dewsbury's imprisonment at Northampton, with which one of the tracts deals, arose in part from fears that the quakers were involved in leveller plots: 'If thou and Fox, had us in your power,' the judge told Dewsbury at his trial, 'you would soon have your hands Imbrued in blood.'[53] Dewsbury Braithwaite accounts 'perhaps the sweetest and wisest of the early Friends'; he found, he says, 'his prison bars served the truth better than any pulpit'.[54] But there was a genuinely levelling spirit in him. 'The Mistris and Maid are Hail-fellow well met', he once said; and continued, '. . . Here is now a New World, and the fashions of the Old World are gone.'[55] The impact on Lilburne of the tract by Nayler, in answer to John Jackson, part of a prolonged controversy between the two men, will have owed something to Lilburne's regard for 'the Grand Treasurer for the Excise',[56] as Richard Baxter calls Jackson; for Lilburne refers to him as 'my indeared friend, and old and long acquaintance'.[57] In a letter written later this year, on 27 October, a copy of which is preserved in manuscript in a printed volume of Jackson's writings in the library of the Society of Friends, Lilburne further describes Jackson as 'the strongest and rationalest that ever I read of the controversies of that

---

51 Lilburne, *Resurrection*, p 4. 52 *Ibid* pp 5, 7, 5.

53 W. Dewsbury, *A Discovery of the Ground from whence the Persecution did arise* (London 1655) p 12; in Braithwaite, *Beginnings* p 175, following Edward Smith, *Life of William Dewsbury* (London 1836) p 95, 'us' is altered to 'it'.

54 Braithwaite, *Beginnings* pp 63, 175.

55 *Concurrence and Unanimity of the People called Quakers* (London 1694) p 22.

56 *Reliquiae Baxterianae* ed M. Sylvester (London 1696) App IV, p 93; see *Acts and Ordinances of the Interregnum 1642–1660*, edd C. H. Firth and R. S. Rait (London 1911) II, pp 1350, 1353, 1424.

57 Lilburne, *Resurrection* p 8.

encountered-with-my-soules-endeared freinds called Quakers'.[58] All
in all, the effect on Lilburne of these tracts, together with his encounter
with Luke Howard, George Harrison and other Friends in Dover
meeting, was, as he says, that, although at first he could not do as
George Fox had done in signing an engagement never again to draw
the sword, 'the true occasion, or real ground of all outward war and
humane busling contest being not taken away, or absolutely crucified
or subdued at the very Root in my soul' – for 'betwixt the Winter-
storms and fierce tempests of conviction, (or rather the beginning of it)
and the pleasant sunshine, dews, and springing days of growth into a
measure of refreshment, there is a vast difference' – now he could do so;
for 'now in my already attained growing up measure . . . I am able to
witness . . . that the true grounds or reall occasions of all outward
wars, and all carnall buslings, and all fleshly strivings within me, is in a
very large measure, or degree, become dead or crucified within me: . . .',
and that the 'spiritual Sword is the only alone weapon that this glorious,
conquering, spiritual King useth to fight withall against all enemies . . .
with which only and alone he conquereth and overcometh carnal
Weapons of any kinde whatsoever . . .'[59]

It is a pity that Lilburne did not live to show, by further writing
or by action or refraining from action just what difference in practice
his convincement made. He knew that 'the strange politick contrivance
of my (largely reputed by them) politique heart in turning quaker'[60]
would arouse suspicion; and in *The Chasing of the young quaking Harlot
out of the Citie*, published soon afterwards, an opponent did in fact ask
if it was not 'easie to discern that J. Lilburnes Resurrection is but a mear
immagination or Quaking Delusion'.[61] The quaker Richard Hubberthorne sprang to Lilburne's defence, claiming that God had 'owned him
in opposing many of the unjust powers of the Nation'; for precedent
for Lilburne's sudden conversion he pointed to Saul of Tarsus.[62] In a
letter to Fox written early in 1657 Hubberthorne describes Lilburne as
'zailus and forward for the truth';[63] and when in August of that year
Lilburne died, 'a croud of Quakers'[64] attended his funeral. This, with a

[58] The MS is preserved between J[ohn] J[ackson], *Strength in Weakness* (London 1655)
and [John Jackson], *Hosannah to the Son of David* (London 1657) in Tract vol 309.
[59] Lilburne, *Resurrection* pp 9–10, 12.
[60] *Ibid* p 9.
[61] R. Hubberthorne, *The Horn of the He-Goat Broken* (London 1656) p 11.
[62] *Ibid* pp 10–11.
[63] Swarthmore MS IV fol 14.
[64] *Mercurius Politicus* for 27 August to 3 September 1657, no 379, p 1600.

letter from Lilburne to Margaret Fell, written in May, in which he refers to 'the strong measur of god dwelling in G. Fox, W. Dusbery, R. Hubberthorne'[65] and other Quakers, is as far as the external evidence will take us.

Internally, however, Lilburne's account of his conversion not only carries conviction but is in line with what we know otherwise of early quakerism. It is clear, in the first place, that what was transformed was not his social and political programme but himself. It confirms what Penn says of the first quakers, that 'they were changed Men themselves before they went about to change others';[66] and the capture of one so 'insatiably vindictive'[67] (it is sir Charles Firth's phrase) as Lilburne is striking evidence of the power of the new movement. Outwardly, what Lilburne's convincement did was to change not his ends but his methods of gaining them. It required that he turn from plots and threats of violence, and accept that over-riding concern for the recovery of the oppressor, as well as of the oppressed, which is the mark of quaker manifestoes throughout the decade. The quakers saw themselves as in the line of the prophets who 'were often sent to pronounce judgement against unjust men, who had the power committed to them' but nevertheless 'never attempted to rayse any violence against them, but used all meanes to perswade them . . . ; for those that be of God, cannot rejoyce in the destruction of any, but would have all to turn to God and find mercy'.[68] So writes Nayler, as early as 1653. 'If His Nature be once brought forth in you', wrote a less well-known quaker, William Tomlinson, in 1656, 'you will finde a saving spirit raised up in you, not a destroying spirit; for Christ and every measure of Him is a Saviour, not a Destroyer; and so from Christ the Saviour spring up many Saviours, Obad. v. 21.'[69] 'I am moved to charge all', writes Fox to magistrates in 1657, 'to be meek, to be humble, to be patient, and not to be rash, nor to be heady, nor to be fierce, but to be gentle.'[70] This is what Lilburne was learning, in his measure. For, thirdly, Lilburne had clearly absorbed another position essential to early quakerism: namely, that a man must not pretend faith or conversion, nor follow any teaching or teacher unless and until he is convinced and persuaded;

---

[65] Friends House Library, Thirnbeck MS II fol 2; *JFHS* 9 (1912) p 53.
[66] Penn, in Fox, *Journal*, ed Ellwood, preface, fo. F1ʳ.
[67] *DNB*, under Lilburne.
[68] Fox and Nayler, *Severall Papers* p 15.
[69] *Copies of Some few of the Papers given into the House of Parliament in the time of Iames Naylers trial* (n.p., n.d.) p 5.
[70] G. Fox, *This is to all Officers . . . and to all Magistrates* (London 1657) p 4.

must not go beyond his measure, or run beyond his Guide, but must *wait* until his convincement and conviction are his own. Even when, as in Lilburne's case, the convincement is sudden, the convictions, and the power to live by them, come only gradually.

Laudable such sentiments may be. To a government already suspicious they seemed evasive in the extreme. When is a quaker not a quaker? There were grounds for uneasiness. Up in the north, in Swaledale, was a company known as the Dales men, who 'in time of the warr did not submit themselves to anie power, neither Civill nor Militarie but stood upon their guard, and for most of them refused to pay tythes. And their was noe cours to be taken to compell them.'[71] So runs the record of a young man who in 1648 took a lease of the sequestrated rectory of Grinton-in-Swaledale, a sprig of the family of Swale Hall above the river and of the Swale chapel within the church; and did not the quakers come from the North? Indeed, was not 'the first out-breaking of that Prodigious and Comprehensive Heresy', asked the author of *Magnalia Christi Americana* fifty years later, (virtually) 'in that very place', causing the vicar of Kirkby Stephen, a few miles west of Swaledale, to write 'the first Book that ever was written against that Sink of Blasphemies',[72] *A Brief Relation of the Irreligion of the Northern Quakers* (1653)? By 1669 quakers were numerous in Swaledale, Grinton alone counting sixty.[73] More than this, Philip Swale was among those converted. He was treasurer of the meeting at Richmond and also held meetings in his own house, and he had not only written off the Grinton church rents due to him but had been fined himself for not paying tithes.[74] The local authorities can hardly be blamed if they saw in the quakers the Dales men under a new name. Coincidence we might call it, or at most say the Dales men had prepared the ground. But the authorities were probably right. For Swaledale also provided one of the two organised communities of those called seekers whose accession to quakerism, at a meeting held on Whitsunday 1652, on Firbank Fell above Sedbergh, first set the movement aflame; and among these seekers was Philip Swale.[75] In September it was the turn of the

[71] N[orth] R[iding] R[ecord] O[ffice], *Report* for 1966 pp 31–2.
[72] C. Mather, *Magnalia Christi Americana* (London 1702) bk III pt ii cap 1 pp 75–6.
[73] *Original Records of Early Nonconformity under Persecution and Indulgence* ed G. L. Turner (London/Leipzig 1911) I p 173.
[74] NRRO, *Report* for 1966 pp 32, 34. For Swale, of whom we may expect a study by Arthur Raistrick, see also [Richard Robinson], *A Blast blown out of the North* (n.p., 1680) p 7.
[75] W. C. Braithwaite, 'The Westmorland and Swaledale Seekers in 1651', *JFHS* 5 (1908) pp 3–10, using the same MS as is reported on in NRRO *Report* for 1966.

minister who, at Swale's invitation, had been ministering to the seekers, Thomas Taylor, to be converted by Fox.[76] In the following May Taylor wrote to Fox: 'Truly frend I finde through the great grace of my God a principle springing up in my soul that doth really give evidence agaynst all the world. . . . I have been a sorer up in the first nature high, but the Lord hath been good to bring me somewhat low.'[77]

Though it is recorded of him that, even while he was still in a living, he 'denyed to receive his maintaineance by that antixtan & popish way of Tyths',[78] Thomas Taylor was no leveller but continued a devoted travelling preacher – twenty years later his financial needs were still being cared for by Philip Swale;[79] but other converts to quakerism besides Lilburne, it seems, had been levellers.[80] Still others, and a considerable number of these – more than a hundred and fifty, it has been calculated[81] – had been soldiers, among them Gervase Benson, Edward Byllinge and George Fox the younger, together with other leaders, including Nayler, Dewsbury and Hubberthorne. They were soldiers no longer, but their leaving the army had not been always of their own initiative. In 1657 general Monck received complaints about a captain lieutenant 'turned one of this sottish stupid generation of quakers'; 'I never saw man soe metamorphosed in my dayes as he is', his major wrote; 'the levelling principle lyes at the bottome';[82] and the man was cashiered, and was soon in prison.[83] So many, in fact, suffered dismissal at this time that they issued an address *To the Generals, and Captains, Officers and Souldiers . . . ; the Innocent Cause of us, who have been turned out of your Army*. Wherever the quakers went, indeed, they met with response among soldiers, especially in Scotland and Ireland. They also published many tracts addressed to the army, in which, so far from concealing it, they make capital of the fact that they had known the army from within. 'Amongst whom I formerly have had my Conversation about thirteen or fourteen years' stands on the titlepage of a *Visitation by way of Declaration* addressed in part unto . . . *Souldiers, that are in Arms* (1659) by Joseph Fuce, 'and that some of the old Officers and Souldiers may very well remember'. Another quaker, Edward Burrough, makes a similar admission; which he then qualifies with the words, 'We are now better informed than once we were, for though we do more than ever oppose Oppression, and seek after

76 Braithwaite, *Beginnings* p 93.
77 Swarthmore MS III fol 29.
78 Penney, *First Publishers* p 253.
79 Braithwaite, *Second Period* p 363.
80 *JFHS* 33 (1936) p 70.
81 Brayshaw, *The Quakers* p 132 n 3.
82 *Thurloe* VI pp 167, 215, 168.
83 Swarthmore MS III fol 146.

Reformation, yet we do it not in that way of outward Warring & Fighting with Carnal Weapons, & Swords.'[84]

Laudable sentiments, again. But when does a warning become a threat? The language of the quakers remained violent, even military. 'Hew down the tops, strike at the branches, make way, that the Axe may be laid to the root of the tree', this same man, Edward Burrough, had written only a year earlier in an address 'To the English Army, to Officers and Souldiers', 'that your sword, and the sword of the Lord, may neither leave root nor branch of Idolatrie, oppressions and tyranie'.[85] How was the claim of the dismissed soldiers to be interpreted, when they wrote in their address *To the Generals*, 'We were never otherwise minded, then to have stood in defence for the Nations against their enemies'?[86] What was to be made of a petition on behalf of quakers in prison, urging 'all Kings, Princes, Rulers, Magistrates . . . to keepe the outward peace, that none may offer violence, or destroy another', in which the signatories, including Edward Byllinge and others who had been soldiers, also expressed themselves thus: 'Long has the beast reigned who vsurped power . . . But now is the lambe risen & riseing to make warr with the great dragon, the beast'?[87]

This imagery regularly expressed the quakers' programme. The phrase 'The Lamb's War', Hugh Barbour observes, 'appears in the writings of almost every leading quaker'.[88] To take a single example from a document that has already been before us: the men the Northamptonshire quakers considered unfit for commission as justices – men such as major-general Butler of Oundle, or John Norton of Cotterstock, whose manor-house remains a fine example of seventeenth-century domestic architecture – they described as those 'who haue all allong giuen ther power vnto the beast and haue fought with the Lambe'.[89] I have sought elsewhere to expound the symbolism with sympathy, in terms of the Lamb of the Book of Revelation seen as one with the Lamb of Isaiah, the Lamb that 'must have the Victory' through 'the Lamb-like nature' of meekness, gentleness and patience.[90] By and large, this is what the quakers meant by it; but it was ambiguous; and the government remained suspicious.

For one thing, this imagery was not a quaker preserve. It was in

[84] E[dward] B[urrough], *Visitation of Love unto the King* (London 1660) p 10.
[85] Edward Burrough, *Visitation & Warning Proclaimed* (London 1659) pp 30–1.
[86] *To the Generals and Captains, Officers and Souldiers of this present Army* (n.p., n.d.) p 7.
[87] Penney, *Extracts* p 43.   [88] Barbour p 1.   [89] Penney, *Extracts* p 8.
[90] G. F. Nuttall, *Christianity and Violence* (Royston 1972) pp 14–15, 38.

constant use by many fifth monarchists, including the more aggressive, such as Vavasor Powell and John Rogers; and from among fifth monarchists,[91] as from among soldiers, the quakers drew many of their converts, particularly in Wales, where 'Powell's congregations provided their most fruitful field of mission'.[92] When, therefore, in 1659 Fox issued a tract entitled *The Lambs Officer Is gone forth with the Lambs Message*, or when, a year later, his namesake George Fox the younger issued from prison in Lambeth House, as the archbishop's palace was then known, an address *To the Called of God, Who believes in the Light of the Lambe*, the government will hardly have forgotten a *Faithfull Narrative . . . to the Faithful Remnant of the Lamb, who are . . . ingaged against the Beast and his Government* published in 1654 in defence of the implacable fifth monarchist John Rogers, then in his turn 'prisoner for the testimony of Jesus at Lambeth'. Rogers was so wedded to the Lamb symbolism that he actually dated a letter from Lambeth 'Lamb i' th' Prison', pleasantly glossing it 'Christ in this Mount with me'; and in this *Narrative* he is described by his friends as telling Cromwell in the course of an interview, 'I am ready to side with just principles in the strength of the Anointed, whether it be *praedicando, precando,* or *praeliando*', and when asked, 'Said you not *praeliando*?' replied, 'Yes.'[93]

The mystics and the militants, that is to say, drew on the same apocalyptic imagery. As 'for my dear Countreyman Mr. Powels preaching,' wrote the mystically-minded William Erbury in a letter to Powell, Rogers and others, after hearing Powell preach in London in January 1654, 'I could not but cleave to his peaceable spirit at the end of his Sermon, perswading his brethren to meddle no more with Civil matters, but to speak of spiritual glories'.[94] Yet this same sermon, as R. Tudur Jones points out in his recent fine study of Powell, was regarded by government agents as so daring a challenge to the authorities that it led to a warrant for Powell's arrest. In an oxymoron such as 'the Lamb's war' much will turn on where the stress falls. As Jones observes[95] of Morgan Llwyd, another Welsh millenarian preacher, from whose

---

[91] G. F. Nuttall, *The Holy Spirit in Puritan Faith and Experience* (Oxford 1946) p 124 n 5.

[92] [R. T.] Jones, [*Vavasor*] *Powell* (Abertawe 1971) pp 132–3; [G. F.] Nuttall, [*The*] *Welsh Saints* (Cardiff 1957) cap 4.

[93] E. Rogers, *Some Account of the Life and Opinions of a Fifth-Monarchy-Man* (London 1867) pp 175, 152, 211–12.

[94] W. Erbury, *An Olive-Leaf* (London 1654), reprinted in his posthumous *Testimony* (London 1658) pp 186–7.

[95] Jones, *Powell* pp 108–9.

people, again, the quakers drew,[96] it was also possible for one and the same person to oscillate between mysticism and militancy.

In the event, the quakers had too little time to demonstrate that the change which had come over them, their motives and their methods of achieving their aims was both genuine and lasting, combining militancy with moral persuasiveness in what came to be termed 'concern'. Before they had succeeded in shaking men's suspicion of their sincerity, let alone in overcoming the world, the restoration shivered their bright hopes to dull endurance of an all-engulfing suffering. Perhaps we, from the vantage-point of knowing their passion for social and political reform by gentle means, consistent through three hundred years, may say that, like Adam as he left paradise, they had *begun* to live

> with good
> Still overcoming evil, and by small
> Accomplishing great things, by things deemd weak
> Subverting worldly strong, and worldly wise
> By simply meek.

[96] Nuttall, *Welsh Saints* pp 84–7.

For access to much of the material used in this paper, and for constant and willing help, I thank the librarian of the Society of Friends, Edward H. Milligan, and his assistants, Robert C. Nessling and Malcolm J. Thomas.

BISHOP JOHN HACKET AND HIS TEACHING ON SANCTITY AND SECULARITY

by R. BUICK KNOX

JOHN HACKET was the son of a Scot who had prospered in business in London and had become a burgess in the city of Westminster.[1] John was born in 1592 and passed through Westminister school to Trinity college, Cambridge, of which he became a fellow in 1616.[2] His later episcopal eminence is attested in the full-scale portrait which adorns the walls of the Wren library in the college and in the bishop's hostel which was founded in the college by his generosity in 1670. He was ordained by bishop King of London on 20 December 1618.[3] By then he had already come under the influence of John Williams, a fellow of the neighbouring St John's college, whose ability and charm were soon to take him to the deanery of Westminster, the bishopric of Lincoln, and the high office of lord keeper of the great seal.[4] He took Hacket into his household as his chaplain and furthered his career by introducing him to the court where he became a royal chaplain. Williams also assisted his rise in the ecclesiastical firmament by appointing him to a prebend in Lincoln cathedral and then to the archdeaconry of Bedford,[5] and by influencing the king to secure his appointment to the rectory of St Andrew's, Holborn, and to the rectory of Cheam.[6] His Holborn pulpit proved to be a position of great influence and he drew a large congregation, especially from

1 [J.] Hacket, [*A Century of Sermons*,] edited with a biographical preface by T. Plume (London 1675) p iii.
2 Hacket p v; [John Venn and J. A.] Venn, [*Alumi Cantabrigienses*, pt I; *Admissions to Trinity College, Cambridge*], edd W. W. Rouse Ball and J. A. Venn (London 1913) year 1608.
3 Hacket pp vi–vii; Venn; [A.] Wood, [*Athenae Oxonienses*] (3 ed London 1813) IV, p 824.
4 R. B. Knox, 'The Social Teaching of Archbishop John Williams', *SCH* 8 (1972) p 180.
5 Hacket pp vi–viii; Venn; [J.] Le Neve, [*Fasti Ecclesiae Anglicanae*] (Oxford 1854) II pp 98, 75.
6 Venn; [G.] Hennessy, [*Novum Repertorium Ecclesiasticum Parochiale Londoniense*] (London 1898) p 90.

the upper classes of society. His prestige among the clergy of London was so high that he was chosen by them in 1634 to be the second president of Sion college, an institution founded in 1633 as a centre where the city clergy could meet and study.[7]

Hacket's Holborn ministry was carried on amid the mounting storm within the nation and though he was critical of the methods used by Laud to flaunt and enforce the government's civil and ecclesiastical policy he was a firm royalist and took a prominent part in debates about the plans to abolish the ecclesiastical hierarchy and to sequester the property of the church.[8] He was driven from his Holborn pulpit at the start of the civil war and he was fined and was imprisoned in November 1642 but he was soon released and was allowed to retire to his rectory at Cheam where he managed to maintain the use of the book of common prayer 'in most parts' until the storm subsided.[9] At the restoration he resumed his work at Holborn but he was an obvious candidate for further preferment. After refusing the diocese of Gloucester he accepted the diocese of Coventry and Lichfield and bishop Gilbert Sheldon presided at his consecration in Lambeth Palace chapel on 22 December 1661.[10] He was bishop of this diocese until his death in 1670.[11] He collected £20,000 for the restoration of Lichfield cathedral which had been badly devastated during the war and by subsequent neglect.[12] He tried to persuade all his clergy to conform, particularly those for whose talents he had a high regard, but when he failed to win them he was much offended by their recalcitrance which he regarded as wilful obduracy and he urged that the full rigour of the law should be brought to bear upon them and upon all dissenting groups, especially the quakers.[13]

[7] E. H. Pearce, *Sion College and Library* (Cambridge 1913) pp 150-1.

[8] Hacket pp xii, xviii-xxiv; Wood III pp 165-7, IV pp 814, 825; Hennessy pp 38, xxxix; Le Neve II p 413 (he was appointed a prebendary of St Paul's on 28 March 1642 as a reward for his royalism).

[9] Hacket p xxv; J. Walker, *The Sufferings of the Clergy*, ed R. Whitaker (London 1863) p 45; A. G. Matthews, *Walker Revised* (Oxford 1948) p 49.

[10] Hacket pp xxix-xxx; *Calendar of State Papers Domestic* (1661-2) p 134; Le Neve, I p 557; White Kennett, [*A Register and Chronicle, ecclesiastical and civil, from the Restoration of King Charles II*] (London 1728, only vol I printed) I p 587; F. Godwin, *De praesulibus Angliae Commentarius*, rev and ed Gul. Richardson (Cambridge 1743) I p 327.

[11] Hacket p liii.

[12] Wood, IV p 825; *Calendar of State Papers Domestic* (1661-2) p 487; *Catalogus Codicum MSS Thomae Tanneri* ed A. Hackman (Oxford 1860.) 44.15, 45.11 and 82, 131.4.

[13] White Kennett, I pp 738, 816, 820, 917, 918; *Calendar of State Papers Domestic* (1667-8) p 478; *Ibid* (1668-9) p 655; C. Harris, *The Wolf under sheeps-clothing discovered, or the Spirit of Cain appearing in the Bishop of Lichfield, reproved* (London 1669).

As a preacher Hacket was at his best in the years before 1642 when he was rector of St Andrew's, Holborn. Here he delivered series of sermons on great biblical themes and especially upon the events in the life of Christ, namely, his birth, his baptism, his temptations, his passion and his resurrection. A hundred of these sermons were collected by Thomas Plume who published them with a biographical preface under the title, *A Century of Sermons*; there is only one other extant sermon outside this collection.[14] Each sermon was designed to last for one hour and there were frequent apologies that limits of time prevented the pursuit of enticing sidelines. They were copiously illustrated by quotations from the writings of the fathers, the medieval writers, the reformers, the writers of the counter-reformation, and the Greek and Latin classical authors.

In these sermons, Hacket reflected the doctrinal outlook of the church of England and helped his hearers to apply it to the conditions of the time. That outlook embodied much of the general tradition of the church's teaching throughout the centuries and it was also inevitably influenced by the medieval tradition. In that tradition there were two attitudes towards life in this world. On the one hand, the doctrine of creation led to a high regard for the beauty of the world and for the rich resources placed at man's disposal; on the other hand, there was a fear of the world as a place filled with snares to allure mankind into an exclusive preoccupation with desires for earthly passions and possessions to the detriment of their eternal destiny. The reformation rejection of much of the medieval teaching did not seriously change this duality, for, if the doctrine of creation became overshadowed by the doctrine of redemption with its emphasis upon deliverance from the lures and evils of this world, the rejection of the monastic ideal led to a revaluation of life in this world in the setting of the family and of social and commercial concerns. These two attitudes are forcefully expounded in the sermons of Hacket, and his teaching sheds light upon sanctity and secularity and their relationship.

The sermons are all permeated by an intense sense of the reality of God who created all things and with whom all men have to do. Hacket was steeped in the church's message of the holiness of God and the wonder of the incarnation of the Son of God. God was so great and glorious that no one could fully grasp all that he was and all that he had planned: 'In this life we must look through a cloud, we must expect to see through a glass darkly; – the restless wit of man runs

14 J. Hacket, *A Sermon preached before the King on 22 March 1660/1* (London 1660/1).

presumptuously upon all uncouth paths of knowledge which he should not tread.'[15] Yet God had graciously made himself known so that it was possible to be 'transported as it were in an ecstasy of devotion'.[16] 'Grace is the celestial water which supplies the root within us; it makes the conscience abundant in good works, and without it it is impossible to bring forth the fruits of righteousness.'[17]

The sanctity of God was so marvellous that none dare approach him with 'a saucy familiarity'.[18] It was the proper exercise of the human spirit to 'laud and magnify our omnipotent creator'.[19] This reverence in the presence of the holy God was bound to have an influence upon the life of the worshipper; the seed of sanctity could not but be planted in those who humbled themselves before God; only 'a most unreclaimable son could run on in lewdness because he knows he has an indulgent Father'.[20] The purifying effect of God's holiness was such as could not be effected by 'the mountebanks in divinity that will promise many sorts of remedies to a sin-sick soul where there is none at all'.[21]

The model of the life of sanctity was to be found in Jesus.

> All treasures of wisdom are his in his age of nonage, all strength in his infant infirmity, all riches in his state of poverty, all righteousness in him that was accused of iniquity, all freedom from bondage in him that was wrapt up in swadling clouts, all felicity in him that was encompassed with weakness and misery.[22]

His sanctity, however, was not cultivated simply for his own benefit but had a transforming power over those who came under his sway; 'there was no disease of sin whereof we were not sick; there was no kind of cure to be invented which was not practised to restore us'.[23] 'What hath he not healed if he will lay the plasters of his passion to our sins?'[24] This was a celestial irradiation and Hacket became lyrical in describing the redeeming power of Christ:

> Christ is the glass in which we see all truth, the fountain in which we taste all sweetness, the ark in which all precious things are laid up, the pearl which is worth all other riches, the flower of Jesse which hath the savour of life unto life, the bread that satisfies all hunger, the medicine that healeth all sickness, the light that dispelleth all darkness.[25]

[15] Hacket p 464. [16] Ibid p 1. [17] Ibid p 904. [18] Ibid p 35.
[19] Ibid p 100. [20] Ibid p 269. [21] Ibid p 38. [22] Ibid p 81.
[23] Ibid p 241. [24] Ibid p 531. [25] Ibid p 110.

Hacket was nevertheless well aware that however exalted the destiny of man, life had to be lived in the world as it is with all the intractable harshness of the natural order and of human nature. The secular order did not obviously bear the imprint of divine control but Hacket had no doubt that there were sufficient intimations of that control to warrant the venture of faith that God was at work in the whole historical process and not just in religious history. In working out his purpose God had both to hide himself and to use many who were far from sanctity. A measure of obscurity was essential, for otherwise people would pursue goodness for the sake of the rewards; 'it suits well with the divine justice and providence not to make the fortitude of his saints effeminate with abundance'.[26] A system of automatic rewards would devalue the gift of human freedom, and further, the final balance sheet could not be measured solely in earthly terms, and trials were 'a dainty lenitive to the soul'. Moreover, many of God's agents were far from being saintly persons. Hacket cited many biblical heroes who were tarnished characters and he stressed that in the genealogy of Jesus in the gospel of Matthew there were only four women included, Tamar, Rahab, Ruth and Bathsheba, and three of these were 'very strumpets'.[27]

Hacket also pointed out the imperfection of all secular government; 'the description of a platonic commonwealth, an Utopia, or a new Atlantis, is to be found in ink and paper, but never among men'.[28] He often dilated upon the sordid record, not only of traitors and tyrants, but also of lawful governors, and he lashed the rapacious courtiers and statesmen of his day and the rampant vices and the gaudy display of 'gurmundising' among the wealthy in London.[29] Yet far from being an advocate of social change he was a zealous defender of the existing order and of the divine right of kings, and especially of the Stuarts. In James I there was a 'concurrence of the best blood in the world'.[30] Even when kings were evil, as had only too often been the case, their subjects were not justified in trying to remove them. In the bible story, the wicked Herod was not liquidated by his subjects nor even by evil angels but by the angel of the Lord; God reserved the punishment of kings to himself.[31] Moreover, evil as kings might be, the prospect of democracy was worse: 'This is the preposterous course of the world when the tail must lead the head; – the greater part are always

[26] *Ibid* p 277.
[27] *Ibid* p 34.
[28] *Ibid* p 537.
[29] *Ibid* pp 298–9, 344, 852–8, 881.
[30] *Ibid* p 688.
[31] *Ibid* p 960.

ignorant.'[32] 'There are such as have thought of a remedy worse than the disease, namely the ratification of all principality should depend upon the voice of the people.'[33] The secular order was thus far from a model of sanctity. Its abuses arose from the perversity of men whose 'mortal appetite' was further whetted by the allurements, the trinkets, the 'petty promotions' and the 'flatteries of this world'.[34] Secular governments were themselves tainted with the evils they sought to curb and yet they were a prime necessity if evil men were to be restrained.

Moreover, the church which was meant to be the school of sanctity within the secular order was often poisoned by worldliness and by 'emulations and heresies'.[35] Yet, just as the civil government was necessary, so the imperfect church was 'the pipe which conveys those sacred mysteries which Christ reveals',[36] and Hacket was sure that the church of England 'doth always follow the steps of pure antiquity'[37] and had the exclusive right to proclaim the gospel and to order all citizens to conform to its ways. Far from seeing the privileges and possessions of the church of England as an embarrassing contrast to the austerity of Christ and of the early disciples Hacket looked upon the sumptuous furnishing of the churches as a deserved compensation for the dishonour accorded to Christ when he was laid in the manger; now he could come among his people amid fitting magnificence.[38] In view of these high claims for the church of England Hacket had no hesitation in arraigning what he regarded as the arrogant intrusions of the church of Rome and the baseless suspicions of those who saw spectres of papal resurgence in the church's seemly regulations and then agitated for a more thorough protestant reform.

Hacket was particularly disturbed by the puritan movement because its emphasis upon preaching echoed so much of his own thought. He loved to preach, and, no less than the puritans, he believed in its efficacy as a converting and edifying practice in the church, but he had to criticise their zeal and justify the measures taken against them. He held that instead of a healthy desire to hear the gospel there had arisen a fanatical ravening which would not be satisfied with a fit proportion of the heavenly manna.[39] In times of darkness there was justification for an intensive programme of preaching but not in England 'where religion is well planted and we rather want obedience than know-

---

[32] *Ibid* p 489.
[33] *Ibid* p 686.
[34] *Ibid* p 350-1.
[35] *Ibid* p 441.
[36] *Ibid* p 474.
[37] *Ibid* p 301.
[38] *Ibid* pp 73, 453.
[39] *Ibid* p 943.

ledge'; familiarity bred contempt and so, excepting some special occasions, 'I would make it Sunday's religion'.[40]

Hacket's exposition of the place of the church of England within the social order of his day raises two issues. First, could there be any genuine call to sanctity within a system where the appeal for commitment to a life of holiness was backed by threats of penalties for refusal to conform? Hacket saw no inconsistency at this point; he did not believe that the mass of people were competent or willing to make a free decision and he saw conformity to the edicts of church and state as itself an act of piety, but he did not think that all who conformed thereby attained the heights of sanctity; conformity was essential, in his view, for the health of both church and state, but the heights of holiness were reserved for the elect who were called in the secret purposes of God.

Second, did the confinement of preaching to Sunday point to a segregation of sanctity and secularity? Hacket would have denied any such inference. The degree of sanctity to which each person could attain through conformity and obedience provided stability amid the vagaries of the secular order, and secularity was the realm wherein sanctity was tested and refined. Sanctity was, for Hacket, a relationship with God to be cultivated in the church, preferably the church of England, and to be sustained within the secular order with its threatening elements of evanescence and compromise.

[40] *Ibid* p 472.

ORTHODOXY, RATIONALISM AND THE WORLD IN EIGHTEENTH-CENTURY HOLLAND

by J. VAN DEN BERG

AS far as the protestant countries are concerned the eighteenth century, the 'age of reason', might as well be called 'the age of revival'. On the one hand, we meet with a strong desire to escape the snares of this world by concentrating upon the mysteries of salvation: the road to sanctity is a narrow road, to be trodden in fear and trembling. On the other hand there are those for whom this world is a world full of new and unexpected possibilities, a world to be explored and to be made instrumental to the fulfilment of the divine plan with regard to the development of humanity in its secular context. Naturally, also in the eighteenth century 'sanctity' and 'secularity' were not seen as in themselves mutually exclusive concepts. While many revivalists looked forward to the enlightenment of this world by the knowledge of God, many men of the enlightenment saw before them the prospect of the sanctification of the world by the combined influences of reason and revelation. Some of the fathers of the enlightenment – notably Locke and Leibniz – were essentially committed to the cause of christianity, while on the other hand protagonists of the pietist and revival movements such as Francke and Edwards cannot in fairness be accused of an anti-rational attitude and of a lack of interest in the well-being of this world. Nevertheless, within the circle of eighteenth-century protestant christianity there were conspicuous differences with regard to the evaluation of and the attitude towards the world in which the christian community, while living in the expectation of the kingdom, still had to find its way and its place.

These differences are connected with a perennial problem in the history of christianity: the question how to interpret and how to deal with the ambivalence of the concept 'world' as it occurs in the sources of the christian tradition. In the Johannine as well as in the Pauline writings, the world is God's good creation, loved and redeemed by Him – the knowledge of this aspect of the world can lead to a form of

173

christian 'thisworldliness' –, but at the same time we meet with the idea that this world is the totality of unredeemed creation, hostile to God, a threat to christian life – to love this world is incompatible with a true love of God.[1] The tension, inherent in the ambivalent character of the concept 'world' in the New Testament, was activated rather than resolved by the concurrence of classical and christian traditions in the period of the renaissance. Especially the seventeenth century was marked on the one hand by a worldliness which had not developed into the secularism of the enlightenment,[2] but did prepare the way for it, on the other hand by a concentration upon the essential qualities of christian life which in catholic as well as in protestant circles could lead to special emphasis on the distance between the christian and the world. Eighteenth-century christianity inherited an unsolved problem. Bunyan's Christian had to find his way in a world which according to at least some of his fellow-christians was not a vale of tears and darkness, but a field full of new light and new promise – almost a heaven on earth.

To what extent do we find this tension in the Dutch eighteenth-century situation? In order to get a clear view of the context of our problem, it is necessary first of all to have a look at the development of Dutch church life in the eighteenth century. The Netherlands were a country with a pluralistic religious situation, although almost until the end of the century the reformed church was the 'public' or 'privileged' church: it made use of the old church buildings, its ministers were paid out of public funds, only its members could hold public offices of some importance in the state. All this gave to the reformed church an influential position in the midst of Dutch society, which it tried to mould by its preaching and its discipline. But it did not lead to the founding of a calvinistic theocracy in the Netherlands: for this the influence of the reformed churches, as a national church structurally weak because of the absence of a national synod during the larger part of the seventeenth century and the whole of the eighteenth century, was not strong enough, the counter-balance of the influence of more or less erasmian magistrates often too strong. Moreover, precisely the public position of the church could make the exercise of a strict calvinistic discipline rather difficult. In this context, the Nijmegen case of 1752–3 is illustrative.[3] When the consistory of the reformed church of Nijmegen refused to

[1] H. Sasse in: *Theologisches Wörterbuch zum N.T*, III (Stuttgart 1938) pp 867–98.
[2] [P.] Gay, [*The Enlightenment*,] I (London 1967) p 314.
[3] S. D. van Veen, *Uit de vorige eeuw* (Utrecht 1887) pp 45–100.

admit to membership two young people of comparatively high rank because of their masonic sympathies – the consistory considered membership of the lodge incompatible with full church membership – the estates of the province of Gelderland successfully intervened; no doubt the most important factor in the attitude of the estates was, that if these young people were not accepted as full members of the church this would wreck their political career. Such an example, which could of course be multiplied, shows the reverse of the reformed church's privileged position: too often the church had to compromise, too often it was forced to take a course which by precisians could be interpreted as a dangerous adaptation to the pattern of this present world. With an implicit awareness of the dangers of this privileged position of the dominant church the Dutch seventeenth-century catholic church leader Neercassel,[4] a precisian with jansenist inclinations, wrote about his co-religionists who were 'without offices in the republic, without a voice in the council, without power in government': 'Let the catholics rejoice, because it has been granted to them to make sure of their salvation in lowliness, in order not to fall into peril in high places.'[5]

In spite of a formal unity in doctrine (ministers had to subscribe to the Belgic confession, the catechism of Heidelberg and the canons of Dordt), within the eighteenth-century reformed church a variety of tendencies was to be found, each of which represented a particular way of thinking as well as a particular type of spirituality. From the seventeenth century, the church of the eighteenth century had inherited the differences between the followers of two leading theologians, Voetius[6] and Coccejus.[7] The voetians were the more conservative party. They combined a scholastic-aristotelian theology with a puritan way of life.[8] In the practice of piety they were deeply influenced by English and Scottish puritan authors, many of whom saw their works translated into Dutch[9] – the voetians were sometimes even nicknamed 'Scottish

---

[4] Johannes Baptista van Neercassel (1623–86) apostolic vicar from 1663.

[5] Joan Baptist (Neercassel), *Bevestigingh in 't Geloof en Troost in Vervolgingh* (Brussels 1670) pp 385 ff, 402 ff.

[6] Gisbertus Voetius (1589–1676). See A. C. Duker, *Gisbertus Voetius*, 3 vols and reg (Leiden 1897–1915).

[7] Johannes Coccejus (1603–1669). See [G.] Schrenk, [*Gottesreich und Bund im älteren Protestantismus vornehmlich bei Johannes Coccejus*] (Darmstadt 1967 1 ed 1923).

[8] See for an analysis of the ideas of the voetian party: W. Goeters, *Die Vorbereitung des Pietismus in der reformierten Kirche der Niederlande* (Leipzig 1911) pp 53–120.

[9] One of the most important translators was the voetian minister Koelman; a list of the works he translated is in A. F. Krull, *Jacobus Koelman* (Sneek 1901) pp 352–7.

clerks'.[10] Like the puritans, they were precisians; their Sunday observance was very strict, and as far as possible they held aloof from worldly pomp and pleasures. In politics, the voetians were strong supporters of the orangist party; socially, they found their stronghold in the lower middle class. The followers of Coccejus were different in more than one respect. Many of them tried to combine the biblical thinking of Coccejus[11] with the philosophy of Descartes. It is difficult to see a direct connection between the unphilosophical theology of Coccejus and the philosophy of Descartes; probably many coccejans followed the French philosopher because his modern outlook was more in accord with their somehow rather open and dynamic thinking than was static aristotelianism.[12] With at least some coccejans, their sympathy for cartesian thinking led to a greater appreciation of the possibilities of human reason than was to be found in the voetian circle. In practical affairs such as Sunday observance and matters of dress and fashion the coccejans were less strict than the voetians; their attitude was more in keeping with the climate of opinion among the higher classes of Dutch society, from which the 'burgher oligarchy' was recruited, although we get the impression that sometimes even coccejan ministers were still too strict for patricians and scholars of the erasmian tradition.

In the course of the eighteenth century, the old cleavage between voetians and coccejans was gradually superseded by other differences. To the average church member, preaching meant more than theological niceties or philosophical speculations. In certain quarters of the church, especially, but not exclusively among the common people of town and country-side those preachers were popular who preached in an 'experiential' way. Of course they were to be found among the voetians, with their traditional sympathy for the 'practice of piety', but

---

10 J. C. Trimp, *Joost van Lodensteyn als pietistisch dichter* (Djakarta and Groningen 1952) p 41.

11 G. Schrenk remarks that the theology of Coccejus preeminently wants to be a biblica theology (Schrenk p 14).

12 See for Dutch cartesianism: J. A. Cramer, *Abraham Heidanus en zijn Cartesianisme* (Utrecht 1889); J. Bohatec, *Die cartesianische Scholastik in der Philosophie und reformierten Dogmatik des 17. Jahrhunderts*, I (Leipzig 1912); M. J. A. de Vrijer, *Henricus Regius* (The Hague 1917); [E. J.] Dijksterhuis [and others,] *Descartes [et le Cartésianisme hollandais]* (Paris and Amsterdam 1950); C. Louise Thijssen-Schoute, *Nederlands Cartesianisme* (Amsterdam 1954); E. Bizer, 'Die reformierte Orthodoxie und der Cartesianismus', *Zeitschrift für Theologie und Kirche* 55 (Tübingen 1958), pp 306–72. Cramer only assumes an external connection between coccejanism and cartesianism, but others are more inclined to assume an internal relationship between both systems.

also among the coccejans there were preachers who appealed to the emotions rather than to the intellect; the people distinguished them from the cartesian coccejans as the 'serious' coccejans, who had strong affinities with the more pietist or 'living' voetians. Among the leading eighteenth-century Dutch pietists we find coccejans (such as the Utrecht professor Lampe)[13] as well as voetians (like W. Schortinghuis, the minister of the village of Midwolda in the province of Groningen):[14] their differences were blurred by their common pietist interest. A remnant, more extremely voetian, whose representatives preferred the name of 'calvinist' to the name of 'reformed',[15] remained vocal until halfway through the eighteenth century; it sympathised with the pietists and took their side in the heated controversies of the day. On the other hand the leading non-pietist coccejans tried to vindicate their own orthodoxy in their discussions with pietists and rationalists. Their most influential spokesman was the Leiden professor Van den Honert,[16] who was not inclined to accentuate the differences between voetians and coccejans. He was a typical theologian of the middle way; while some pietists accused him of rationalist traits in his theology, the more liberal theologians saw in him an intolerant defender of the calvinist system. However this may be, the reformed pietists as well as their theological opponents considered themselves orthodox: in their sometimes sharp discussions, both sides once and again appealed to the reformed confessions. Their struggles took place within the circle of an unmistakable loyalty to the calvinist tradition, which, however, in the heat of the controversy was not always mutually recognised.

A more liberal and rationalist tendency mainly revealed itself within the circle of the protestant dissenters, especially the mennonites and the remonstrants or arminians. In this context, it is necessary to make some preliminary remarks. In the first place: in spite of the leniency of the Dutch spiritual climate, the Netherlands did not prove a fertile soil for the development of radical enlightenment ideas; Holland did not produce a Toland, a Tindal, a Voltaire, a Rousseau. Furthermore, in

---

[13] Friedrich Adolph Lampe (1683-1729); see: [G.] Snijders, [*Friedrich Adolph Lampe*] (Harderwijk 1954).

[14] Wilhelmus Schortinghuis (1700-50); see: J. C. Kromisgt, *Wilhelmus Schortinghuis* (Groningen 1904); M. J. A. De Vrijer, *Schortinghuis en zijn analogieën* (Amsterdam 1942).

[15] [N. Holtius en A. Comrie], *Examen van het Ontwerp van Tolerantie* X (Amsterdam 1759) p xli.

[16] Johannes van den Honert (1693-1758); see: *Biographisch Woordenboek van Protestantsche Godgeleerden* IV (The Hague 1931) pp 232-46.

eighteenth-century Holland there existed an ecletic attitude with
regard to various philosophical systems; in its turn, this attitude
strengthened the tendency towards a moderate rationalism which had
affinities with and was influenced by the thinking of the German
philosopher Christian Wolff.[17] The precarious balance between
reason and revelation in the wolffian system coincided with what has
been called the moderately rationalist doctrine of religion of John
Locke.[18] From this it follows, that a rationalist influence on theology
often led to what Peter Gay, speaking of Wolff, called a 'gently
modernized Protestant orthodoxy'.[19] But some went further; their
mixture of christian thinking and rationalist influences led to a form
of christian rationalism which placed them somewhere outside the
circle of traditional orthodoxy. As we shall see, even with regard to
them the word 'rationalists' must be used with all proper reserves:
although their world-view as well as their spirituality were not in-
considerably influenced by the spirit of the enlightenment with its
more optimistic appraisal of the possibilities, hidden in man's reasonable nature, their rationalist inclinations did not imply a rejection of the
value of divine revelation and of the necessity of man's striving for
sanctity with the help of God's grace. Moreover, the boundary lines
between a more orthodox and a more rationalist way of thinking
often were not so clearly drawn as to allow of a facile classification
within the well-defined framework of any particular group: deep
cross-currents and unexpected affinities sometimes blurred the image.

That a more liberal attitude towards traditional values and a greater
openness towards new tendencies first of all appeared in the circle of
the dissenters is connected with their specific historical development.
The mennonites, divided as they were among a number of sometimes
conflicting groups, had not been able to achieve a united stand with
regard to matters of doctrine and practice. While some eighteenth-

17 See for the influence of the philosophy of Wolff in the Netherlands: A. W. Brons-
veld, *Oorzaken der verbreiding van het rationalisme in ons land* (Rotterdam 1862) pp
115–29; H. H. Zwager, Nederland en de verlichting (Bussum 1972) p 76.
18 See the title of the chapter on Locke in: [E.] Hirsch, [*Geschichte der neuern evan-
gelischen Theologie*] I (3 ed Gütersloh 1964) pp 271–92. Compare Hazard's remark on
the eighteenth-century alliance between rationalism and empiricism: ' . . . l'esprit du
XVIIIe siècle, tel qu'il prend ses racines dans le XVIIe, est rationaliste par essence, et
empiriste par transaction', P. Hazard, *La crise de la conscience européenne* II (Paris
1961) p 10.
19 Gay I p 331; compare the Dutch philosopher F. Sassen on the orthodox protestant
enlightenment in his: *Johan Lulofs (1711–1768) en de reformatorische verlichting in de
Nederlanden* (Amsterdam 1965).

century mennonites still clung to the strictest traditions of their six-teenth-century ancestors, others had moved into a different direction. Their far more liberal doctrinal outlook was attended with the loss of much of the traditional strictness of life, much in line with the development in the latter part of the seventeenth century which made an unknown critic remark in a satirical poem: 'Formerly the Men-monites were in the world, but now the world is in their midst.'[20] As a matter of fact, those more modern followers of Menno Simons usually did not call themselves 'mennonites', but preferred the more formal name of 'doopsgezinden' ('baptists'). Their shift towards a new outlook and a new way of life had some connection with the social changes which had taken place in the mennonite circle: while the early mennonites mostly belonged to the lower strata of society,[21] many of their descendants had attained positions of wealth and social influence. One of the leading spokesmen of the more rationalist wing of the mennonite community was the Frisian preacher Stinstra,[22] well known in the English-speaking world because of his heavy attack on the revival movement of *c* 1750. When John Wesley had read his *Pastoral Letter against Fanaticism*, the English translation of a tract in the form of a warning letter to the Frisian mennonites,[23] he wrote in his *Journal*: 'He is doubtless a well-meaning man, but deeply ignorant of the subject he treats of; and his arguments are of no force at all. . . . They utterly overthrow many of the grand arguments for Christian-ity. . . .'; many years afterwards, Wesley wrote: 'In truth, I cannot but fear Mr. Stinstra is in the same class with Dr. Conyers Middleton. . . . The very thing which Mr. Stinstra calls fanaticism is no other than heart-religion.'[24]

The remonstrants had been even more accessible to liberal opinions. The eighteenth-century descendants of those who had been ejected

---

[20] [N.] van der Zijpp, [*Geschiedenis der Doopsgezinden in Nederland*] (Arnhem 1952) p 152.

[21] See for this (with a correction of the traditional mennonite view with regard to this point): A. F. Mellink, *De Wederdopers in de Noordelijke Nederlanden* (Groningen 1953).

[22] Johannes Stinstra (1708–1790); see: [C.] Sepp, [*Johannes Stinstra en zijn tijd,*] 2 vols (Amsterdam 1865–6).

[23] J. Stinstra, *Waarschuwinge tegen de geestdrijverij vervat in een brief aan de Doopsgezinden in Friesland* (Harlingen 1750). I quote from the first English translation: [John] Stinstra, *A Pastoral Letter* [*against Fanaticism, Address'd to the Mennonists of Friesland*] translated from the original Dutch by Henry Rimius (London 1753). See for the English translations: [*The Richardson-Stinstra Correspondence and Stinstra's Prefaces to Clarissa,* ed W. C.] Slattery (Carbondale etc 1969) pp 214 ff.

[24] J. Wesley, *Journal* (3 ed London 1960) IV p 72 (8 June 1753) V p 426 (12 Aug 1771).

from the reformed church by the synod of Dordt of 1618–19 formed a small group in which, due to its erasmian traditions and the high intellectual level of its leaders, there was a lively interest in new currents in European thinking. In particular, John Locke's ideas found a ready response among the leading arminians: together with his colleague Jean le Clerc (Clericus), the editor of the *Opera* of Erasmus, the Amsterdam professor Philippus van Limborch, who in the winter of 1683 had first met Locke when both men had been invited by a medical doctor in Amsterdam to be present at the dissection of a dead lioness, became the protagonist of Locke's philosophy in the Netherlands.[25] Eighteenth-century remonstrant theology as a whole was deeply influenced by the spirit of the enlightenment.

The leading remonstrant theologian of the second half of the century, the Amsterdam professor Van der Meersch may serve for an example. He was on the cross-roads of German and English influences. In a cultural and theological review, the *Algemeene Bibliotheek*, he introduced German christian rationalist authors like the lutheran abbot Jerusalem[26] to the Dutch. Bishop Warburton, whose *The Divine Legation of Moses* was also translated by Van der Meersch, thought very highly of the arminian Dutch professor and of the remonstrant fraternity in general. In a letter of 21 March 1762 he wrote to his Dutch friend: 'For ever since I could distinguish right from wrong, I have had a predelection for the Arminian Church, founded on the true principles of Christian liberty, by a succession of heroes; I would call them saints, tho' not of the roman fabric, yet made of better stuff, of Erasmus's own texture; but stronger. . . .' , and nine years later (4 April 1771) he wrote, referring to the 'persecuting spirit of Calvinism': '. . . though the ministers of the Calvinistical church of Holland do not, nor are ever likely to abate their *intolerant* principles, yet in this inlightened age (for which it is principally indebted to your heroes), it is to be hoped, your magistrates will no longer add terror to their *brutum fulmen*'.[27]

The spirit of the Dutch protestant enlightenment is vividly epitomised in the works of two women authors: Elizabeth Wolff, a minister's

---

[25] P. J. Barnouw, *Philippus van Limborch* (The Hague 1963) p 33.

[26] Abraham Arend van der Meersch (1720–92); Johann Friedrich Wilhelm Jerusalem (1709–89); see for the latter's theological radicalism: Hirsch IV pp 31 ff.

[27] J. Tideman, 'Briefwisseling tusschen den Hoogleeraar A. A. van der Meersch en den Bisschop van Gloucester, William Warburton (1761–1771)', *Kerkhistorisch Archief* 3 (Amsterdam 1862) pp 417–25. See also: C. W. Roldanus, 'Nederlandsch-Engelsche betrekkingen op den bodem van "Arminianisme" ', *Tijdschrift voor Geschiedenis* 58 (Groningen 1943) esp p 21.

wife, and her friend Aagje Deken, who together wrote some novels in which the whole spectrum of Dutch life in the second half of the eighteenth century is reflected. We are confronted with various types: the hypocrite pietist brother Benjamin but also the genuinely pious Stijntje Doorzicht ('Christine Discernment') – she went to church with Mr Peiffers, an Amsterdam minister who recommended the works of Doddridge and other English theologians to the Dutch public –; the tolerant minister Redelijk ('Reasonable') and the mildly orthodox professor Maatig ('Moderate'), probably the Leiden professor Hollebeek, Elizabeth Wolff's much-admired brother-in-law, who tried to introduce the 'English way of preaching' into Holland,[28] and with them quite a number of other characters, taken from life, who together form a cross-section of the Dutch protestant population of those days. How did they all, orthodox people and rationalists, followers of Calvin and people of erasmian texture, conservative theologians and daring innovators, pietist and anti-pietist christians, deal with the problem of the christian's relation to the world?

This question has a twofold aspect, a theoretical as well as a practical one. We may ask, whether their view of this world with its light and its shadows was – contrary to the spirit of the age – of a more pessimistic, or – in accordance with contemporary feeling – of a more optimistic nature. But we may also ask what was their answer to the many practical questions with regard to the christian's participation in the social and cultural life of his own enlightened eighteenth-century surroundings. These two aspects are so closely interwoven that it would be inadvisable to treat them separately.

Let us first of all turn to those of a strong pietistic bent. We have already mentioned the Utrecht professor Lampe, who showed a combination of the spirituality of the seventeenth-century voetian circle in Utrecht and the reformed pietism of north-west Germany – two forms of spirituality which in spite of their different background yet had many elements in common. Lampe was known and respected as a man of a deep and genuine piety. A remarkable instance of the esteem in which Lampe was held by congenial spirits can be found in a work which appeared anonymously in Denmark in 1742–3 under the title: *Menoza, en Asiatisk Printz.*[29] It was written by the Danish pietist Erik Pon-

---

28 Ewald Hollebeek (1719–96): see for him: L. Knappert, *Geschiedenis der Nederlandsche Hervormde Kerk gedurende de 18ᵉ en 19ᵉ eeuw* (Amsterdam 1912) pp 131 ff, 153 ff.
29 I used the German translation: *Menoza, [Ein Asiatischer Prinz . . .,]* Aus dem Dänischen übersetzt, 3 vols (Hollstein n.d., probably 1746).

toppidan,[30] and it contained the story of the travels of an imaginary Asian prince who, converted to christianity, went out in search of real christians, of whom he only found a very few. Lampe was one of them; here the story has an authentic ring, because Pontoppidan himself had visited Lampe on his travels to England and Holland in 1720-1; partly at least, the story of Menoza's travels is founded upon Pontoppidan's own experiences. After visiting England, where he had come into contact with some pious presbyterians and had made the acquaintance of archbishop Wake, Menoza came to Holland, a country which could be called a *compendium universi*. A Dutch minister told him, that the kingdom of Christ still had many true adherents in Holland, although they formed a small number, compared with those who served the God of this world. In Amsterdam and again in Utrecht he met Le Clerc, who was rather critical of his Utrecht colleague Lampe: he thought him too stern a moralist, and besides somewhat sectarian, and too much of a zealot. This, however, did not deter our Indian prince; he thought it might be with Lampe as with other spiritual people in Europe, whom Satan made objects of slander in order to promote his own kingdom; he would be a stupid devil if he did not act like this! Menoza noted that Lampe's adherents were called 'ijnen' (the precise people) – a common nickname for Dutch precisians; according to Menoza it was invented by Satan, who incites his instruments to point out those who are not prepared to walk on the broad highway of this world. In this context, Menoza mentions a conversation with Lampe with reference to a story he had heard from his landlord, whose brother-in-law had joined the precisians and consequently had neglected his affairs to the extent that he now had to eat the dry bread of poverty. Was there indeed, as popular opinion would have it, a connection between his religious attitude and his economic failure? No doubt many seventeenth-century Dutch puritans would have denied such a connection; Lampe however answered the question in the affirmative: now that the merchant let himself increasingly be guided by his conscience, he also suffered in a material sense, but the cross he had to bear was a noble cross. Formerly, our merchant had been guilty of various nasty tricks, which in Holland are called 'the soul of commerce', but since the love of Christ had taken possession of his soul, all this had changed. To be among the wolves without being

---

[30] Erik Pontoppidan (1698–1764). See *Dansk Biografisk Leksikon* XVIII (Copenhagen 1940) pp 458–66, and J. W. Vink, 'Erik Pontoppidan en zijn stichtelijke roman "Menoza",' *Tijdschrift voor Geschiedenis* 68 (Groningen-Djakarta 1955) pp 33–58.

able to howl with them, to live in the midst of a wicked generation without being able to go along with them, all this makes the christian's path a thorny one. He, who follows Christ must be prepared to suffer worldly loss – yet a blessed loss, when we turn our eyes to the future economy in the world to come.[31]

It is all in line with what Lampe remarks in his best-known work, an exposition on the mystery of the covenant of grace, written in 1712, which, translated into Dutch, became a popular work of edification in the Netherlands. Satan often makes use of this world as a means to stir up persecutions against the children of God or to arrange such objects as may stimulate the evil which is in them. Therefore, the world is the second main enemy of God's children. It is like a tempestuous sea, where flood follows flood in order to devour the little ship of the faithful.[32] Naturally, this view of the world has its consequences for daily practice: 'Let all worldly entertainments be as nothing in your eyes. Make it manifest by utterly despising these things that now you have found something which is better. They who have tasted the heavenly Manna no longer take delight in the fleshpots of Egypt. . . .'[33] In his sermons, too, Lampe was uncompromising with regard to the world and its vanities: as man is but ash and dust, and his body is but a maggot's bag, why would people bother about appearances and pleasures. Fashion is but a 'livery of Satan', beauty is but a passing thing: let the bones in the grave be your mirror. – One may wonder whether according to Lampe it still would be possible for a christian to live in high places in the midst of the world. Lampe does not go so far as to deny the possibility altogether, but in a sermon preached before the dowager princess of Orange at Soestdijk he remarked that because of the dangers of court life it had become well-nigh impossible to combine life at court with true christianity.[34]

The same spirit of ascetic, world-denying christianity is met with Schortinghuis, one of the most outspoken and controversial eighteenth-century Dutch pietists. His work on 'Inner Christianity',[35] which appeared in 1740, aroused a storm of protest – not only from the side of more rationalist opponents, but also from theologians who were akin to him in their emphasis on the spiritual experience of

---

31 *Menoza* III pp 3–23.
32 [F. A.] Lampe, [*De Verborgentheit van het Genaade- verbondt*] (Amsterdam 1735) p 490.
33 Lampe p 627.
34 Snijders pp 24 ff.
35 [W.] Schortinghuis, [*Het Innige Christendom*] (Groningen 1740) I used the fourth ed (Groningen 1752).

the inner man, like the redoubtable Groningen professor Antonius
Driessen, who shortly before had written: '... grace is experiential. ...
It is experience which awakens the hope of a better life. ...'[36] The main
point of attack was Schortinghuis's supposed sympathy with what used
to be called: 'corrupt mysticism'; however, some of the most conservative voetians like Alexander Comrie, a minister of Scottish descent
defended his orthodoxy.[37] Schortinghuis had strong affinities with
German reformed pietism and accordingly with Lampe, while in his
main work he also mentions a number of English and Scottish authors,
amongst whom were John Bunyan and William Guthrie.

For Schortinghuis,[38] the true church is the inner church, true knowledge inner knowledge, true sanctity inner sanctity. Everything is
concentrated on the heart of man and on man's inner contemplation
of Jesus' heavenly glory. With great approval he quotes Van Lodensteyn's poem – dear to Dutch pietists –: 'High, on high, my soul, fly
upwards, for it is not here below. ... All that you see on earth, all
that you hear on earth, ... all that you wish on earth, is not worth
your costly heart.'[39] One of the persons in his dialogues is 'man without
grace', who in fact stands for the more moderate orthodox; this
person remarks that he has not much sympathy with the narrow precisians, who want to appear in angelic purity; man lives in this world
and must converse with the world, rather than wanting to be holier
than others. But of course his remarks evoke a heavy protest: those who
reject the precisians' attitude condemn themselves and are hostile to
inner sanctity and its outward fruits.[40] The great sin of conformity to
this world is not only a matter of external conduct, but of a wrong
orientation of inner man. People may be outwardly religious, while
yet their roots and their whole natural state are vicious.[41] If they knew,
what a profound comfort the beloved of the Lord often experience,
it would make them truly zealous 'to change all the foolish and idle
joys for those blissful, joyful tears. ...'[42]

Between the predominantly pietistic and the more moderate
orthodox there was a difference of emphasis rather than a fundamental
difference with regard to the general pattern of life. In 1746 Van den

[36] A. Driessen, *Oude en Nieuwe Mensch* (Groningen 1738) p 459.
[37] A. G. Honig, *Alexander Comrie* (Utrecht 1892) p 281.
[38] An analysis of Schortinghuis's language in an unpublished paper of Miss G. Recter
(Free University, Amsterdam): 'Een onderzoek naar het pietistische taalgebruik van
ds. Willem Schortinghuis in zijn boek "Het Innige Christendom" uit 1740'.
[39] Schortinghuis p 549.
[40] *Ibid* p 256.   [41] *Ibid* p 136.   [42] *Ibid* p 233.

Honert published his *The Church in The Netherlands considered and admonished to conversion*[43] – a lengthy complaint about and protest against the decline of religion and the defection of the country; in this it was in a line with earlier works like Hondius's *Black Register of a thousand Sins,*[44] Witsius's *The Lord's Dispute with his Vineyard*[45] and Fruytier's *The Struggles of Zion.*[46] As we have seen, Van den Honert was a staunch opponent of the Dutch pietists; however, with regard to the practice of daily life his strictness, although different in some respects, was not essentially less than that of those he opposed. In this the non-pietist orthodox could hardly afford to be outdone by their more pietistic brethren, whose views of sanctity and sanctification they thought to be one-sided and even dangerous; in this context, Van den Honert himself remarked that an emphasis on practical theology and evangelical morality would be a good remedy against an influx of enthusiasm into the church.[47]

The tone of Van den Honert's work is different from that of Schortinghuis. Though he, too, used the word 'inner experience' in a positive sense, he was critical of the way this element was emphasised by the pietists.[48] He paid due attention to the many questions with regard to man's personal relation to Christ,[49] but he was also deeply interested in the christian's responsibility for public life. On this point, the contrast between Van den Honert and Schortinghuis was of a relative character. In Schortinghuis's work we indeed find something like a 'regent's mirror', but it is only marginal and is mainly concerned with the inner life of pious and impious magistrates.[50] Van den Honert is less inner-directed than Schortinghuis, whose pietism he disliked and who even became one of the main targets of his theological attacks. He does not address himself first of all to the small circle of the godly remnant, but rather to the much larger group of confessing reformed christians in general, many of whom bore the burden of responsibility in high places. In his *The Church in The Netherlands* he draws a very vivid picture of eighteenth-century Dutch social life, particularly in the

43 [J.] van den Honert, [*De Kerk in Nederland Beschouwd, en tot Bekeering vermaand*] (Leiden 1746).
44 [J.] Hondius, [*Swart Register van duysent Sonden*] (Amsterdam 1679).
45 H. Witsius, *Twist des Heeren met syn Wijngaert* (Leeuwarden 1669).
46 J. Fruytier, *Sions Worstelingen* (Rotterdam 1713).
47 Van den Honert p 215.
48 *Ibid* pp 220 ff, 273.
49 His work 'Man in Christ', *De Mensch in Christus* (Leiden 1749) gave testimony of a genuine interest in the matter of man's personal salvation.
50 Schortinghuis pp 47–59.

upper middle classes, of which he had a rather poor opinion: 'Truly, when we observe the country, we find it filled with impieties.' Van den Honert tries to show, that those who have not been able to conquer the country by the force of their weapons have now conquered it by their morals. The Dutch 'have become ridiculous copies of ridiculous neighbours. . . . To be a Dutchman is an original sin according to the men of this world.'[51] The cultural influence of catholic France manifests itself in many ways – it is a threat, not only to the stability of Dutch life in general, but most of all to a life in the true spirit of reformed christianity. People rightly complain about the decay of life with the common people, the so-called 'small congregation', but the attitude of the rich and the prominent is no better: they take no measures against the desecration of the Sabbath, against the taverns and brothels where even on the Lord's day the rich spend their time.[52] Nor do they know the world which they serve, nor God whom they should serve; they do not know that the world lies in wickedness, that it is a deceiver. A choice has to be made: 'to go to Sohar, and to look back to Sodom; to travel to Canaan, and to look back to the flesh-pots of Egypt . . . these are incompatible. . . .'[53] Indeed, much of what Van den Honert remarks sounds like the complaints and the warnings of the pietists, although the differences in context and in background should not be overlooked.

As we noticed before, on a number of practical points all orthodox agreed. Of course, they were opposed to the theatre. In 1711 the liberally minded Utrecht professor of history, literature and civics Petrus Burman gave a public lecture *Pro Comoedia*, in which he openly defended theatre-visiting. This was soon published in Latin and Dutch and created a stir in ecclesiastical circles.[54] The Utrecht ministers were unanimous in their protest, whereupon Burman ironically wrote, that he thought it a pleasure to be the peace-offering which brought together the parties, once deadly opposed to each other.[55] A theatre-visiting minister seems to have been so rare that it could be used as an additional point of reproach in a heresy-case.[56] And as late as 1772, the struggle around the theatre broke out anew after the terrible fire at the Amsterdam theatre, which according to at least a number of orthodox

[51] Van den Honert p 24.   [52] *Ibid* pp 332 ff.   [53] *Ibid* p 380 ff.
[54] See H. C. Hazewinkel, 'Professor Burman, de kerkeraad en het tooneel', *Jaarboekje van 'Oud-Utrecht'* 1927 (Utrecht 1927) pp 120–54.
[55] P. Burman, *Redevoering voor de Comedie* (3 ed Amsterdam 1772) p **5.
[56] *Examen van het Ontwerp van Tolerantie* X, p xxxv.

people was clearly an act of God's judgement.[57] In the same circles, dancing too was strictly prohibited. There is the notorious Groningen, case of 1771–2, when an elder of the reformed church was attacked by his consistory because of the opportunity given to dance at his daughter's wedding-party.[58] The offended elder argued, that if it were true that the old rules forbade elders to dance, the ministers themselves were equally guilty because they wore periwigs. The whole affair inspired Elizabeth Wolff to write her satirical poem: 'The Menuet and the Minister's Periwig'.[59] In this case, too, ministers of various parties joined hands to defend the traditional way of life. A third point on which the orthodox were uncompromising was that of card-playing; in an early eighteenth-century sermon, which was reprinted several times, a Middelburg minister, De Frein, remarked that playing cards sprang from the devil himself and that it was a sin against all God's commandments.[60] But of course there were still many other things, large and small, which were seen as manifestations of an attitude of conformity to this world. Those who wanted to know the strict orthodox rules regarding all matters of a practical nature could find them in alphabetical order in Hondius's *Black Register*, where under the heading 'World' we read: 'such people are sinning who, being members of the congregation, nevertheless are worldly minded, love the world above God and more attend to what belongs to the earth than to what appertains to heaven. . . .'[61]

We may ask how eighteenth-century christians, who leaned towards rationalism, regarded the world, what expression they gave to the christian ideal of sanctity, how they reacted to the secularising tendencies which revealed themselves in the age of enlightenment. While orthodox christians – and in particular the pietistically minded – considered themselves involved in a dramatic struggle between God and Satan, and believed the devil to be ever personally present to ensnare them by the temptations of this dark and evil world, more enlightened christians lived in a disenchanted world, in which the night of ignorance, disorder, intolerance and superstition gradually gave way to

[57] In a poem by J. C. Mohr, *Ontzaglijke doch nuttige Beschouwing van het akelig treurtooneel* (Amsterdam n.d., it appeared shortly after the fire), we read (p 3): 'I sing, though trembling, Jehovah's majesty, manifested in the exercise of his justice.'
[58] See S. D. van Veen, *Historische Studiën en Schets en* (Groningen 1905) pp 279–310.
[59] *De menuet en de domineespruik*, ed P. Minderaa (Amsterdam and Antwerp 1954).
[60] H. de Frein, *Het Spelen Met de Kaart Den Christenen Ongeoorlooft* (Amsterdam 1720) pp 32, 58 ff.
[61] Hondius p 444.

the light of reason and virtue. In his work *The Enchanted World* the Amsterdam minister Bekker, who because of the consistent use of the cartesian method of reasoning had been led to a more rationalist attitude than we find with most contemporary theologians,[62] had blazed the trail for a more undramatic, almost secular understanding of the processes going on in this world: much of what formerly was ascribed to the devil could be explained in a rational way. According to Bekker, it was mostly common people, children and old women who were deeply impressed by the stories told about the devil's activities.[63] Stinstra, the Frisian mennonite preacher mentioned earlier, also dealt with the problem of the devil and his work, although he approached it from a different angle. In his *Sermons on the Nature and Condition of the Kingdom of Christ*,[64] which made him the object of the dangerous charge of socianism,[65] he emphasised the spiritual character of the kingdom of God, which can only be propagated by love of truth and virtue into the hearts of men.[66] In this, he followed the argument of bishop Hoadly's well-known sermon on *The Nature of the Kingdom or Church of Christ* (1717); no doubt, the spiritualist element in his mennonite heritage made him the more responsive to the much debated ideas of the bishop of Bangor.[67] In accordance with the thinking of the English latitudinarians, whom he so much admired, the Frisian preacher saw a close connection between truth and virtue. Truth is always combined with virtue, because it is moral truth, marked by moderation, justice and piety, while virtue is indissolubly connected with truth: God's grace is in harmony with perfect, pure and most holy reason.[68] Christ has been manifested that he might destroy the works of the devil and might overcome the power of darkness. This must not come to pass by force, but through the light of truth, which expels the darkness and recommends true virtue in its natural beauty: 'The kingdom of Satan cannot be conceived as opposing the kingdom of God violently, but only morally . . .'[69] Stinstra sings the praises of freedom, equality and tolerance;[70] in this, he is the

62 See for Bekker (1634–98): W. P. C. Knuttel, *Balthasar Bekker* (The Hague 1906); for his philosophical emphasis: W. Reuning, 'Balthasar Bekker', *Zeitschrift für Kirchengeschichte* 45 (Gotha 1927) pp 562–96.
63 *De Betoverde Weereld* (Deventer 1739) I p 137.
64 [J.] Stinstra, [*De Natuure en Gesteldheid van*] *Christus Koningrijk* (2 ed Harlingen 1741).
65 See for this accusation and its fateful results: Sepp I pp 238–68, II pp 1–265.
66 Stinstra, *Christus Koningrijk* p 37.
67 See for his views: G. R. Cragg, *Reason and Authority in the Eighteenth Century* (Cambridge 1946) p 196.
68 Stinstra, *Christus Koningrijk*, p 59.   69 *Ibid* p 77.   70 *Ibid* pp 176 ff.

exponent of the spirit of a new age, which for obvious reasons was more readily accepted in the circle of enlightened dissenters than in that of orthodox members of the privileged church; half a century later many of the more liberal mennonites would find themselves in the vanguard of the patriot movement, looking forward to the blessings of 'liberty, equality and fraternity', sometimes even taking up arms in the defence of the ideals of the revolution.[71]

We should not attribute to Stinstra an undue optimism with regard to the state of affairs in this world. In a sermon on Ps. 90: 12, he remarked that life is transient, uncertain and short and that therefore man has to be wary of the enjoyment of worldly and temporary pleasures and of the temptation of the benefits which life offers to us: these things could possibly turn him away from his highest and most excellent good. Without any delay man has to enter seriously upon the work of sanctification and the practice of virtue.[72] All this, however, should be seen against the background of an image of man and of God, which differs much from that which we find in orthodox, and especially in pietist circles. In his *Pastoral Letter* he writes:

> That which the Fanatick calls the *Work of Regeneration*, consists in sensible Alarms, cruel Agitations of the Soul, arising from a Consideration of the Misery and Corruption of our Nature, (which he supposes a great deal more dreadful than they really are) and in a kind of dreadful Amazement and Terror for God, (painting this adorable Master as a barbarous Tyrant) which sometimes throw the Soul into the greatest Horror.[73]

The way that Stinstra pointed out to his Frisian mennonites was quite different from the arduous journey of Bunyan's Christian and the narrow road of the pietists: it was the road of a religion, based on sound reason and demanding what is perfectly reasonable, honest and decent.[74] He knew that among the enthusiasts, antinomians excepted, there also were people who strongly insisted on moral virtues, but all too often their idea of virtue was defective; while pressing some duties too far, they were inclined to overlook other duties. Stinstra stood for 'a manly Piety': 'Let us make appear by our Conduct, that a reasonable Faith has no less Power and Influence over us, than Superstitions and chimerical Opinions have over others.'[75]

---

[71] Van der Zijpp p 177.
[72] Johannes Stinstra, *Bedenkingen over des menschen leeftijd* (Harlingen 1744).
[73] Stinstra, *A Pastoral Letter* p 18.   [74] *Ibid* p 32.   [75] *Ibid* pp 85, 88.

How far these fundamental views affected Stinstra's attitude with regard to what the pietists used to call 'worldly pleasures' may be seen in the preface to his translation of the third and fourth volume of Richardson's *Clarissa*.[76] Stinstra sees the search for pleasure and re-creation as in agreement with the loving intentions of our Creator. Naturally, that which induces to evil inclination and crimes has to be avoided, the right measure has to be respected and the useful advantage of pleasure has to be kept in view – but given all this, there is ample room for various forms of 'gay pleasure and light relaxation'. The reading of novels is one of them, but from Stinstra's line of argument it appears that he is not opposed to other forms of relaxation either, whose 'essential usefulness' does not detract from the 'sweet pleasure' they may offer. 'If you dance, if you take a pleasant walk for relaxation or enjoyment, you would not say that the enjoyment loses something of its power to refresh you because at the same time you have in mind protecting or promoting the fresh and well-kept health of your body.' Stinstra was far from being a libertine; he, too, shows a certain restraint with regard to the pleasures of this world; but still, how much more open, how much less grim is his attitude towards the world than that of so many of his orthodox contemporaries. And even when he too is critical of some forms of relaxation he remains moderate and urbane: his slightly ironical treatment of the question of card-playing is strikingly different from the vehement denunciations of De Frein's sermon on the subject. In all this, the social factor may neither be overlooked nor unduly stressed: of course, Stinstra stands for much that was customary in upper middle classes, although there, too, besides a more liberal and latitudinarian attitude an almost methodist strictness could be found, as John Wesley noticed when he visited Holland in 1783 and 1786.[77]

Stinstra is the almost perfect example of a Dutch moderate. Some, however, went even further: their world-view was marked by an optimism which was in striking contrast to the often pessimistic world-view of the pietists. Perhaps it is best summarised in a review, probably written by Van der Meersch, in the *Algemeene Bibliotheek* of a work by the abbot Jerusalem –

> Could we not, when we regard the gradual progress of arts and
> sciences in former times, and their amazing progress in this

[76] *Clarissa of de Historie van eene Jonge Juffer*, III (Harlingen 1753). I follow the translation, given by Slattery, pp 129-55.

[77] See: J. van den Berg, 'John Wesley's contacten met Nederland', *Nederlands Archief voor Kerkgeschiedenis*, n.s, 52 (Leiden 1971) p 82.

present century, deduce with rightful expectation, that this enlightenment will spread further and further? Once this is realised
it is highly probable that eventually it will have a salutary influence on human morality. . . . With civilisation spreading, society,
virtue and sound morals will necessarily improve, although it is
beyond doubt that there will always be people unable to overcome
their corrupt nature. To this ever spreading civilisation and
improvement of morals, Christian religion can be a strong
impetus.[78]

Those, who looked at the world with such almost unbounded optimism, were fighters for a new society, in which freedom and tolerance would be dominant concepts. Amongst them was Van der
Meersch, whose great ideal was a free and open society, in which
there would be no privileged church and no infringements upon the
great principle of religious liberty. Yet he did not stand for a secular
society in the modern sense of the word: while he agreed with Hoadly
and Stinstra that the kingdom of God is not of the world, he, too,
believed that the christian religion would have a wholesome influence
on life in civil society, which in its turn would advance the influence
of religion as much as possible.[79]
It is a far cry from men like Lampe and Schortinghuis, who lived
in the darkness of a world where Satan raged and sin abounded, and
Van den Honert, who stood in the *clair-obscur* of a nostalgic longing
for a better more godly past, to people like Stinstra and Van der
Meersch, who rejoiced at the mild light of a morning full of promise.
And yet, Lampe, Schortinghuis and Van den Honert also looked forward, each in his own way, to the coming day when the kingdom of
God would fill the whole world – while Stinstra and Van der Meersch
were also conscious of the distance between this world and the kingdom
of Christ. There is much ambivalence – as there was in the men and
women, who are described in the novels of Wolff and Deken. They
lived in a small rather parochial world, as so many Dutchmen did:[80] it
is strange that, apart from the small group of Moravians and a few

---

[78] *Algemeene Bibliotheek* 4 (Amsterdam 1784) pp 270–2. The review deals with Jerusalem's best-known work: *Betrachtungen über die vornehmsten Wahrheiten der Religion*;
the first vol of a Dutch translation had appeared in Amsterdam in 1783.

[79] In his anonymously published work *De Vryheid van Godsdienst in de Burgerlyke Maat-
schappy betoogd en verdeedigd* (Amsterdam 1774) pp xxxiv ff.

[80] See for Dutch social life in the eighteenth century: J. Hartog, *De Spectatoriale Geschriften
van 1741–1800* (2 ed Utrecht 1890) and L. Knappert, *Het zedelijk leven onzer vaderen
in de achttiende eeuw* (Haarlem 1910).

others especially in the closing years of the century, eighteenth-century Holland was almost completely unaware of the missionary dimension of the word 'world', once so important in Dutch protestantism. They lived in a world full of innocuous and dangerous pleasures, as the girl Sara Burgerhart did: religious, but rebelling against the fetters of a narrow orthodoxy and striving for a life of which the end would be free, gay and beautiful.[81] They wished each other a 'heaven on earth',[82] but yet they knew that there was more than this present world – the world beyond the grave with which this generation was so much concerned.[83] They were children of their own age, full of a remarkable optimism with regard to this world, but they also knew their bible and were sensitive to the tensions inherent in the word 'world'. And in the great spiritual struggles of the next century, which would so thoroughly plough the Dutch soil, it appeared how much the problems the eighteenth century had left behind were still unsolved.[84]

---

[81] See for the meaning of the word 'gay' in this context: P. J. Buijnsters, *'Sara Burgerhart' en de ontwikkeling van de Nederlandse roman in de 18^e eeuw* (Groningen 1971) p 28, n 70.

[82] E. Bekker and A. Deken, *Historie van Mejuffrouw Sara Burgerhart*, ed L. Knappert (Amsterdam 1906) II p 269 (letter 173).

[83] See for the influence of English literature of death and the grave in the Netherlands: P. J. Buijnsters, *Tussen twee werelden* (Assen 1963).

[84] I thank dr M. van Beek, Amstelveen, for his kind assistance with regard to linguistic problems.

'HOLY WORLDLINESS' IN NINETEENTH-CENTURY ENGLAND

by HADDON WILLMER

IF it had ever been coined, the slogan 'holy worldliness' would
have been welcomed in nineteenth-century England. So many of
the longings, and half-formed visions of the period seemed to be
pressing in that direction. And yet the fact that it never appeared, so
far as I know, suggests that the thinking of the time was somehow
deeply inhibited. In this paper, I wish to try to show how close theologians and popular religious thinkers came to framing the concept of
'holy worldliness', and how and why they were held back.

My reading has unfortunately been inadequate and this paper can
be no more than a first impressionistic sketch. I have not taken the
well trodden highroad of F. D. Maurice and Charles Kingsley and the
like. This is not to deny their importance, but given a limited space, I
want to explore some of the by-paths, if only to keep open the historian's rights of way. Only as we walk them well shall we be able to
understand the merits and demerits of the highroad. To speak plainly,
figures like F. D. Maurice are studied too much in isolation from their
context; even when this procedure does not lead to positive error, it
cannot help but reduce claims for their special significance to mere
assertions. To judge whether a man had a unique or seminal role
involves comparing him with his competitors, and that means, doing
equal justice to them all. By itself, the biographical method – the hero
against a backcloth – gives no grounds for estimating the hero's significance, since it has already been prejudged by the biographical form.
But this reflection is no doubt an inaptly grandiose apology for the
deficiencies of what I have to offer.

From the beginning the christian concept of worldliness had an
ambiguity which could hardly be removed, at least within christian
limits. The world comes from God. It is his by creation and redemption
and yet it has been usurped by fallen man, who makes it reflect and
embody his opposition to God. Though the word 'worldliness' was
invariably pejoratively used, there sprang from faith in God a long

tradition of affirmation of the world. George Herbert had the secret of an elixir which made for holy worldliness of a kind:

> A man that looks on glasse
> On it may stay his eye;
> Or if he pleaseth, through it passe,
> And then the heav'n espie.

> All may of thee partake:
> Nothing can be so mean,
> Which with his tincture (for thy sake)
> Will not grow bright or clean.

> A servant with this clause,
> Makes drudgerie divine:
> Who sweeps a room, as for thy laws,
> Makes that and th' action fine.

> This is the famous stone
> That turneth all to gold:
> For that which God doth touch and own
> Cannot for less be told.

Within this ancient tradition, consider Mrs Humphrey Ward's novel, *Robert Elsmere*, published in 1888. Catherine Leyburn, who became Elsmere's wife, represented what Mrs Ward thought an out-moded but honourable conception of sanctity.[1] In Catherine, drudgery was divine; her holiness set high value on supplying the real needs of others; but it feared passion and pleasure. Such was the ambiguity of George Herbert that Catherine could, in a crisis, quote his words, 'Thy Saviour sentenced joy!' Elsmere argued with Catherine about this, not only because he wanted her to have the joy of marrying him, but also, that her sister Rose might be set free for her passion for the violin. Elsmere, we are told, had a 'more modern sense' which, though deeply christianised, assumed almost without argument the sacredness of passion and its claim.[2]

Catherine asked: 'How was it lawful for the Christian to spend the few short years of the earthly combat in any pursuit, however noble and exquisite, which merely aimed at the gratification of the senses, and implied in the pursuer the emphasising rather than the surrender of self?' According to Mrs Ward, Elsmere here argued very much as

[1] [Mrs Humphrev] Ward, [*Robert Elsmere*] (London 1888) p 104 cap vii.
[2] Ward p 112.

Kingsley would have done; amongst other things, he pressed 'the natural religious question: How are the artistic aptitudes to be explained unless the Great Designer meant them to have a use and function in His world?'

The principle that what man can do with the world, he may do, or that the whole world was given as the field of man's self-extension was essential to Herbert's spirituality.

> More servants wait on Man,
> Then he'l take notice of . . .
> for,
> . . . Man is one world, and hath
> Another to attend him.

> 'For us the windes do blow.
> The earth doth rest, heav'n move, and fountains flow.
> Nothing we see, but means our good,
> As our delight, or as our treasure:
> The whole is, either our cupboard of food,
> Or cabinet of pleasure.'³

Again in Herbert's view, creation is the *act* by which God sets a value upon earthly things which outweighs any unworthiness: the soul says to welcoming Love, 'I cannot look on thee.' Then,

> Love took my hand, and smiling did reply,
> Who made the eyes but I?⁴

> For that which God doth touch and own
> Cannot for lesse be told

The love of God in creation and redemption, thus provides for a life in the world which is uncrippled by a sense of worthlessness or sin. But Catherine's spirituality did not enable her to make this deduction from the fact of creation. Mrs Ward hints that she resisted Elsmere's advances partly because she could not, or even 'in a kind of terror' would not 'believe in her own love-worthiness, in her own power to deal a lasting wound'.⁵ In this, as in so much, she was her father's daughter. He, so Catherine said, 'was always blaming, scourging himself. And all the time he was the noblest, purest, most devoted . . .'⁶ Now, according to Mrs Ward, such ascetic tortured misrepresentation of one's own

³ [George] Herbert, *Man*.   ⁴ Herbert, *Love*.
⁵ Ward p 102.   ⁶ Ward p 96.

goodness came from St Augustine, and in the 'tragedy of our time' it clashed with another estimate of life, which is 'the offspring of the scientific spirit, and which is for ever making the visible world fairer and more desirable in mortal eyes'.[7] But in view of George Herbert, it seems likely that the spirit of 'the pious cavalier', to use a phrase of R. H. Hutton's,[8] had anticipated that of the modern scientific approach to the world. Though the crisis of faith hid it from Mrs Ward's and Catherine's eyes, there was in the christian tradition through Herbert to Keble and Kingsley, T. T. Lynch, who wrote *The Rivulet* and R. W. Dale, a repeated witness to man's being free, by God's creative love, to live before Him in the world.

Yet clearly, though the possibility of worldliness had long been present in the christian tradition, it was always seriously inhibited. And the tension between possibility and restraint increased in the nineteenth century. There is fierce strife between those who affirmed the world and those who insisted on the inhibitions. The kind of worldliness that could grow from a treatment of creation, like Herbert's, was limited, first, by a prevalent view of the church's relation to the world. To be made holy it was commonly thought that the world needed to be controlled by the church or by christianity. So Thomas Arnold thought that without a church establishment England would be 'wholly a kingdom of the world, and ruled according to none but worldly principles'.[9] So Newman preached, 'In all things then we must spiritualize this world . . . when a nation enters Christ's Church, and takes her yoke upon its shoulder, then it formally joins itself to the cause of God, and separates itself from the evil world . . . You must either conquer the world, or the world will conquer you.' He admitted that like other earthly things, christianity might die, but he then dared to say, 'The world's duration is measured by it. If the Church dies, the world's time is run. The world shall never exult over the Church.'[10] Nonconformist attitudes were not dissimilar. As far as I can find, R. W. Dale came nearer to using the actual words, 'holy worldliness', than anyone else when he gave a lecture entitled 'Christian Worldliness'. But his thought had its limits. He spoke in terms of the kingdom of God – 'The ideal Christian life is a life in God – a life under the absolute

---

[7] Ward pp 129–30.

[8] R. H. Hutton, 'Christian Worldliness', [*The*] *Spectator* (London) 7 March 1885 p 212.

[9] Thomas Arnold, *Principles of Church Reform* edd M. J. Jackson and J. Rogan (London 1962) p 142.

[10] [J. H.] Newman, *Sermons*, [*bearing on Subjects of the Day*] (London 1843) pp 142, 124–6, 115.

control of the laws of an invisible, eternal and Divine Kingdom.'[11] And his christian worldliness means fighting the world's evils in alliance with God. 'God made [the world], and Christian men have to win it back to God again.'[12] Hugh Price Hughes and C. S. Horne had similar attitudes. Although a radical free churchman and a Liberal member of parliament, Horne could still say,

> Some spiritual power must be found to unify society. Christianity must do it or die. It is her unaccomplished mission . . . To those of us who believe that the Church of Christ is still the real, if unacknowledged mistress of the world, and who do not despair of her fulfilling her destiny, the lines of cleavage that run everywhere through society are at once a reproach and a challenge.[13]

The sense of the indispensable and dominant role of christian faith in the life of the world was as strong in Horne in 1913 as in Newman in 1843. Neither was unaware of the weakness of the church – indeed it spurred them to action – but neither had lost the belief that, if the right action were taken, there was still time for the church's destiny to be fulfilled. This points to one real difference between their thinking and that of Bonhoeffer's *Letters and Papers from Prison*. Outside the churches, too, ecclesiasticism still beguiled many in the nineteenth century, like comteans and spiritualists. Robert Elsmere, having given up his parish when he lost his faith in orthodox christianity, was faithful to one aspect of T. H. Green when he set about founding 'The New Brotherhood of Christ'. He exhorted his working-class company: 'Be content to be a "new sect", "conventicle" or what not, so long as you feel you are something with a life and purpose of its own, in this tangle of a world.'[14] So the separateness of church from world is cultivated because it helps men to a sense of identity and purpose. Even in this form, ecclesiasticism draws a sharp line between the little flock and the tangled world. Talk of 'holy worldliness' is unlikely in such a context.

Another reason why the concept 'holy worldliness' did not grow out of christian belief in creation was that this world, however good, was regarded as the ante-chamber of the next. It was not an end in itself, autonomous or self-sufficient. The eye must not stay on the glass, but

11 [R. W.] Dale, *Laws [of Christ for Common Life]* (7 ed London, 1893) p 217.
12 Dale, *Laws* pp 233–4.
13 C. S. Horne, *Pulpit, Platform and Parliament* (London 1913) p 7,
14 Ward p 554.

pass through it to see heaven. The beauty of the earth and the dignity of worldly life are affirmed by John Keble in *The Christian Year*, but he hardly accepts the world simply as itself.

> New every morning is the love
> Our wakening and uprising prove,
> Through sleep and darkness safely brought
> Restored to life, and power, and thought
>
> . . .
>
> If on our daily course our mind
> Be set to hallow all we find,
> New treasures still, of countless price,
> God will provide for sacrifice.
>
> . . .
>
> We need not bid, for cloister'd cell,
> Our neighbour and our works farewell,
> Nor strive to wind ourselves too high
> For sinful man beneath the sky.
>
> The trivial round, the common task,
> Would furnish all we ought to ask –
> Room to deny ourselves; a road
> To bring us daily, nearer God.[15]

The worldliness of the pilgrim whose way leads through the hard low and dreary places is genuine, but it sufficiently transcends or transfigures or leaves behind the world to make 'holy worldliness' an unlikely thought.

Nonconformists, on the whole, were similarly inhibited. Thomas Binney's positive lectures to young men, *Is it Possible to Make the Best of Both Worlds?* went through many editions in the 1850s and met much contradiction.[16] We are told Binney himself came to regret having published the book.[17] Clearer evidence comes from Dale, who qualified his argument for christian worldliness thus:

> And yet we shall not be Pagans, finding our rest in visible and transitory things. They will satisfy the powers and capacities to which they are related, and we shall not in a spirit of querulous discontent refuse to enjoy the satisfactions they are intended to

15 John Keble, *The Christian Year* (Oxford 1827) 'Morning', pp 2–4.
16 T. Binney, *Is it Possible to Make the Best of Both Worlds?* (10 ed London 1856).
17 C. S. Horne, *A Popular History of the Free Churches* (London 1903) p 399.

bring. We shall take them, being thankful for them, acknowledging them as proofs of the Divine love and care. But over the common earth will bend the Heaven of God. The streams of earthly joy, beautiful in themselves, will carry us onward to the ocean of eternal blessedness.[18]

In some ways, idealism, a popular replacement for christian faith in the nineteenth century, was less able to be worldly, to let the world be itself, than orthodox christianity. As uncertainty grew about the next world and about another world above the sky, so the distinction between two worlds, preserved largely for ethical reasons, was made wholly internal to this one world. Men spoke of higher and lower, of real and unreal, true and false, human and brutish. Robert Elsmere, a disciple of T. H. Green, was an optimist who to the end saw the world through the haze of a romantic imagination and, as the sceptical squire Wendover and his old tutor Langham both thought, with an incurably religious anti-empirical temperament. So, even when he was no longer a christian, he could sound like Newman as he preached against the world. That wickedly seductive woman of the world, Mme de Netteville, offended by his diatribes against worldliness, told him: 'What you religious people call the ' world" is really only the average opinion of sensible people which neither you nor your kind could do without for a day.'[19] His axiom was that miracles do not happen but it proved to be no guarantee of worldliness: when he was dying, 'the only realities to him in a world of shadows were God-love-the soul'.[20]

Again, the controversy in 1907 about the new theology with its immanentism might seem to promise something of 'holy worldliness'. R. J. Campbell joined the independent labour party, arguing that since it was the business of the church not to prepare souls for heaven, but to turn earth into heaven, the party was the true catholic church. *The British Weekly* from the traditionalist otherworldly side asked 'How can earth be heaven while death remains?'[21] Robert Blatchford, editor of *The Clarion*, who saw the world with atheist realism said 'Mr Campbell calls nature God. I call nature nature. Mr Campbell thinks we ought to have some form of supernatural religion, and that we ought to associate it with Christ. I prefer a religion of humanity without idolatry.'[22] So Campbell's theology was attacked as being either

---

[18] Dale, *Laws* p 237. [19] Ward p 524. [20] Ward p 600.
[21] *The British Weekly* (London) 4 April 1907 p 694.
[22] *Ibid* p 696.

insufficiently holy or insufficiently worldly. P. T. Forsyth showed his quality by attacking from both sides at once.[23]

Now we must turn from the side of the christian idea of the world derived from the doctrine of creation and consider the word as it referred to the social human reality of fallen man in the world he makes rather than the world he is given. Despite the influences of the doctrine of creation, of Wordsworth and of the scientific spirit, the pejorative language of worldliness survived because of the priority of ethical concern, because of the weight of evil. Many tried, in a phrase, to safeguard the goodness of the world as created but overwhelmed it with ethical generalisations about the wicked state of society. Newman for example:

> The whole visible course of things, nations, empires, states, politics, professions, trades, society, pursuits of all kinds, are, I do not say directly and formally sinful (of course not), but they *come* of evil; they hold of evil; they have in them the nature of evil . . . all of them, every thing in the world is in itself alien from God, and at first sight must be regarded and treated as being so . . .[24]

As he wrote in a famous passage in the *Apologia*, it was in 'this living busy world' that Newman saw 'no reflection of its Creator'.[25]

Such a gloomy view could be repressed but not wholly obliterated. Tom Paine preached a deist kind of holy worldliness which had great influence throughout the nineteenth century. He claimed to see the world more happily and more clearly than christian orthodoxy, which he criticised from a positive worldly standpoint: 'Christian mythology gives most of the world to the devil, who is deified, having a power equal if not greater than the Almighty's . . .' This view must be rejected, since, in truth, 'there is a fair creation to be grateful for'. 'How different is Deism! One Deity: and his religion consists in contemplating the power, wisdom and benignity of the Deity in his works, and in endeavouring to imitate him in everything moral, scientifical and mechanical.' He thought the quakers approached nearest to this in the moral and benign part, but they were too narrow; they left the works of God too much out of their system. 'What a silent and drab coloured creation it would have been if the taste of a quaker could have been con-

[23] *The Old Faith and the New Theology*, ed C. A. Vine (London 1907) pp 47 ff.; P. T. Forsyth, *Socialism, the Church and the Poor* (London 1908) pp 44, 47-9, 54.

[24] Newman, *Sermons* pp 119-20.

[25] J. H. Newman, *Apologia pro Vita Sua* (London 1912) p 217.

sulted at the creation.'[26] So Paine sought to interpret this living busy world in direct relation to the Creator's work, without the interposition of fall and redemption. Yet in his way he too saw the world's evil as plainly as Newman and so worked for revolution. In his deist mythology of despots and priests, who invented christianity and imposed it on men out of lust for power and wealth, he found his devils and his fallen race and was driven to think in terms of redemption by revolution and reason. It is difficult to give no foothold to the pejorative language of worldliness when the living busy world of men is out of joint.

Paine attempts to ground value on the goodness of creation, and on it to build his protest against the evil of the social world. A worldliness that is in accordance with nature is unworldly in relation to society. He called on men to imitate God the worker, the Mechanic; his God was the Doer of the Deed rather than the Word. True religion was not a matter of opinions but 'the endeavouring to make our fellow-creatures happy'.[27] Though the holy is not here profoundly felt, this approach points to holy worldliness of a kind, except that, as I have suggested, it then becomes the basis of a new discrimination between holy and worldly, between God and man, between the real, the serious and the false and frivolous. In this idiom, unworldliness is still a high value.

Such thinking was not a deist monopoly. William Penn had written directions for the education of his children on this basis:

> For their learning be liberal. Spare no cost; for by such parsimony all is lost that is saved: but let it be useful knowledge, such as is consistent with truth and godliness, not cherishing a vain conversation or idle mind, but ingenuity mixed with industry is good for the body and mind too. I recommend the useful parts of mathematics, as building houses or ships, measuring, surveying, dialling, navigation but agriculture is especially in my eye, let my children be husband men and housewives; . . . This leads to consider the work of God and nature, of things that are good, and diverts the mind from being taken up with the vain arts and inventions of a luxurious world.[28]

Elsewhere, he wrote: 'The country life is to be preferr'd; for there we see the Works of God; but in cities little else but the works of Men;

---

[26] [Thomas] Paine, [*The*] *Age of Reason* [*being an Investigation of True and Fabulous Theology*] (Paris/London 1794) pp 8–10, 39.   [27] *Ibid* p 2.
[28] Quoted in John W. Graham, *William Penn* (London 1917) p 147.

And the one makes better subject for our contemplation than the other.'[29]

William Cowper is representative of much evangelicalism in his celebration of the goodness of God's creation, and his looking to its eschatological renewal. But by the world he often means the world of man joined together by frivolity, as in the theatre or in card playing – 'the world's time is time in masquerade'[30] – or in evil, for though man's faculties only reach their proper use in society, it is also in society that man engages in war, or in commerce –

> Hence merchants, unimpeachable of sin
> Against the charities of domestic life,
> Incorporated, seem at once to lose
> Their nature, and disclaiming all regard
> For mercy and the common rights of man,
> Build factories with blood . . .[31]

Cowper found the simple domestic values of God's creation more in the country than in the town; hence his alarm when he saw that 'the town has tinged the country'.[32]

In F. W. Robertson of Brighton, whose name is often coupled with F. D. Maurice's, the tradition continued. An admirer of Wordsworth, Robertson insisted that 'unworldliness' was indispensable for understanding him.[33] The explanation of this apparently odd demand may be found in his criterion for judging female beauty. 'I admire the beauty which God made – health – immeasurably above the counterfeit which man procures. A country girl, modest and neat, is not my *beau idéal* of beauty; but I admire her far more than a pale languid girl of fashion . . .'[34] Robertson gives the impression of a man between duty and desire, for he is not really attracted by the country girl. But by the basic criterion of health, God's making, the town girl is worldly, with her artificial fashion and, no doubt, her French novels.[35] Unlike Cowper, Robertson will defend worldly occupations 'for work, rightly done, is a man's religion'. The law, for example, sifts right from wrong; it is therefore working against worldliness which is 'Attachment to the outward – attachment to the transitory – attachment to the unreal: in

---

[29] *Ibid* p 209.
[30] [William] Cowper, *The Task* bk iv line 213.
[31] *Ibid* lines 676–81.   [32] *Ibid* line 553.
[33] Stopford A. Brooke, *Life and Letters of Frederick W. Robertson, M.A.*, 2 vols (London 1865) II, p 175.   [34] *Ibid* II, p 224.
[35] F. W. Robertson, *Sermons on Religion and Life* (London 1906) p 148.

opposition to love for the inward, the eternal, the true . . .'[36] The basic value of health is found again in Dale and in Bonhoeffer and clearly is on the brink of holy worldliness. One more example will suffice: Maurice's colleague, J. M. Ludlow, had a distaste for consumer cooperation, on the ground that 'If you appeal to consumption you appeal to the belly; God is the eternal producer.'[37] Repeatedly, then, the affirmation of God's creation and its values was the springboard for hostile criticism of the kind of urban world that most people were being compelled, willy-nilly to make the best of.

Dale, the pastor of a large Birmingham congregation, wanted to give ethical guidance to his members engaged in the world's business. Like Robertson, he wanted all lawful worldly occupations to be understood as vocations, as religious. Further, maybe because he was no mean theologian, Dale was aware of the negative effects of the traditional preference for the language of unworldliness. All the same he did not break completely with that language or succeed in creating a new one. His talk of christian worldliness emerged from that tradition and was fairly soon sucked back into it. The consequent inconsistency of language is plain, when, for example, he said 'Of all secular affairs, politics rightly considered, are amongst the most unworldly, in as much as the man who is devoted to political life ought to be seeking no personal private good. The true political spirit is the mind that was in Christ Jesus, who "looked not on His own things, but also on the things of others".'[38] Politics are secular, but their true nature calls for unworldly participants.

He remarked that it had long been the custom to preach about the righteousness of God in punishing national sins whenever cholera or bad harvests or wars befell the country. Dale thought it wrong not to extend this preaching so as to specify these national sins and to show what policies would be 'more righteous and Christian'.[39] This extension was resisted on the grounds that it was a profanation or secularisation of the pulpit. The inconsistency exposed here is so obvious that its wide currency needs explanation. Political preaching was a longstanding issue between anglicans and dissenters. Anglicans thought that loyal, tory sermons were not political, because the constitution was

36 *Ibid* pp 155-6.
37 Quoted in N. C. Masterman, *John Malcolm Ludlow, the Builder of Christian Socialism* (Cambridge 1963) p 115.
38 A. W. W. Dale, [*The Life of*] R. W. Dale [*of Birmingham*] (London 1899) p 250.
39 *Ibid* p 250-1.

203

above politics; so they felt free to put on dissenters the responsibility for introducing politics into the pulpit. Dissenters retorted that the mere existence of the church of England was a political question. In anglicanism, then, Dale had already come across a political preaching artificially curtailed; as a nonconformist he was well aware of its illogicality.[40]

A similar artificial limitation arose when political action was held to be justified only in so far as it was based on an explicit scriptural command. For example, when William Brock, a baptist minister in Norwich tried in 1844 to stop the selling and buying of votes at election time, his congregation asked whether the bible had condemned the practice. If it had not, the matter should be left to men's sense of the expedient. They clearly thought in terms of a sharp distinction between the gospel and politics; like Dale later, Brock answered by admitting that scripture is against worldly-mindedness, but if this were to be interpreted as proscribing politics, then philosophy and literature and 'even commerce' must also be excluded.[41] All series of proscriptions were vulnerable to this kind of argument; they could only be made consistent if they applied to all activity in the world. Going out of the world, however, was impracticable and unscriptural. William Cowper in *The Love of the World Reproved; or, Hypocrisy detected*, had recognised the problem, but offered no solution, and so long as no theological reinterpretation was undertaken, preaching against worldliness was bound to be illogical and nullified by the practice of the community.[42] It may not be wrong to see Dale's *Christian Worldliness* as a theological response to pressures of this kind. Essentially Dale tried to get away from defining sanctity by the exclusion of the worldly, and wished to find a worldliness which would be christian because it rested on God's affirmation of the world in creation and redemption, understood in keeping with the orthodox tradition.

In Dale's view, the solution of the theological problem of worldliness had been found before the rise of deism or the modern scientific spirit. The world denying form of sanctity was, he thought, a legacy of the traditional roman catholic idea of the saint.[43] Since protestants had given up the theology of Rome, they ought also to free themselves from its religious ideal. This was possible, thanks to Luther, who

[40] R. W. Dale, *The Politics of Nonconformity* (Manchester 1871) pp 5–9.
[41] C. M. Birrell, *The Life of William Brock, D.D.* (London 1878) p 143.
[42] F. J. A. Hort, *The Way The Truth The Life* (Cambridge 1893) pp 160–4.
[43] Dale, *Laws* p 225.

'rediscovered God; with God he rediscovered the Gospel'.[44] The protestant spirit was

> the antithesis of the despondency which had prevailed in Christendom for many centuries. It taught every man to have unmeasured confidence in the Divine mercy for the forgiveness of his past sins, and unmeasured confidence in his Divine inspiration for the strength he needed in the future to live devoutly and righteously.[45]

> The ideal Catholic saint is the monk, and monasticism in its best times and in its highest moods sprang from a noble despair. The world was so full of evil, that for a man who wanted to live in God the only safety seemed to be in flight . . .[46]

Catholic sanctity fled the world out of fear that it might succumb to its charms; it believed in the sanctity of misery. By contrast Luther

> was a man, and did not try to be anything else: God made him a man, what was he that he should quarrel with God's work? He had flesh and blood; he could not help it. He did not desire to help it. He ate heartily and enjoyed seeing his friends at dinner. He married a wife and loved her; and he loved God none the less . . . He had a genial humour as well as deep devoutness. He was a brave man, strong and resolute, with abounding life of all kinds; a saint of a type with which, for many evil centuries, Christendom had been unfamiliar.[47]

Such a contrast between the lutheran and the catholic ideals was not Dale's invention. He came to speak of Luther by way of quoting J. B. Mozley's review of Stanley's *Life of Arnold*. Mozley found it a deficiency in Arnold's character that it was 'too luscious, too joyous, too luxuriant, . . . too happy to be interesting', or, it appeared, to be holy.[48] Arnold was not wounded where wounding tells, and had been left 'heart-whole, unhumbled'. It was particularly offensive that Stanley made Arnold's happiness almost a part of his religion: 'a sort of deep mysterious language with respect to it seems to convert the sensation of pleasure into a positive religion (on the principle that religion is the deepest part of us), and give the intensity of eternal essence to present life'. Behind this, the anglican reviewer detected 'genuine religious

---

44 *Ibid* p 229.   45 *Ibid* p 232.
46 *Ibid* p 233.   47 *Ibid* p 234–5.
48 [J. B.] Mozley, *Essays* [*Historical and Theological*] 2 vols (2 ed London 1884) II pp 24–5.

Germanism'; Arnold was a lutheran albeit a very good one. 'The Lutheran and the Catholic systems have been ever, under one form or other, fighting for the possession of man's goodness. His goodness is recipient of either form, and may be refracted into either atmosphere'[49]. Speaking of Arnold's clash with Hurrell Froude, Mozley wrote:

> The Catholic system, as it advanced from the worlds beyond the grave, came with some of the colour and circumstances of its origin. It contrasted strangely with the light, hearty, and glowing form of earth, that came from wood and mountain, sunshine and green fields, to meet them. And the unearthly, supernatural dogmatic Church opposed a ghostly dignity to the Church of nature and the religion of the heart.[50]

It is not surprising that this irritated a nonconformist like Dale. The problem of holy worldliness evidently went to the roots of theological options and styles of the day, and was much affected by ecclesiastical, social and national divisions. The strength of the other worldly catholic cult of sadness was not simply in the stalwarts of an older generation – Mozley had written his essay in 1844. Dale's talk of christian worldliness in 1885 was judged worthy of comment in the *Spectator* by its editor, R. H. Hutton.[51] He argued that Dale's christian worldliness was less true to the teaching of Jesus and the apostles than the catholic idea of sanctity. Paul indeed had taught exulting confidence in God, but not exulting enjoyment of all human blessings. Both Paul and John constantly feared lest the richness and joy of this life should absorb too large a part of the soul's energies. Hutton confessed that he would have liked to believe that Dale's was the true idea of saintly life; but, since it was unscriptural, he could not. Here again we meet a man divided between duty and desire.

Hutton advised Dale to look at Newman's sermon on the apostolical christian, one of the *Sermons, bearing on Subjects of the Day* from which I have already quoted. Dale wrote to Hutton confessing the spell Newman's sermon cast over him – 'the beauty of his vision of the saintly life is enough to tempt the angels from their thrones'.

> But, frankly, the vision does not seem to me to have been suggested by the four Gospels, the Acts of the Apostles, or the Epistles . . . I sometimes tell my people to try the health and soundness of their spiritual taste by asking whether any devotional

[49] *Ibid* p 26.　　[50] *Ibid* p 51.　　[51] *Spectator* 14 February 1885 p 212.

206

book or life seems to them to have a fascination which they cannot find in the four Gospels. If it has, there is something wrong in it.

My faith in the Trinity and the Incarnation – where I find the root of all ethics and of all politics . . . – prevents me from yielding to the charm of the Catholic ideal. It is in the air. It touches earth too lightly, and misses heaven. The Christian ideal is near to both and touches both.[52]

Dale thus demands an ideal that does justice to both heaven and earth in their otherness. As in Bonhoeffer, holy worldliness is dialectical. This is interesting, because Mozley, from the other side, had criticized Arnold on the same principle that Dale directs against Newman. Arnold the latitudinarian went for compromise, mixture. 'He exhorts his boys to be "Christian gentlemen", and he wants an undermaster who must be a "Christian gentleman". We would rather see this combination implied than expressed. Expressed in this way, it seems to have a lowering influence on both characters – to tend to secularize the Christian and to puritanize the gentlemen.'[53] The language and criteria in this theological debate were uncertain and slippery. Dale himself told Hutton: 'On the larger question of the true Christian ideal, I suppose that the answer comes out of the innermost life of a man, and discussion is unavailing.'[54] It is not altogether surprising that little came of it. As far as I know, no one after Hutton talked about christian worldliness, and Dale's writing was forgotten.

Though Hutton could not find apostolic warrant for making enjoyment of the world part of sanctity, in the face of atheism he grasped what might be called the essential worldliness of God. As befitted a friend of F. D. Maurice, he maintained that the atheist was not deprived of the God he denied, and that the theist must interpret the rise of modern atheism without compromising his grasp on the reality of God by atheist thinking.[55] Holy worldliness could, in this situation, come into view because here men on one hand really believed in God yet on the other could not but feel that the world was autonomous, self-sufficient, allowing God no room and maybe having no need of Him. If holy worldliness were spoken of in this context, the word 'holy' would, of course, denote not so much a style of human goodness, but an essential quality of God. The question then becomes whether

52 A. W. W. Dale, *R. W. Dale* p 532.
53 Mozley, *Essays* p 45.
54 A. W. W. Dale, *R. W. Dale* pp 531-2.
55 R. H. Hutton, *Theological Essays* (3 ed London 1888) pp 342-4, 353-4, 360-1.

and how God is so committed to the world that he is inescapable in it. The question raises the possibility that man, simply by being in the world, is holy; or, at least, that holiness is a mode of worldliness, not its opposite.

The concept of holy worldliness did not arise in this situation partly because the autonomy of the world was almost invariably seen as a threat to faith by those most likely to use the word 'holy'. Worldliness seemed to be close to the abyss of final loss of faith – indeed many thought it was the sure way to it. The self-sufficient world made apologetic necessary, not simply to prove the existence of God in Himself, but to show that the present world was still open to Him. The common apologetic of the eighteenth century argued for miracles as occasional suspensions of the laws of nature, proving that God could intervene if He wished. In its protestant form, at least, the argument compromised with the practical atheism that feared enthusiasm, by restricting miracles to the apostolic period; there was thus evidence both of God's power and freedom and of His endorsement of the orderly routines of modern society and thought. But ardent, worried believers could not be content with the report of ancient miracles, or with anything that held God at arm's length. Their quest for religious life, their desire to silence the Hune and the Gibbon in their own minds made them seek anxiously for 'a present God'.[56] 'What hath God wrought!' was the principle on which Wesley presented the history of his own work as up-to-date evidence to doubters. The progress of the missionary movement was celebrated in the same spirit. In these events God was presently active in the world. The interpretation of biblical apocalyptic in the decades after the French revolution had the same intention. George Müller raised money for his orphan house solely by prayer, 'that in this way before the world and the church there might be another visible proof, that the Lord delights in answering prayer'.[57] J. H. Newman sought for a church to speak with the present authority of God, and, according to Liddon, Pusey valued the sacraments, in his 'zeal for the defence of Revealed Religion', because they are 'with us now; each time they are administered they challenge a verdict as to their precise worth and power; and thus it is that unbelief, which could mask its real attitude towards an ancient and inspired literature, is obliged to display itself when dealing with them'.[58]

[56] Cowper, *The Task* bk vi lines 199–210, 247–54.
[57] George Müller, *A Narrative of some of the Lord's Dealings with George Müller* (3 ed London 1845) p 192 (entry for 28 May 1837).
[58] H. P. Liddon, *Life of Edward Bouverie Pusey* 4 vols (London 1893) I p 344.

In all these ways, men sought for the presence of God in the world as the determining power of life and the convincing answer to the threat of atheism. These examples are limited by their preoccupation with the church as the place of God's presence, but the quest evident in them all could become more worldly. James Anthony Froude tells us:

> It had always struck me as odd that, if to think rightly of religion was the thing of greatest moment to us, the principles on which we were ruled by Providence should not be found, like all other knowledge, in the present reality of our actual life and experience. For our knowledge of astronomy we were not referred to Hipparchus or even to Newton but to the visible heavens that envelop us . . . Things, not books, were our real teachers – while theology seemd to possess every time but the present. It told us of what was; it told us of what would be. Even the mysterious privileges of the Church and the present virtues of the sacraments were not known to us by experience. . . .

Faced with Pusey's challenge, then, Froude would declare himself an unbeliever; but

> Across these perplexities Carlyle's books passed like a flash of lightning. In the French Revolution, in which my brother had seen Antichrist, Carlyle saw the visible revenge of God upon human wickedness. . . . Laws had been laid down in the constitution of things for human conduct, and enforced in this world by awful penalties. It was an answer to the sick question of every thinking soul: Why, if God exists, are there no signs of him? Why do the affairs of this world go on by natural force as if there were no God at all? The natural, Carlyle said, was the supernatural; the supernatural, the natural; and in his *Heroes and Hero Worship* he showed how the great course of the world had been directed by great gifted men who could see this truth and dared to speak it; and to act upon it; who had perceived the Divine presence and the Divine reality, and the truth which they had taught had embodied itself in Norse Gods, in Mahomet, in Luther and Knox, the rule of the gods being for a time or times made visibly recognizable.[59]

Certainly no one in the early nineteenth century detected godlessness and witnessed against it like Carlyle. But since, for him, the churches,

[59] W. H. Dunn, *James Anthony Froude* 2 vols (Oxford 1961) I pp 72–3,

still clothed in their dogmas, the rags of Houndsditch, partook of the atheism of the age, it was not surprising that orthodoxy treated him with some reserve. The formula, 'the natural is the supernatural, the supernatural is the natural' is essentially unstable. It may be a short and easy way of reducing all to the natural. Carlyle, gifted with historical imagination and living in a transitional period, was really in touch with both the old age of faith and the present sense of nature. But the synthesis, or dialectic, easily fell apart. T. H. Green was self-conscious about the duties of a conscientious man of faith in a period of transition between old and new faiths; he thought in terms analogous to the kind of holy worldliness I am concerned with now. But in his religious as in his political thought, Green offered a synthesis that disintegrated rapidly after his death, and the possibility of holy worldliness was not realised.[60]

The fragility of the synthesis of the holy and the world's life is made plain in the creed professed by the comtean layman, Frederic Harrison. At the end of his life, he wrote

> I have at no time . . . lost faith in a supreme Providence, in an immortal soul, and in spiritual life; but I came to find these much nearer to me on earth than I had imagined, much more real, more vivid, and more practical. Superhuman hopes and ecstasies have slowly taken form in my mind as practical duties and indomitable convictions of a good that is to be. I feel that I possess a real, vital, sustaining, unfailing and inseparable *religion*: part of my daily life. . . . This is no metaphysical thesis about the Origin of the Universe, but the present sense of touch with a Providence that enters into every side of daily life . . . Our Providence is no Sabbath visitant; we need no Church or Chapel to contain it; . . . it can be found and heard in the busiest crowd about us, in the commonest intercourse of trade, or society, even of artistic enjoyment. . . .[61]

This seems, at first sight, to be simply holy worldliness. It rejects christian faith, but it lives in touch with providence whose scope is the whole worldly life. But Harrison goes on:

[60] *Works of Thomas Hill Green* ed R. L. Nettleship 3 vols (London 1906) III pp 248, 269–76; Ward pp 411–13, 493; M. Richter, *The Politics of Conscience* (London 1964) pp 293, 340–3, 375–6.
[61] F. Harrison, *The Creed of a Layman* (London 1907) p 1.

It may be that this Providence is neither omnipotent nor omniscient, but most imperfect, often erring, like any one of us. But then for that very reason, it is so close to us, so much akin to us in every want, so perfectly in sympathy and touch with us. It is no purely ideal symbol of perfection. It is the most undeniable fact we know; it is the largest living power on earth.[62]

So the dialectic collapses: providence is simply nature; it is close to us because it is human nature. Elsewhere he said that the only providence we can know is that which 'the whole human race is to its members'.[63] So once more on the brink of holy worldliness we are held back.

The apologetic question of the reality of God in an autonomous world has brought us closer to 'holy worldliness' than direct concern with sanctity. But, even here, the nineteenth century was unable to arrive at the concept. The autonomy of the world was made inescapable by the rise of atheism, but for this reason it was felt as a threat to faith. Holy worldliness became possible in Bonhoeffer's thinking only as he ceased to worry about the apologetic problem, and gave up seeking so to prove God to the world that it had to surrender its autonomy. On the other hand, those who felt the world was no real threat to faith in God found that they were more or less separated from traditional christian language and the christian community. They were driven to regard both as hostile to the world, more hostile than perhaps they really were. And outside the christian tradition they either adopted an idealist approach which can be worldly only within ideal limits, or they seemed, with Harrison, to be affirming simply what the world is. Either way, Robert Blatchford could make them uncomfortable with his 'Mr. Campbell calls nature God. I call nature nature.'

[62] *Ibid* pp 54–5.   [63] *Ibid* p 57.

THE BUSINESS OF BELIEF:
THE EMERGENCE OF 'RELIGIOUS'
PUBLISHING

by PATRICK SCOTT

IN 1863, when a London printer, called Collingridge, produced a handbook for the aspiring author, he made it clear that one particular class of aspiring author was of dominant commercial importance:

> We may venture to assert that no other profession produces so *many* works as the clergy. This is no more than might be expected from a body of gentlemen having the advantages of sound learning and well-regulated minds . . . there are thousands of clergy who neither know, nor desire to know, the toils, the anxieties, or the pleasures of authorship; yet even they, if in active duty, require the services of the printer. Special sermons, schools, and other local institutions in the parish or district, necessitate an outlet for printing.[1]

No one who frequents theological libraries, or second-hand bookshops, would be inclined to dispute Collingridge's assertion about victorian clerical productivity. It is interesting, though, that he links clerical authorship with the commercial, jobbing printer, rather than with more specialised modern publishing activities, because, quite early in the century, mainstream publishing had become independent, of bookselling on the one hand and printing on the other. I want in this paper to give some outline of the religious market, and then to explore some of the reasons why victorian religious publishing stood apart from the broad trend to specialisation, and kept links with both producers and distributors. Two figures may suggest the general picture. Of the thirty-five publishers who took a page or more of advertising in the Christmas number of the *Publisher's Circular* for 1859, twelve were advertising only religious or juvenile-moral works.[2] At the

---

[1] *Collingridge's Guide to Printing and Publishing* (London 1863) p 1.
[2] *Publisher's Circular* 22 (London 1 December 1859).

same time, the proportion of religious works in the list of a general publisher was rapidly declining: religion formed a third of Macmillan's list in 1849, a fifth in 1869, and only a seventeenth in 1889.[3] Since at the beginning of the century theology had formed a dominant part of any ordinary publisher's list, and since throughout the century religious sales remained enormous, it is surely remarkable that religious publishing should show the separatism which is a response to secularisation, so long before the church and chapel pews began to empty.

Statistics about religious publishing are scattered, but not lacking. One crude guide lies in the output of titles published each year. Exactly comparable figures are only available for the last thirty years of the century, but there are usable figures for a much longer period (see Appendix). In the eighteenth century, under 500 titles were published in the average year, and between a third and a half of those were theology or sermons.[4] The nineteenth century saw an absolute growth in the number of annual titles, to over a thousand a year by the eighteen-fifties, which was the high-point of religious publishing, but this growth took place against a much greater growth in general publishing. The trade as a whole published fifteen times as many titles annually by the end of the century as it had at the beginning. The religious publisher S. W. Partridge wrote about this publishing expansion:

Alas, they come like locusts, or like frogs;
'Tis the eighth plague, that Egypt never knew:
And Shallowness, Conceit, Ambition, Greed,
Deluge the land with most unmeaning trash,
And hug themselves as authors. . . .
To have no books is undesirable,
To have too many is almost as bad.[5]

From the eighteen-sixties onwards, religious publishing has formed a shrinking proportion of the year's publications, while the literature of idleness has continued to grow.

Titles, however, give no guide to circulation figures, which are often

3 [A] Bibliographical Catalogue [of Macmillan and Company's Publications 1843 to 1889] (London 1891).
4 Ian Watt, The Rise of the Novel (London 1957) p 49, gives an average of two hundred religious titles a year throughout the century. The 1749 figures break down as 58 sermons or volumes of sermons, and 98 titles of controversy and divinity.
5 [S. W. Partridge,] Upward and Onward[: A Thought Book for the Threshold of Active Life] (London 1857) pp 73–4.

terrifyingly high. We are accustomed to think of Tennyson's *In Memoriam* as a central victorian document, and it sold about sixty thousand copies over twenty years; yet Keble's *The Christian Year* had sold three hundred and seventy-eight thousand copies by the expiration of copyright in 1873.[6] We are accustomed to think of Dickens's novels as making an immediate impact on the reading public, and his *Bleak House* sold some thirty-five thousand in the year of publication; yet Catherine Marsh's *Memorials of Captain Hedley Vicars, Ninety-Seventh Regiment* sold seventy-eight thousand within a year, partly perhaps because of its Crimean interest, but also because it was a suitable gift for pious or erring youth.[7] For many years, such biographies were the long-term big-sellers, but, later, religious novels intended for children outstripped them in sheer quantity: two of the Religious Tract Society's books, Hesba Stretton's *Jessica's First Prayer* (1868), and *Christie's Old Organ* (1873) sold over a million copies each in hard cover, after periodical serialisation. These enormous sales reflect their popularity as Sunday school prizes, though other titles, such as Legh Richmond's *The Dairyman's Daughter* also topped the million mark from their original publisher, and were also reprinted by other firms.[8]

In the first half of the century, sermons, separately or in volume form, could have a substantial sale. The twenty-one-volume set of Charles Simeon's *Horae Homileticae* ran to eight editions in fourteen years, while Newman's *Parochial Sermons* (1834–43) were popular enough for the ailing firm of Rivingtons to reprint them in 1868.[9] A really controversial or newsworthy sermon, in pamphlet form, could also get heavy short-term sales. W. F. Hook's sermon before queen Victoria in 1838 ran to twenty-eight editions in a year, and sold over a hundred thousand copies.[10] The publication of sermons had been a steady proportion of religious publishing, and had usually involved

---

6 R. D. Altick, [*The English Common Reader, A Social History of the Mass Reading Public 1800–1900*] (Chicago 1957) pp 386-7. On pp 99-128 Altick has a full discussion of religious books.

7 Figure from title-page: on its use for presentation see E. E. Kellett, in G. M. Young (ed) *Early Victorian England* (London 1934) II p 95; [J. S.] Reynolds[, *Canon Christopher of St Aldate's Oxford*] (Abingdon 1967) p 280; John Pollock, *The Cambridge Seven* (London 1955) p 46.

8 Gordon Hewitt, *Let the People Read, A Short History of the United Society for Christian Literature* (London 1949) pp 39, 61.

9 [Septimus] Rivington, [*The*] *Publishing Family [of Rivington]* (London 1919) pp 117, 149. Newman had been paid £100 for the copyright in each edition of 1000 volumes.

10 Amy Cruse, [*The Victorians and their Books*] (London 1935) p 119: C. J. Stranks, *Dean Hook* (London 1954) pp 68-70.

publishers in very little risk: the publisher had simply acted as agent for the author, charging a percentage on the cost of publication. This was especially the case with sermons 'published by request'. In the more competitive mid-victorian publishing situation, some publishers took the risk themselves, and went on to a half-profits system, or bought the copyright outright or in a stated edition-size. William Sewell was given £90 by Parker of Oxford for the rights in a single university sermon of 1845, *The Plea of Conscience*.[11] With reprints which were a doubtful risk, publishers still occasionally insisted on the old-fashioned pre-publication subscription list.[12] Some sermons, of course, were more difficult assignments to handle than others; preachers in a time of controversial reviewing, and theological change, often insisted on extensive revision between editions, precluding the use of stereotype plates and so cutting profit-margins.[13] An example of this, happily untypical, is Adam Sedgwick's commemoration sermon at Trinity in 1833, which he expanded to twice its original length for publication: for the fifth edition of 1850, Sedgwick added a preface of 450 pages, and an additional supplement to the appendix, which ran to 145 pages, making his original sermon into a book of over 750 pages.[14] Closer study of the various editions of famous victorian theological works would probably provide many small details about the evolution of victorian thinking.[15] There is no doubt that it was commercially sounder, if less prestigious, to publish in book form authors whose thought did not evolve. The sermon market was effectively ended by the growth in the number of religious periodicals, because they printed weekly sermons for devotional reading, and the controversial sermons were reported in the growing number of

---

11 Lionel James, *A Forgotten Genius: William Sewell of St Columba's and Radley* (London 1945) p 54. The sermon only ran to four editions. For his book *Christian Morals*, Sewell got £70, and for articles in the *Quarterly Review* £50 or £60 each.

12 [Septimus] Rivington, [*The*] *Publishing House* [*of Rivington*] (London 1894) p 24. Compare also Rivington, *Publishing Family*, pp 142–3, and *A Memorandum respecting the connection between Oxford University Press and the Family of Parker of Oxford* (Oxford 1863) p 7.

13 Rivington, *Publishing Family* p 144: 'Few books were stereotyped in those days, especially in the case of theological works, where evolution in thought is usually going on in the author's mind.'

14 J. L. Madden, in Adam Sedgwick, *A Discourse on the Studies of the University* (Leicester 1969) p 26.

15 There were for instance at least six differently printed versions of the first *Tract for the Times: Guardian* (London 1 August 1894); Rivington, *Publishing Family* pp 122–30. The only variorum editions of victorian religious works known to me are Martin Svaglic's edition of Newman's *Apologia* (Oxford 1968), and R. H. Super's *Complete Prose Works of Matthew Arnold* (Ann Arbor, Michigan, 1960–   ).

newspapers. This had been affecting the pamphlet market (by piratical short-hand reporting) since the eighteen-forties, but the cheapening of periodicals in the eighteen-sixties, after the end of paper duty, meant the end of sermon publishing in volume form. There were three exceptions to this: publishing on commission at the author's risk; publishing the sermons of an established literary preacher such as Liddon; and publishing a controversial course of sermons such as F. W. Farrar's series *Eternal Hope* (1878).[16]

Much steadier sales could be expected from the relatively new market in hymn-books, at first often locally produced, but increasingly centralised. The extent of undenominational victorian religious activity, and the emphasis on family devotions and hymn-singing round the cottage piano or harmonium, meant that this market was not simply the preserve of denominational committees, though the congregational union sold forty thousand copies of its hymn-book in the first three years after publication, and so gained some financial freedom for the central secretariat from the suspiciously independent member chapels.[17] But a really big seller had to combine sales for congregational use with sales for home use, as with Sankey's *Sacred Songs and Solos*. This had a bigger sale than any other book I've come across, selling ninety million copies in its first seventy years. It had the further advantage over more staid competitors that, in the complicated international copyright situation before 1911, the publishers, Morgan and Scott, had been able to establish copyright in a number of American hymns, as well as in Sankey's own compositions, and these were then no longer freely available for inclusion in other hymn-books.[18] Hymn-books, once finally edited, are a long-run publication with steady sales, usually printed from stereotype plates.

These circulation figures, like the figures for published titles, refer only to books. The picture is yet more overwhelming when more ephemeral material is considered. Bishop Ryle's tracts circulated twelve million copies; in the eighteen-sixties, the Religious Tract Society

---

[16] *Eternal Hope* was delivered as sermons in November and December 1877, and widely reported in the newspapers: it was stereotyped for first book publication in February 1878, and went through eight editions that year (with minor revisions in March, and heavier ones in April). There were six more editions in the next ten years. *Bibliographical Catalogue* p 335.

[17] Owen Chadwick, *The Victorian Church* I (London 1966) pp 401–2.

[18] For sales see J. Edwin Orr, *The Second Evangelical Awakening* (London 1949) p 261: Orr uses figures supplied by the publishers. Morgan and Scott had previously published *The Revival Hymnbook*, *Heart Melodies*, and *Songs of Love and Mercy*. Compare Ira D. Sankey, *Sankey's Story of the Sacred Hymns* (London 1906).

was producing thirty-three million items of literature each year; the Wesleyan Book Room issued one million three hundred thousand items in 1841 alone; the Scripture Gift Mission distributed over forty-three million New Testaments and separate Gospels, with appropriate bindings and service crests, during the years 1914–19.[19] As Richard Altick says, those figures are more numbing than illuminating. But one can get comparable figures for much less well-known authors or publishers. Edmund Gosse's mother wrote a tract during the Crimean War, called 'The Guardsman of the Alma', of which more than half a million were sold.[20] Canon Christopher of Oxford, who smuggled tracts in his boots to garden-parties when his family forbade him to take any, could sell ninety-five thousand of a much less catchy title, 'Salvation in the Lord Jesus'.[21] A Kingston-upon-Hull publisher, J. W. Leng, advertised a relatively expensive tract series in 1864, selling in shilling packets of thirteen assorted titles (such as *Angel Lilly: or, Do you love Jesus*, and *Carletta: or, Going to sing in Heaven*), and could state in the advertisement, 'Upwards of eight hundred thousand of these interesting little works have been circulated.'[22] Successful tract distribution probably ended much earlier than the production of tracts did, partly because as the century went on, there was much more literature available anyway, and because periodicals supplanted pamphlets as the characteristic non-book publication; as early as the eighteen-twenties, tract societies and publishers began to publish magazines cheaply in quantity for free distribution, giving an excuse for regular district visiting.[23] The pattern set up by tract distribution and by tract magazines was developed in the parish magazine, whether locally printed, or merely a localised form of centrally prepared tract material.[24] The thought behind the free distribution of literature was

---

19 Altick pp 100–2: for the Scripture Gift Mission, see Ashley Baker, *Publishing Salvation* (London 1961).

20 Edmund Gosse, *Father and Son* (London 1907 ed of 1969) p 19.

21 Reynolds p 273.   22 *Publisher's Circular*, 27 (London 8 December 1864) p 826.

23 The Religious Tract Society started the *Tract Magazine* (1824), followed by *The Visitor* (1828), but there were many publishers working on the same pattern: for instance, in 1904 John Ritchie of Sturrock, Kilmarnock, published the *Localised Gospel Messenger* at 1s. 6d. per hundred, the *Gospel Messenger* at 1s. 0d. a hundred, and *Good Tidings* ('district gospel literature') at 2s. 0d. a hundred. Compare P. G. Scott, '*Zion's Trumpet*: Evangelical Enterprise and Rivalry 1833–36'. *Victorian Studies* 13 (Bloomington, Indiana, 1969) pp 199–203, and 'Richard Cope Morgan, Religious Periodicals, and the Pontifex Factor', *Victorian Periodicals Newsletter*, 15 (Amherst, Mass Summer 1972).

24 See J. M. Swift, *Parish Magazines* (London 1939); Alan Webster, 'Parish Magazines', *Theology* 46 (London 1943) p 156; 'The Man who started it all', *Home Words* Centenary Issue (London 1971) pp 1–2.

not always clear, and the operation was often more a self-validation
for the distributor than a communication to the recipient, but the
contemporary justification is given in a mid-victorian hymn:

> Work in the wild waste places
>   Though none thy love may own;
> God guides the down of the thistle
>   The wandering wind hath sown.
> Sow by the wayside gladly,
>   In the dark caverns low,
> Where sunlight seldom reacheth,
>   Nor healthful streamlets flow.
> Watch not the clouds above thee,
>   Let the whirlwind round thee sweep;
> God may the seed-time give thee
>   But another's hand may reap.[25]

This concept of tract distribution, 'sowing by the wayside', though
common enough, must be modified by remembering the victorian
emphasis on parochial visitation, and district responsibilities.[26] It
implies a very much clearer difference in religious attitude between
distributor and recipient than the much more moralistic tracts of the
eighteenth-century SPCK had done. The criticism is frequently made,
and was made at the time, that the tracts' 'inflexible style of phraseology,
together with the uniform mould of thought, imparts a technical and
exclusive character to the whole teaching, and effectually bars its
access to any mind unfamiliar with the teaching of the sanctuary'.[27]
A contemporary discussion of this, in the *Christian Observer* for 1855,
argued: 'the language of the Gospel is emphatically a technical and
peculiar language, to be discerned only by those who are taught of
God . . . Yea, the self-same words which fall so repulsively from the
mouth of the canter, may be the consecrated vessels of the most
important and soul-cheering truths.'[28] The chief effect of the huge
tract trade on publishing was to keep religious publishers involved in

25 [J. A.] Wallace, [*Lessons from the Life of James Nisbet, Publisher*] (Edinburgh 1867) pp
  67–8.
26 There is a fictional description of tract distribution in Dickens's *Bleak House* (1852–3),
  chap viii; and non-fictional ones in Reynolds pp 115–19, 233–4, 356–9. There is a good
  discussion of the tract philosophy in Brian Harrison, 'Early Victorian Temperance
  Tracts', *History Today* 13 (London 1963) pp 178–85.
27 S. G. Green, in 1850, quoted by R. K. Webb, *The British Working Class Reader 1790–*
  1848 (London 1955) p 28.
28 E.C.A., 'On Religious Cant', *Christian Observer* 214 (London 1855) pp 662–3.

the direct sale of quantities of literature to individual customers, or to
non-commercial tract repositories, at reduced prices; this was against
the general publishing trend of selling only to retailers, and later wholesalers, and against the trend to a net price agreement for sales to the
public.

A similar difference from general publishing arose on the production
side. The book trade as a whole was separating from general printing.
The printing of ephemera, handbills or single sheet pamphlets, was
jobbing printing which could be accomplished on a small handpress
such as an Albion or a Columbian, while that of books, especially long-
run books, was increasingly a matter for machine-printing. The two
sides of the trade had separated in secular publishing, but the fact that
many religious publishers had started by printing their own tracts, that
is as jobbing printers, and the overwhelming importance to religious
publishing of ephemera, meant that the religious publishers kept links
with the ordinary printing trade long after other sections of publishing
had lost them.

One minor production factor keeping religious publishing apart
from general publishing was the importance of special and 'extra'
bindings, in ivory, morocco, or heavy-gilt bevelled-edge cloth boards,
for devotional books and hymn-books: general publishing in the
victorian period was relying more and more on the standard publishers'
cloth binding, even if decoratively stamped in gilt or, later, colours.[29]
It is difficult to prove, but one suspects that with Sunday school prize-
books the binding often accounted for a very high proportion of the
total production cost, the printing being on miserably poor paper.

Separation from general publishing was further encouraged by the
growing importance of the publisher's imprint as a kind of seal of
approval on the theological content of religious books. This factor, of
course, affected those general publishers who also published religious
books: one expected Macmillan books to be theologically liberal.
But it operated much more strongly among religious booksellers,
especially when they were first building up a business. James
Nisbet's imprint meant low, later free, church of Scotland, and

29 J. F. Shaw, for instance, could advertise Cumming's *The Life and Lessons of Our Lord* in
three different bindings (7s. 6d.; 9s.; and 10s. 6d.) as 'the cheapest gift-book of the
season' (*Publisher's Circular* 27, 31 December 1864 p 47); while the *Poems of A. H.
Clough*, though going through thirteen Macmillan editions, were only available in
a plain cloth binding. On this topic see Michael Sadleir, *The Evolution of Publishers'
Binding Styles* (London 1930). On extra bindings see Rivington, *Publishing Family*
p 148, or any catalogue for Samuel Bagster's *Biblia Sacra Polyglotta Bagsteriana*.

therefore evangelical books. Morgan and Scott's books were usually the product of writers connected with the interdenominational evangelicalism of the later part of the century. Hodder and Stoughton, particularly when W. R. Nicoll was their literary editor, 'while perhaps losing a little of the ebullient evangelicalism, . . . became the acknowledged leader in the publication of progressively conservative religious thought'.[30] Too precise a theological label could be an embarrassment: R. C. Morgan had been a member of the Plymouth brethren in the 1850s, co-operating with William Yapp of Hereford, but by the sixties Morgan kept himself and the firm free of denominational alignment, and so out of a very over-crowded field.[31] When James Burn, who had built up a business publishing the more popular tractarian books of the eighteen-forties, followed Newman over to Rome in 1846, he lost his business, and had to be helped in restarting by Newman's hurriedly written novel *Loss and Gain*.[32] Rather similarly, the old-established firm of Rivingtons, which had had a large theological and sermon business since the early eighteenth century, lost most of its evangelical customers by remaining unenthusiastic in the eighteen-tens; then, by publishing on commission the *Tracts for the Times*, Rivingtons became identified as a high church imprint. As a result, although their authors included Pusey and Christopher Wordsworth, by the eighteen-fifties their business was declining sadly; they responded by launching the lighter-weight Rivingtons Devotional Series in the sixties, but the firm was only saved by building up an educational textbook trade, which eventually replaced religious publishing altogether.[33] By the eighteen-sixties, Emma Jane Worboise could make a fictional lady novelist remark: 'If I write a red-hot Puseyite story, I know exactly to whom it ought to be confided; if a Low Church novel, where it would receive a hearty welcome.'[34] This limitation of publishers by partisan attachment served

[30] [G. H.] Doran [,*Chronicles of Barabbas*] (London 1935) p 62. Hodder had an early success with Henry Drummond's *Natural Law in the Spiritual World* (London 1883), which sold 141,000 (41 editions) by 1905: Doran p 63 discusses the theological qualms of the older members of the firm over Drummond's books. See also T. H. Darlow, *William Robertson Nicoll* (London 1925).

[31] [G. E.] Morgan, [*Veteran in Revival: Richard Cope Morgan, his Life and Work*] (London 1909).

[32] Meriol Trevor, in J. H. Newman, *Loss and Gain* (London 1962) p v.

[33] Rivington, *Publishing House* pp 17–24; *Publishing Family* pp 142–4, p 166.

[34] Quoted by Amy Cruse p 60: on religious novels see Margaret Maison, *Search Your Soul, Eustace* (London 1961). F. W. Farrar's books were various in kind but always appeared with a suitable imprint; his novels were published by A. and C. Black, his *Life of Christ* from the 'popular' Cassells, *Social and Present Day Questions* from Hodder,

a useful function for purchasers in the bewildering variety of victorian belief, but it reduced a religious publisher's chance of appealing to a general audience. Only one *caveat* needs to be added, and that is that two big firms, S. W. Partridge and the wholesalers Simpkin Marshall continued to do a lot of private commission publishing (what is now called 'vanity' publishing), and so their imprints cover some fairly eccentric theology, as well as the relative normality of their own publications.

The four reasons so far suggested (production, distribution, bindings and imprint significance) would make it good sense commercially for religious publishing to be distinct from general publishing. There is, though, a fifth, and possibly the chief, factor operating to effect the separation: particularly in the first half of the century, publishing was affected by the individual publisher's own self-image or commitment. Several of the publishers seem to have set out deliberately to run 'religious' firms, uncontaminated by the worldliness of arts, science or politics. James Nisbet, for instance, 'made it a matter of conscience to exclude from his stock every book that was not of a moral or religious character'.[35] Of James Burn, his biographer tells us that he was 'no latitudinarian in life, and no latitudinarian in the literature he set forth'.[36] G. H. Doran commented on the stock of the Willard Tract Depository; 'We handled only religious books. Novels were anathema, in fact everything that did not teach the necessity of repentance and the punishment of sin. We sold Christmas cards, New Year's cards, and birthday cards only if they had Scripture texts as messages.'[37] S. W. Partridge advised the aspirant to the commercial life:

> Thy business
> Must not be such as will debase thyself.
> 'Tis a poor bargain that – a fortune made
> By a soul's ruin. Nor must thou so trade
> That thou become a mean and cunning knave,
> An over-reaching and unconscienced thing,
> Laying thy goods off to thy customers,
> And foisting trashy things on ignorance
> With well-dissembled candour.[38]

R. C. Morgan's son wrote: 'My father never failed to ascribe the success and growth of his work to the Divine Hand: he listened for the

---

Solomon: his Life and Times from James Nisbet, *Eternal Hope* from Macmillan, and *Protestantism: its Peril and its Duty* from J. A. Kensit.   [35] Wallace p 91.

[36] Wilfred Wilberforce, *The House of Burns and Oates* (London 1908) p 23.

[37] Doran p 10.   [38] *Upward and Onward* pp 141-2.

Voice that said, "This is the way, walk ye in it".'[39] These publishers would be running firms in the same spirit and on much the same pattern as the non-commercial tract societies and denominational book-rooms. Firms like Rivingtons which had been going for many years, or the second generation of managers and editors in large religious publishers (men like Ernest Hodder-Williams or W. R. Nicoll or G. H. Doran) do not seem to have been nearly so single-minded in the pursuit of their business: in the interests of expansion Hodder-Williams moved into general publishing with a large list of cheap novels, but the firm remained under the stigma of being a 'religious' publisher because of its backlist.[40] The personal disregard for a general culture by the religious publishers of the thirties, forties and fifties helped to fix the continuing pattern of separation.

There are many other trends in victorian religious publishing which could have been selected for discussion. It would be possible to show that works with a high circulation tended to be biographical or devotional, rather than strictly theological or even controversial; that they tend to be books which would be bought for other people, children or the poor, rather than for oneself; and that they tend to be evangelical in theology, rather than high or broad church. It would be possible to suggest that the growth in the number of books and periodicals affected the way in which people read, away from careful scrutiny to a more emotional skimming of fragmented material, a kind of religious light reading. The growth of religious periodicals, and the impact on them of the rise of fiction, and the cheapening of newspapers, shows a much more complicated relationship between religious and general publishing than the overall pattern suggested here. The separation of religious publishing could also probably be connected with the concept of 'Sunday reading': by the eighteen-eighties, only one seventh of new book titles were religious. Commercial religious publishers would be influenced on the distribution side by the pattern set up by the earlier tract and literature societies. But the process of commercial separation that I have sketched is significant, I think, as demonstrating that in the great flowering of victorian religious publishing, the very production and distribution processes indicate a sharp division between the religious and the secular. When religious publishing was statistically dominant, the pattern was set, or perhaps chosen, for its continuance as a minority, specialised service.

[39] Morgan p 47.   [40] Doran pp 30–3, 66, 312–13.

APPENDIX

RELIGIOUS BOOKS AND GENERAL PUBLISHING, 1699–1935

	1	2	3	4	5	6	7	8	9	10	11	12
	1698–9	1749	1801–35	1836–63	1849	1859	1869	1879	1889	1899	1921–5	1931–5
Annual total of books published (in thousands)	0·43	0·47	1·60	2·30	4·45	4·54	4·57	5·83	6·07	7·57	12·0	15·2
Religious books	199	156			1086		1047	1086	764	693	865	953
Religion as a percentage of total	46	33	22·2	33·5	28·5	31·1	33·3	17·1	12·7	9·2	7·2	6·2
Fiction and juvenile books as a percentage							21·4	19·5	31·9	34·1	27·7	39·3

Sources

col 1 is derived from *Bibliotheca Annua* (1700), in [D. F.] Foxon [(ed)] *English Bibliographical Sources Series I,*] I [London, n.d.]

col 2 is derived from the *London Magazine*'s Monthly lists for 1749, in Foxon VI

cols 3 and 4 are based on a sample in *English Catalogue of Books 1801–35* (1914); 1836–63 (1864)

col 5 is based on a sample in *Publisher's Circular catalogue* XII (1849)

col 6 is based on a sample in the *British Catalogue* (1859)

cols 7, 8, 9 and 10 are derived from *Journal of the Statistical Society*, 33 (1870) p 157; 43 (1880), pp 114–16; 53 (1890) pp 151–3; 63 (1900) pp 135–46

cols 11 and 12 are from summary tables in *English Catalogue of Books 1921–25* (1926); 1931–5 (1936)